THE
BEAST

THE
BEAST

by
Judge Ben B. Lindsey
OF THE JUVENILE COURT OF DENVER

and
Harvey J. O'Higgins
AUTHOR OF "THE SMOKE-EATERS," "DON-A-DREAMS," ETC.

Foreword by
Stephen J. Leonard

UNIVERSITY PRESS OF COLORADO

Published by the University Press of Colorado
5589 Arapahoe Avenue, Suite 206C
Boulder, Colorado 80303

Previously published by Doubleday, Page & Co., 1910

 The University Press of Colorado is a proud member of
the Association of American University Presses.

The University Press of Colorado is a cooperative publishing enterprise supported, in part, by Adams State College, Colorado State University, Fort Lewis College, Mesa State College, Metropolitan State College of Denver, University of Colorado, University of Northern Colorado, and Western State College of Colorado.

∞ The paper used in this publication meets the minimum requirements of the American National Standard for Information Sciences—Permanence of Paper for Printed Library Materials. ANSI Z39.48-1992

Library of Congress Cataloging-in-Publication Data

Lindsey, Ben B. (Ben Barr), 1869–1943.
  The beast / by Ben B. Lindsey and Harvey J. O'Higgins.
    p. cm. — (Timberline books)
  Originally published: New York : Doubleday, Page & Co., 1910.
  Includes index.
  ISBN 978-0-87081-953-7 (pbk. : alk. paper) 1. Political corruption—Colorado. 2. Juvenile courts—Colorado. I. O'Higgins, Harvey Jerrold, 1876–1929. II. Title.
  JK7845.L55 2009
  364.1'323097809041—dc22

                                                                    2009014003

Design by Daniel Pratt

18 17 16 15 14 13 12 11 10 09   10 9 8 7 6 5 4 3 2 1

To those who have helped:
the hundreds whose names I have not had room to mention;
the thousands whose names I do not even know.

B.B.L.

"And they fling him, hour by hour,
Limbs of men to give him power;
Brains of men to give him cunning; and
*   for dainties to devour*
Children's souls, the little worth; hearts
*   of women, cheaply bought:*
He takes them and he breaks them, but
*   he gives them scanty thought."*

THE BRUTE
by William Vaughn Moody

NOTE

In the winter of 1908, the editor of *Everybody's Magazine* obtained from Judge Lindsey the manuscript of a series of articles of an auto-biographical nature. The articles had been dictated hurriedly to a stenographer in Judge Lindsey's intervals of leisure, and they were not in a form in which they could be published. The editor sent Harvey J. O'Higgins to Denver to work with Judge Lindsey on them; this book is the result. It is a joint work, but the autobiographic "I" of Judge Lindsey's first draft has been preserved, because the voice is still Judge Lindsey's, though the pen that reports it is another's.

CONTENTS

FOREWORD

BENJAMIN BARR LINDSEY:
THE BEAST AND AFTER

You are one of the few men who has [*sic*] done the most for the
moral awakening of our people. When you wrote "The Beast
and the Jungle," you rendered a service that hardly any other
man would have had the courage and knowledge to render. You
attacked evil in the concrete, not merely in the abstract. Plenty
of people are willing to attack it in the abstract, for no courage
is necessary in such a diffuse assault. But very few are willing to
face the intense bitterness of counter-attack which follows upon
assailing evil in the concrete.

THEODORE ROOSEVELT TO BEN LINDSEY,
September 18, 1913, Lindsey Papers, Library of Congress

Denver, a city little more than half a century old in 1909, gave
its boosters ample room to brag. They boasted of its popula-
tion of more than 200,000. They boasted of its nearby mountains, its sunshine, its U.S. Mint, and its new Municipal Auditorium,

site of the 1908 Democratic National Convention. When not busy touting their town, the yeasayers flayed the naysayers—reformers such as feisty Benjamin Barr Lindsey. Ben was bad for business. Ben had a "withered soul."[1] Ben was "illy-balanced, erratic, and emotional."[2]

At five foot five and ninety-eight pounds, Ben Lindsey hardly seemed a threat to anyone. Did plump David H. Moffat, the president of Denver's First National Bank, fear the pint-sized jurist? Did portly William Gray Evans, king of the Denver Tramway Company, pale when he heard Lindsey's name? Did solid Robert W. Speer, Denver's mayor and Evans's pliable friend, tremble at the thought of little Lindsey?

Evans and Moffat with a small circle of associates owned Denver's water company, its street railway company, and its most important bank. The political machine they greased with the help of the underworld, bossed by men such as Edward Chase, ensured their rule. They made Lindsey a county judge in January 1901. They supported him as he crusaded for creation of a juvenile court and the humane treatment of young offenders. They made him. No doubt, they thought they could unmake him.

They demonstrated their power in 1906 when Lindsey challenged Democrats, Republicans, and Socialists by running as an independent reform candidate for governor. Evans's candidate, the Republican Henry Augustus Buchtel, a Methodist minister and chancellor of the University of Denver, trounced the little judge. The Evans-Speer crowd squirmed a bit in 1908 when the judge, assisted by newspaperwoman Ellis Meredith, wrote *The Rule of Plutocracy in Colorado: A Retrospect and a Warning*, a long pamphlet detailing local corruption. Yet *Plutocracy* was a mere lady-finger firecracker compared to the dynamite in Lindsey's next work, "The Beast and the Jungle."

"THE BEAST AND THE JUNGLE"

Upton Sinclair, noted for his 1906 exposé of the meatpacking industry, *The Jungle*, took credit for sparking publication of "The Beast and Jungle." In his autobiography, Sinclair remembered his summer 1908 visit to Denver: "Denver, and Ben Lindsey, judge of the Children's Court; a new idea and a new man. . . . He revealed to me that he had written an account of his war with the organized corruption of Denver. I took the manuscript, read it on the train, and telegraphed *Everybody's Magazine* about it."[3]

Sinclair served Lindsey well. With a readership of half a million, *Everybody's* ranked high among the nation's most influential publications. It and a few other magazines, such as *McClure's* and *Cosmopolitan*, boosted sales by exposing venal politicians, greedy corporations, and assorted malefactors of great wealth. Jacob Riis, Lincoln Steffens, Upton Sinclair, and others let America know about its warts. Branded as "muckrakers," they quickly transformed the put-down into a badge of honor.

Everybody's editor, John O'Hara Cosgrave, recognized that Lindsey's manuscript had muckraking merits, but he also realized that chunks of the judge's prose could choke readers. Cosgrave sent Harvey J. O'Higgins, a college-educated professional writer with four novels to his credit, to Denver to help Lindsey spin his flax into gold. The duo worked fast. On the afternoon of Saturday, September 18, 1909, the October issue of *Everybody's* with the first installment of "The Beast and the Jungle" hit the newsstands.

Denver knew the shape, if not all the details, of what was coming. Lindsey had waged his war against corruption since shortly after he became a judge. His creation of a juvenile court, his campaign against child labor at the cotton mills in south Denver, his exposure of rigged county printing contracts, his brief jailing of utility magnate Henry L. Doherty, and his race for governor all bespoke a man committed to reform. *Everybody's*, anxious to increase its circulation, advertised in *The Denver Post*.

> *When you open Judge Lindsey's "BEAST AND THE JUNGLE" in the October EVERYBODY'S MAGAZINE you will begin to read the most amazingly concrete revelation of cussedness—political and municipal—that has ever been told by a man who knew what he was talking about. The application is for every city in the United States big enough to know the meaning of the word graft.*

Everybody's urged everyone to rush out and buy a copy at 15 cents per issue.[4]

Rush they did. "LINDSEY STIRS DENVER; CITY IN SCRAMBLE FOR EVERYBODY'S MAGAZINE" read the page 1 headline in the *Rocky Mountain News* on September 19. Reporting on the "targets" of the revelations, the *News* noted, "A few were swift to deny what the judge charges, but most of them considered silence the better part of discretion." The amused *News* added, "The announcement of the author that the opening chapter is mild compared with those that are to follow did not serve to calm the politicians' nerves."

The *News*, which under its reform-minded publisher Thomas M. Patterson had often sided with Lindsey, told of the nervous plutocrats' efforts to derail the series. In July 1909 they sent an "agent" to New York where he gave John O'Hara Cosgrave a forty-page slur charging Lindsey with "political trickery, treachery, judicial unfairness, . . . lunacy, degeneracy, and degrading immorality."[5]

Fearful that publishing the work of a supposedly degenerate lunatic might open his magazine to a lawsuit, Cosgrave visited Denver to interview the judge's friends and enemies. He concluded that "survivals of the old despotic upholders of privilege" had fabricated the charges. The *News* reported: "Reputable people not allied with the interests . . . assured Mr. Cosgrave that Judge Lindsey was honest as he was brave; that he would not lie about his worst enemy, and that it would be difficult to exaggerate the rottenness of the conditions his story set forth."[6] Reassured, Cosgrave damned the libel suits and published.

The appearance of "The Beast and the Jungle" challenged *The Denver Post*. It could not ignore the sensational story, but it shrank from offending the "interests" by siding with Lindsey. Cleverly, *The Post* ginned up a September 19, 1909, headline to make it appear that Lindsey had foolishly attacked everyone.

THE ENTIRE COMMUNITY IS CHARGED WITH
SATURNALIA OF CRIME AND OPPRESSION

Supreme Court, Judges, Juries, Lawyers of Standing and
Distinction, and Citizens, All Alike, Accused of Endless Infamies.

The next day *The Post* boiled Lindsey, a man with a "withered soul," for subjecting Denver to "the scorn of the world." Who would read "The Beast and the Jungle"? "Abnormal minds, loving to dwell on the self-dissection of abnormal minds, will doubtlessly find here their pleasure. . . . The thing pulsates like torn flesh quivering under the knife; it reeks of *post mortem* inquisitions."[7] Recognizing that "abnormal minds" also read newspapers, *The Post* did not let its fulminations stand in the way of capitalizing on "The Beast and the Jungle." It, like the *News*, published excerpts, and it, like *Everybody's*, named the accused corrupters.

Among them was Fred W. Parks, once Lindsey's law partner, who Lindsey accused of selling out to the plutocrats. In "The Beast and the Jungle," he gave Parks the name "Gardener," but Denverites easily sorted out identities. Parks grumbled: "Why, that man Lindsey is a liar and a perjurer, and I can prove it. He not only is all of these things, but an ingrate as well." Archibald "Archie" M. Stevenson, described by Lindsey as a lackey for the Denver Tramway Company, also fumed: "Lindsey is a lying, crazy little scamp, who should not be allowed to talk to sane men. It's a flat, vicious lie that he tells. That's all."[8]

That was not all. Seven issues of *Everybody's* followed. Month after month, readers throughout the United States learned about the web of graft and corruption that entangled some of Colorado's business leaders, governors, U.S. senators, supreme court judges, legislators, and city councilmen. Month after month, they saw courageous Lindsey battling for honest elections, good government, humane treatment of juvenile offenders, and enforcement of child labor laws. Finally, in May 1910, they read the last chapter of the judge's heroic struggle, and soon after they were able to buy the whole story in book form— its title shortened to *The Beast*.

The Beast's popularity as a magazine series and its survival as a hardback published by Doubleday, Page & Company rested at least as much on Harvey O'Higgins's talents as it did on Lindsey's story. O'Higgins, blessed with an eye for drama and detail, created memorable Dickensian characters. For O'Higgins, Archibald M. Stevenson was not simply a tool of the Denver Tramway Company. He was that and more, "a heavy-jowled, heavy-waisted, red-faced bulk of good humor—looking as if he had just walked out of a political cartoon." When Big Steve visited Lindsey, "[h]e sat down and threw a foot up on the desk and smiled at us with his inevitable cigarette in his mouth—his ridiculously inadequate cigarette. (When he puffed it, he looked like a fat boy blowing bubbles.)"[9] Readers might forget a tool of the interests, but they would likely remember a cigarette-puffing fat boy blowing bubbles.

O'Higgins and Lindsey also flavored *The Beast* with pinches of sarcasm and dashes of irony. Explaining why he had accepted money for the Juvenile Improvement Association from Edward B. Field, head of the Colorado Telephone Company and reputedly the brains of the beast, Lindsey said that he separated the evil that people did from the people that did the evil. For example, he took money for good causes from the keeper of a "disorderly house." "Madam," Lindsey said, "I want to thank you for your good deeds and I want to tell you how I despise your evil ones." He commented, "She was a procuress, but her business was no worse than that of the corporations."[10]

The book's dominant image comparing a camouflaged beast lurking in the jungle to the sinister shadowy power of corrupt corporations pulling politicians' strings was likely O'Higgins's creation. As a literary device, it allowed him to pit brave Lindsey against the fierce tiger. O'Higgins humanized his hero by focusing on Lindsey's happy early childhood, his family's descent into poverty, his attempt at suicide (the gun failed to fire), his eventual rise to a judgeship, and his ensuing empathy for and defense of the poor kids among whom he once counted himself. In O'Higgins's hands, Lindsey's life became a Horatio Alger saga in which Ben went from rags to the richness of helping others—from mistreated children and poverty-ridden mothers to good citizens in general.

Missing from the book's portrayal of young Lindsey was his father's suicide. Despondent and ill, Landy Lindsey slashed his throat with a razor, leaving eighteen-year-old Ben to discover the body in the coal cellar. He probably found that memory too traumatic to recount, or too private to publish.[11]

Readers also appreciated *The Beast* for its point of view. Unlike many muckraking exposés, such as Lincoln Steffens's *Shame of the Cities* (1904), written by outsiders looking in, *The Beast* told the story as seen by an insider at war with the plutocrats. The little judge avoided portraying minnows as morally reprehensible. Rather, he excused minor grafters, like wayward kids, as victims of a corrupt system. Lindsey condemned the system and its architects, not those caught in its net.

The *Everybody's* series included dozens of illustrations. Unfortunately, when the series became a book it contained only one photograph and no index. Those deficits have been redressed in this University Press of Colorado's Timberline edition, which includes photographs and illustrations captioned by Thomas J. Noel and an index compiled by Amy Zimmer.

REFORM AT HIGH TIDE

In mid-May 1910, shortly after *The Beast* ended its run in *Everybody's*, Denverites went to the polls where they dashed William Gray Evans and his fellow investors' hopes of securing a favorable, long-term franchise for the Denver Union Water Company. "Amazed, confused, baffled, impotent," the *Rocky Mountain News* crowed, "the bosses stared at each other desolately."[12] In late August, former president Theodore Roosevelt spoke at the Municipal Auditorium. Local bigwigs, stung by Lindsey's barbs, denied him a seat on the platform. Spying the judge in the crowd, Roosevelt exclaimed, "Here is the man I've been demanding to see all day."[13] Roosevelt then invited Lindsey to occupy a place of honor.

In November 1910, Colorado voters again whacked the beast by reelecting John F. Shafroth, the state's most politically effective reformer, to the governorship and by approving three amendments to the Colorado constitution that progressives saw as highways to good government. One gave voters the right to pass laws without going through the state legislature. Another allowed the legislature to refer proposed statutes to the people for their consideration. The third allowed citizens to remove elected officials from office.

For a few more years, the tide of reform vindicated Lindsey's courage. Banker David H. Moffat's death in March 1911, and the revelation that his empire was smoke, mirrors, and bankrupt, weakened William Gray Evans and others among Denver's moneyed overlords. In 1912, Mayor Robert W. Speer, Evans's cat's-paw in City Hall, bowed out of office. A year later Denver adopted a commission government, the reformers' cure-all for the ills spawned by boss mayors and their shady supporters.

Lindsey may have exaggerated his role in Evans's downfall, but there was truth in the judge's ebullient October 17, 1913, letter to Harvey O'Higgins. "Boss Evans is licked. The old gang of privilege grabbers are actually turning against him." Lindsey said that John Evans, William Gray's son, "told me that his father was in bad physical condition—a thousand times worse than I was, and instead of having to be in a sanitarium two months, he said the doctors had advised his father that he must go to a sanitarium for two years to get his health back."

The blow to Evans went beyond wrecking his health. "It seemed from [John's] talk that 'The Beast and the Jungle' had been held responsible for the defeat of the water franchise . . . and it also interfered with them in their financial deals in Wall Street." Lindsey probably did not know the particulars of the Evans-Moffat debacle that left the First National Bank in shambles and the fortunes of some community pillars, including Evans, shattered. Yet, the little judge knew enough to recognize that he and O'Higgins had wounded the beast.

As a tiger hunter, Lindsey added sparkle to his already lustrous national reputation, which he had gained largely through his work to protect and rehabilitate juvenile offenders. As the preeminent and best-known crusader for the humane treatment of young miscreants in the United States, he cultivated other reformers including Lincoln Steffens and Upton Sinclair. They in turn touted him. Jacob Riis, whose book *How the Other Half Lives* (1890) graphically introduced

Americans to the realities of urban poverty, arranged for Lindsey to confer with President Theodore Roosevelt in 1904, cementing a bond between them that proved valuable to both. Lincoln Steffens also promoted the judge by featuring him in a series of *McClure's* articles that began appearing in 1906. Three years later Steffens's *The Upbuilders* devoted nearly 150 pages to "Ben Lindsey, The Just Judge."

Celebrity could not shield Lindsey from criticism, overwork, and exhaustion. Despite his hard work, Progressive candidates were defeated in the November 1912 state elections. In the spring of 1913, he suffered a "sort of general nervous breakdown after ten years without any vacation whatever," which forced him to recuperate at Dr. John Harvey Kellogg's Battle Creek Sanitarium in Michigan.[14] There he had an X ray taken of his heart, which he had framed. "I am . . . sending it to the Juvenile Court," he wrote his mother, Letitia, on June 24, 1913, "so if I should never go back there, my heart will be there— the picture of it."

Writing to journalist Paul U. Kellogg on November 7, 1913, Lindsey, then back in Denver, reported that he had "not yet entirely recovered," that his fight for reform "has really been a source of much suffering and hardship to me." The "old gang . . . keep up a constant warfare and attack against me. This is sustained principally by the 'eminently respectables' of the community. Many of the Lady Bountifuls . . . the ultra fashionables, and four hundred of society . . . are among the most bitter of my foes."

Fortunately, Lindsey found a helpmate far superior to the "Lady Bountifuls." In late 1913, he married Henrietta Brevoort of Detroit, a woman twenty-five years his junior.[15] She brought him stability and support until his death in 1943 and she guarded his memory and legacy until her own death in 1969. They adopted a daughter whom they named Benetta.

THE LUDLOW MASSACRE

Henrietta accompanied Ben on his next great adventure as he jousted with the Rockefellers, the richest family in the United States. Their far-flung empire included the Colorado Fuel and Iron Company (CF&I), operator of a huge steel mill in Pueblo, Colorado, and of numerous coal mines including those at Ludlow seventy-five miles south of Pueblo. At Ludlow, on April 20, 1914, Colorado state militiamen, acting to protect Rockefeller property, fired upon a tent colony of striking coal miners and their families. When the smoke cleared and the bodies were counted, Colorado and the nation were horrified to find that the troopers, who suffered one fatality, had killed two women and eleven children.

Speaking at a mass meeting held at the state capitol in Denver on May 15, 1914, Upton Sinclair challenged his audience: "There has recently been committed in this State the most horrible public crime in the entire history of our country. What do the people of Colorado intend to do about it?"[16] Recognizing that Lindsey's fame would ensure good press coverage, Sinclair persuaded the judge to take a delegation of women, including Mary Petrucci, who had lost two of her children in the Ludlow fire, to Washington, D.C., to enlist the aid of President Woodrow Wilson.

Wilson listened politely, but he did little. Lindsey and his party then went to New York City, hoping to meet with John D. Rockefeller Jr. He refused. In a May 22, 1914, letter, Lindsey lashed John Jr.: "Violence produces violence. The silent, but most terrific of all violence is promoted by you and the system you stand for. It is bound to provoke the explosive kind of violence that we have faced in our state and other states."

For helping to focus the national spotlight on Ludlow, Lindsey paid a price. Coloradans whose fortunes flowed from King Coal, Coloradans fearful that labor unions would cut into their profits, and Coloradans loyal to the state militia came, if they had not done so already, to see Lindsey as their enemy. Philip S. Van Cise, a National Guard captain who participated in the board of inquiry that investigated the Ludlow killings, objected to Lindsey's characterization of the inquiry's report as a "huge joke." Van Cise, once a supporter of Lindsey, wrote him on June 11, 1914, asking, "Did you ever consider that possibly in all scrapes there are two sides to the question, and that all the right is not on one side?"

REFORM EBBS

As Lindsey's opponents waxed hot, the fires of progressive reform that sustained him cooled. Thomas M. Patterson, who normally had supported Lindsey, sold the *Rocky Mountain News* in 1913 and died in 1916. Edward P. Costigan, a brilliant orator and the darling of Colorado reformers, failed in his 1912 and 1914 bids as the Progressive Party's candidate for the Colorado governorship, after which he left the state for a long tenure as a Federal Trade commissioner in Washington, D.C. Another Lindsey ally, journalist George Creel, also decamped Denver for Washington during World War I to head the Office of War Information, the U.S. government's propaganda arm. Former governor John F. Shafroth went to the U.S. Senate in 1913 where he served until 1919. His successor in the Senate, Lawrence C. Phipps, was a multimillionaire who Lindsey described as "one of my bitterest enemies."[17]

In 1916, Denver scuttled the commission government and brought back its strong mayor system and its old boss mayor, cigar-chomping Robert W. Speer. Beholden to the "interests," Speer repaid them handsomely by helping engineer the city's 1918 purchase of the Denver Union Water Company for more than $13 million. Two years later, strikebreakers hired by the Denver Tramway Company killed seven people, one of them sixteen years old and all of them innocent bystanders. None of the trigger-happy strikebreakers was prosecuted, but District Judge Greeley Whitford ordered labor leaders to jail. Memories of Ludlow bedeviled Denver as the beast stirred.

Surprisingly, the kids' judge survived for a time. Poor people whose children got in trouble and middle-class and wealthy people whose children also got in trouble appreciated his humanity. Election after election he found strong support from voters in the Jewish precincts along West Colfax Avenue and in other poor areas of city where Irish, Italians, and other immigrants concentrated. Such support became a liability in the early 1920s when Denver fell under the spell of the Ku Klux Klan.

KU KLUX KLAN

Originally conceived in the post–Civil War South to keep African Americans "in their place," the Klan reinvented itself in 1915 as an organization dedicated to "100 percent Americanism" and to the proposition that African Americans, Jews, Roman Catholics, and various immigrant groups endangered the republic. Spreading from its Southern base, the Klan began recruiting in Denver in 1921. Within a couple years, the hooded empire had attracted thousands of men, women, and even children. In *The Dangerous Life*, which he wrote with Reuben Borough in 1931, Lindsey recalled talking with a youngster proud of his membership in the "Juniors." Lindsey asked, "Junior what?" The boy replied, "Junior K.K.K. . . . . We are out to clean up the Micks and the Sheenies."[18]

The Klan soon flexed its political muscle. In early August 1924, Mayor Benjamin F. Stapleton, a Klan member and heir to Speer's political machine, pledged, "I will work with the Klan and for the Klan in the upcoming election, heart and soul."[19] In November's statewide elections, the Klan endorsed Clarence Morley for governor, Rice Means for U.S. senator, William Louis Boatright for attorney general, and John T. Adams for the Colorado Supreme Court. All won.

Lindsey himself might have seemed a likely recruit for the Klan. His father, Landy, had been a Confederate captain in the Civil War. Ben was born in Jackson, Tennessee, in 1869, three years after the original Klan was founded at Pulaski in the same state, and he spent part of his boyhood in the South. Although raised for a time as a Roman Catholic, he found that his grandparents, with whom he lived for a few years, preferred that he become a Southern Baptist, a denomination he eventually shed to become a Methodist.

If his background gently bent him toward the Klan, his sympathies strongly pulled him in the opposite direction. As he explained in *The Dangerous Life*, he could not abide "Negroes run out of town,

Jewish merchants boycotted, Catholics in fear of their lives. Beatings, kidnapings [*sic*], tar and feathers—all the vicious instrumentalities of mob 'justice.' "[20] In a November 12, 1924, letter to journalist William Allen White, Lindsey reported that his friends urged him to mute his criticism of the Klan in order to dampen their opposition to him. "But, I felt that I had to hit this thing and hit it as hard as I could because it was, to my mind, the most infamous, unAmerican, dangerous thing that has appeared in my time."

With courage bordering on recklessness Lindsey waged war: "I fought the klan [*sic*] with all the power that was in me. I boldly asserted that its members were more like sadistic savages than followers of the great teacher they claimed to represent." When he reminded audiences that Christ was a Jew, Klan adherents would "rise by the scores and even hundreds and march out of the audience."[21]

LINDSEY OUSTED FROM THE JUVENILE COURT

In 1924, the Klan, at the height of its power, targeted Lindsey, who was running for reelection to the Juvenile Court. Seeing in the attack the claw of the beast, he wrote his old ally Edward P. Costigan on August 16, 1924, to report that Lawrence C. Phipps, then seeking reelection to the U.S. Senate, "is tied up here with the Ku Klux Klan." He added, "[A]t present the Ku Klux Klan has the entire sympathy of the privileged interests and is being used right and left for their purpose in robbing the people."

Klan tactics ranged from spreading a lie that Henrietta Lindsey and her friend Ruth Vincent had been bounced out of Baur's Restaurant for smoking to dirty tricks at Lindsey campaign events. In a November 3 letter to journalist Wainwright Evans, the judge described raucous meetings:

> I have been speaking on an average of from three to seven times a night, depending on how many meetings I can make and how big a fight I have getting through the barrage set up by the Kluxers' hoodlums who pursue us with their savagery. . . . At one meeting wild, fanatical women like maniacs hissed in my

face, "You dirty cur, etc." All this, after a lifetime of struggle to get maternity laws, mothers' compensation laws, and fifty other laws for the protection of women and children, to be called a dirty cur. I paused long enough to ask one of these infuriated creatures why she called me a dirty cur. With a demonical laugh, she screamed, "You are not 100% American. You are against the Klan."

Surviving harassment by "infuriated creatures," Lindsey seemingly won the November 1924 election, defeating Klan candidate Royal R. Graham by little more than a hundred votes.[22] Graham challenged the outcome. A Denver court reviewed the complaint and declared Lindsey the winner. Graham, accused of fraud in another matter, committed suicide in 1925, but his widow kept the case alive by appealing to the Colorado Supreme Court. In late January 1927, the justices held Lindsey's election invalid and ordered him to pay Graham's widow the salary her dead husband would have collected had he taken office. Appeals delayed Lindsey's ouster, but by the end of June 1927, he was no longer juvenile judge.

Before he left office, Lindsey, fearing that his confidential notes would fall into Klan hands, took his files to his home at 1343 Ogden Street where he, Henrietta, and friends Ruth Vincent and Josephine Roche shredded the documents. In a vacant lot near Thirteenth Avenue and Umatilla Street, he doused the papers with gasoline and incinerated the tattered remains of the sins of many young people.[23] He also apparently arranged for many court employees to depart with him, temporarily leaving the court in chaos.

LINDSEY DISBARRED

The judge's flaming exit angered Philip S. Van Cise, a Denver district attorney in the early 1920s who attacked organized crime and battled the Klan—a man Lindsey praised in a September 24, 1924, letter to William Allen White as "the finest District Attorney in the history of Denver." Not withstanding Lindsey's admiration for Van Cise and their common fight against the Klan, there were rifts between them dating back to the aftermath of the Ludlow Massacre when Van Cise bridled at Lindsey's attacks on the National Guard and continuing into the 1920s when Lindsey resisted Van Cise's efforts to limit the jurisdiction of Lindsey's court.

Van Cise's complaint against Lindsey for destroying records came to nothing. Many people rejoiced knowing that the missteps of their sons, daughters, and themselves would not fall into Klan hands. Not easily bested, Van Cise found a more effective way to rid Colorado of the ex-judge.

Helen Ellwood Stokes, a longtime friend of Lindsey, was the estranged wife of W.E.D. Stokes, a wealthy businessman who on his death in 1926 left nothing to his and Helen's two children. She contested the will and asked Lindsey to appear on her children's behalf at a New York probate court hearing. He did and he facilitated a settlement that satisfied Helen, her children, and Stokes's son by an earlier marriage. For his help, Helen gave Ben $37,500 and Samuel Untermyer, her attorney, sent him $10,000.

Colorado law stated, "The Judge of the Juvenile Court . . . shall receive no other compensation for his services as such judge save the salary herein provided; nor shall he act as attorney or counselor at law." Another statute provided, "A judge of a court of record shall not act as attorney or counsel in any court or any cause."[24]

Van Cise, contending that Lindsey had violated the Colorado statutes, asked the Colorado Bar Association to initiate action to disbar Lindsey. Lindsey contended that his services in New York, where he was not an attorney licensed to practice law, were not those of an attorney but of a mediator and that Stokes and Untermyer had, as they themselves said, given him a gift, not paid a fee. He also pointed out that before he accepted the money he had asked Denver judge George Luxford about the propriety of doing so and that Luxford had assured Lindsey that it was proper and had signed the order authorizing the payment. Luxford confirmed that account. Moreover, Lindsey was able to argue that since the Supreme Court in 1925 had invalidated his 1924 election to the Juvenile Court judgeship, he could not be considered to have been a judge when he assisted Mrs. Stokes in 1926.

The Bar Association disagreed. It recommended that Colorado attorney general William Louis Boatright request the state Supreme Court to rebuke Lindsey. Boatright sailed farther. He asked the high court to disbar Lindsey, thereby keeping him from practicing law. Lindsey's attorneys—Morrison Shafroth, son of Governor John F. Shafroth, and Philip Hornbein Sr.—defended the ex-judge, arguing in part that Van Cise harbored a grudge against Lindsey.

Some members of the Supreme Court probably winced at the grudge argument for they risked the same criticism if they ruled against Lindsey. For years, the little judge had roasted big judges. He devoted an entire chapter in *The Beast* to exposing connections between corporations and the Colorado Supreme Court. For more than five years, he battled the state Supreme Court as he resisted its order for him to testify in a murder case that would have forced him to violate the confidence of a juvenile. He lost the battle, but he won the public relations war as newsboys across the country collected pennies to pay the fine imposed on the kids' judge who would not snitch.

Lindsey and his supporters could fault the Supreme Court's objectivity on other grounds. Justice John T. Adams had been elected with Klan help and Chief Justice Greeley Whitford, anti-union to the bone, had long been at odds with pro-union Lindsey.[25] Such considerations did not deter the justices. On December 9, 1929, they disbarred Lindsey. Lincoln Steffens wrote him on December 22, "The Beast has got you."

Although sympathetic to Lindsey, the *Rocky Mountain News* admitted that "to say the least he was exceedingly indiscreet" in accepting money from Stokes and Untermyer. Yet the *News* thought the high court had gone too far. "He was always a poor man, struggling against debt fighting to raise funds for his numerous election campaigns. . . . He didn't graft. He refused to take advantage of the intimate files of his court, of the favors, which he might have received and the obligations that many people owed him." The *News* concluded: "At least some charity could have been shown him. His record of service entitled him to that."[26]

The Denver Post, which twenty years earlier had called Lindsey a "withered soul," defended him more strongly than the *News* did. Arguing that "political animus was behind the charges which were filed against Lindsey," *The Post* accused the legal establishment of selectively targeting the ex-judge. "The bar association must know of lawyers of this state who have as much moral character as wolves. Why doesn't it move to disbar them? If the Supreme Court should disbar every lawyer who has violated a law of this state, there wouldn't be enough attorneys left to wad a shotgun."[27]

Lindsey explained his disbarment in a February 12, 1930, letter to an old acquaintance, Lawrence Richey, confidential secretary to Herbert Hoover, then president of the United States. Back in 1909, Richey had helped John O'Hara Cosgrave investigate the truth of the allegations in "The Beast and the Jungle" before the magazine series was published. After it was published, Richey had assisted Lindsey in successfully fighting a libel suit. "Every daily newspaper in Denver is on my side, and our powerful *Denver Post*, the largest newspaper in the inter-mountain states, is not only with me, but its owner has declared that the action of the Supreme Court against me is one of the most brutal and outrageous cases of injustice in the history of the state."

Newspaper outrage had no immediate effect on the Supreme Court, although it may have contributed to the November 1930 defeat of Justice Whitford. In 1933, Lindsey—supported by a list of luminaries including one of Colorado's U.S. senators, Edward P. Costigan—asked the court to lift the disbarment. The court refused, citing Lindsey's unwillingness to apologize for saying that the 1929 action had been politically motivated. "Not Justice, But Wounded Vanity," ran a headline in the *Rocky Mountain News* as the wounded justices stuck to their guns.[28] Two years later, on November 25, 1935, Lindsey's sixty-sixth birthday, the court reinstated him to the Colorado bar with no apology asked of him, nor any given.

CALIFORNIA

Lindsey had won a moral victory, but his reinstatement was of limited value to him because he had been living in California since the early 1930s. His friends and fellow muckrakers Upton Sinclair and Lincoln Steffens lived there. There he could practice law because he had been admitted to the California bar despite objections from his Colorado enemies. However, before he permanently left Denver, he again won national attention by wrestling with a bishop.

In *The Companionate Marriage* (1927), which he coauthored with Wainwright Evans, Lindsey advocated birth control and, in certain cases, no-fault divorce. Those ideas cost him much of the support he had enjoyed from Roman Catholics and some other denominations, but they also brought him speaking invitations. While lecturing in New York City in late 1930 he learned that Episcopal bishop William T. Manning intended to attack his views in a sermon slated for Sunday, December 7, 1930.

Ben attended church that Sunday at the cavernous Cathedral of St. John the Divine. Manning spoke for most of an hour. Lindsey listened, glared, and took notes. When the prelate finished and continued with the service, Lindsey added a few feet to his height by leaping on a table near the pulpit. "'Bishop Manning,' I cried . . . 'you have falsely represented me. If this is not a house of justice, it is not a house of God. I ask for five minutes to answer your unjust attack.'"[29]

He did not get those five minutes. As he remembered the scene, all hell broke loose in church. "I found myself being roughly shoved by ushers down a side aisle. . . . Blows rained upon me—about my head, my back, and legs. Three thousand men and women in the fashionable congregation were in an uproar. As I was briskly catapulted toward an exit, hostile eyes glared at me, angry voices pierced the tumult: 'Kick him . . . punch him . . . throw him out.'" Police who "conducted him from the savagery of the bishop's cathedral to the safety of a jail cell" saved him.[30]

Had it been London in 1555 or Salem, Massachusetts, in 1692, he might have been burned at the stake or hanged. As it was New York in

1930, a magistrate dismissed the complaint against the former judge. Neither Manning nor Manhattan, unlike Denver, wanted a martyr.

His "banning by Manning" renewed interest in two of Lindsey's 1920s books—*Revolt of Modern Youth* and *The Companionate Marriage*, both coauthored by Wainwright Evans. However, the Manning blow up did little to bolster *The Dangerous Life*, published in 1931. Reuben Borough, a Los Angeles newspaperman who came to Denver to serve as co-author, tried to organize Lindsey's free-flowing thoughts. "I am bewildered by his conflicting moods—his elations, doubts, despairs, his driving and at times almost hysterical bursts of energy."[31] Despite Borough's work and Lindsey's energy, *The Dangerous Life*, a book of less literary merit than *The Beast*, sold poorly in depression-ridden America.

CALIFORNIA YEARS

In Los Angeles, Lindsey fished for a government job. Edward P. Costigan, who had toiled with Lindsey in the reform vineyard in the days of *The Beast*, was elected to the U.S. Senate in 1930. After Franklin D. Roosevelt became president in 1933, Oscar L. Chapman, who had served Lindsey's court as a probation officer, landed a platinum-plated post as Assistant Secretary of the Interior. Josephine Roche, a Lindsey protégé and friend, became Assistant Secretary of the Treasury, making her the second-highest-ranking woman in Roosevelt's first administration. For the controversial Ben Lindsey, the pickings were slimmer. Not until 1934 did he secure a second-tier position in California as an attorney with the National Recovery Administration, a New Deal agency.

That same year Upton Sinclair rescued Lindsey from the bowels of bureaucracy. Running for California governor on the End Poverty in California (EPIC) platform, Sinclair built a political movement that he used to help elect Lindsey to the Superior Court of the County of Los Angeles. There Ben chafed as his fellow judges, perhaps fearing his penchant for the limelight, refused to let him hear juvenile cases. His greatest success came in 1939 when the California legislature, in large measure because of his lobbying, created a conciliation process in an attempt to save troubled marriages. His peers allowed him to sit on the Conciliation Court. Ben Lindsey, faulted for backing easy divorce in *The Companionate Marriage*, spent the last years of his life trying to patch up marriages.

The Denver Juvenile Court, where the kids' judge's heart remained, enjoyed thirty-three years of service (1940–1973) from Phillip B. Gilliam, a jurist sensitive to Lindsey's legacy. Gilliam, a judge far less controversial than was Lindsey, was honored for his work when Denver's principal juvenile detention facility at Twenty-Eighth Avenue and Downing Street was named for him. At other times, however, the court became a political football. In a 1970 campaign reminiscent of some Lindsey had faced, voters removed Judge H. Ted Rubin from the court because his support for rehabilitation and due process for juveniles angered those anxious to get tough on crime.

DEATH AND REPUTATION

Still working at age seventy-three, Lindsey died in Los Angeles of a massive heart attack on March 26, 1943. President Franklin D. Roosevelt sent a tribute to Henrietta:

> Among Ben Lindsey's accomplished tasks were the development of our modern juvenile court system and a constructive approach to the whole problem of juvenile delinquency. He is remembered by thousands of Americans who today have reason to feel a direct, personal indebtedness. The memory of Ben Lindsey is best honored in the name of youth. In so honoring him, I speak for those young Americans who now face supreme sacrifice that the ideals of this nation might live.[32]

Praise from Franklin Delano Roosevelt did nothing to redeem Lindsey in the eyes of his Colorado detractors. Samuel Johnson, a local jurist, wrote of Lindsey in 1960: "He had a super ego and there was no one that he acknowledged as his equal in any undertaking. . . . I doubt if there ever lived a man who thought more of himself and his own ideas than Lindsey."[33] In 1966, Charles Larsen, a historian at Mills College then writing a biography of Lindsey, talked with an elderly Denver attorney who asked Larsen, "How could a little guy have been such a big son of a bitch?"[34]

Even some of his fans found the judge difficult. William L. Chenery, once a *Rocky Mountain News* editor and a Lindsey supporter, recalled: "A very skillful journalist, Harvey O'Higgins, wrote Judge Lindsey's story, or what Judge Lindsey thought was his story after its publication. Having assumed the role that O'Higgins had picked for him, Lindsey was in a fight all the rest of his life. . . . The fascination of a newspaper headline or the applause of an audience is the undoing of many politicians. Ben Lindsey was one of them."[35]

Chenery's and Johnson's assessments contain elements of truth. Lindsey sought publicity that he adroitly used to advance his causes. Was his love of the limelight a reprehensible character flaw, or merely his understandable delight in recognition of a job well done? The charitably minded observer might excuse the judge for seeking publicity. It is more difficult to understand why Lindsey sometimes seemed to go out of his way to make enemies. For example, in a September 13, 1924, letter to Colorado governor William Sweet, one of Lindsey's allies, he wrote, "I think you one of the ablest governors we have ever had . . . but I shall always know you for what you are personally—a very selfish, egotistical man who finds in the cause you are working for a means of adding to a kind of glory that I am glad that some men seek because it is a sort of enlightened selfishness from which we all profit." Ironically, Lindsey's criticism of Sweet could easily have been applied to Lindsey.

Morrison Shafroth provided additional insight into the judge's character. Attorney Shafroth represented both Lindsey and Margaret Tobin Brown, the well-known survivor of the 1912 *Titanic* sinking. Sometime in the early 1920s, Shafroth and his wife, Abby, invited the Lindseys and Mrs. Brown to dinner. "Mrs. Shafroth and I had a wager as to which one would out-talk the other. I was betting on Mrs. Brown to recount her story of the sinking of the *Titanic*, which she told us many times. Mrs. Shafroth was betting on Judge Lindsey who was a dramatic story teller." Shafroth reported that after dinner as they gathered around the fireplace, Mrs. Brown spent her time knitting a tie—"she always carried her knitting and was always knitting"—while Lindsey, who had recently seen some New York plays, "not only told us about the plays but acted them out." Mrs. Brown "didn't get a word in edgewise."[36]

Like a daydreaming ten-year-old, Ben participated in a dime-novel drama in which he played all the heroic parts. For the little judge the struggle against the beast was not simply an allegory; it was a reality that sustained him, even as it consumed him.

ACCOMPLISHMENTS

Whatever his faults may have been, Lindsey's accomplishments remain. Theodore Roosevelt's praise for the judge's crusade against political corruption and his effectiveness in promoting "the moral awakening of our people" was not a hollow compliment.[37] Lindsey and O'Higgins's *The Beast* remains one of the most important works of twentieth-century muckraking. They did not slay the beast. Denver did not formally limit its mayors' ability to fill city jobs through political patronage until the 1950s, some years after interminable Benjamin F. Stapleton left the mayor's office in 1947. Still, as a milestone along the long and bumpy road of progressive reform in the United States, *The Beast* endures.

Even more importantly, as Franklin Roosevelt recognized, Lindsey's advocacy of juvenile courts did much to change the way Americans treated wayward young people. He was not the nation's first juvenile court judge and he was not the only jurist who valued rehabilitation more than punishment. However, through numerous nationally circulated articles and tireless lecturing across the country, Lindsey, more than any other, championed and sold the ideals of rehabilitation and merciful juvenile justice. The *Rocky Mountain News* aptly summarized his career on March 27, 1943, the day after he died. "Judge Lindsey's character was full of paradoxes. The friendliest of men, he made many bitter enemies. Denied children of his own, he became as he loved to be called, the 'the kids' jedge [*sic*],' who accomplished more for the children of America than has any other American. He knew spectacular triumphs and bitter humiliations—and, at last, wore himself out in the cause he loved."

To his muckraking and juvenile justice triumphs should be added a victory that at the time seemed to be a defeat. In 1927, it appeared that his enemies had crushed him by ousting him from office. Had he compromised with the Klan he might have retained his judgeship and avoided disbarment. Yet he did not back down, despite sometimes lukewarm support from those he was trying to protect.

During the 1924 election, for example, Lindsey had asked Samuel Untermyer, later Stokes's attorney who was an influential New York attorney and a leader in the Jewish community, for help in raising campaign money. Untermyer replied on September 15, 1924, "Strange to say, the Jews are keeping out of this [KKK] controversy as far as it is possible for them to do so. They feel that the issue is at best transitory and will die of its own inequity and unAmericanism [*sic*]."

In the mid-twentieth century, such dodging and inaction became increasingly unacceptable. The World War II concentration camp deaths of millions of Jews and the recognition of the evils of segregation in the United States alerted many people to the horrors of racism and made them realize that the Ku Klux Klan was more than a transitory gathering of banal bigots in bedsheets. Those who courageously resisted the Klan, people such as Ben Lindsey and Philip Van Cise, eventually won more than elections. In a nation looking for heroes, Lindsey's defeats became badges of honor, his crusades and his sacrifices worthy of remembrance.

A BELATED MEMORIAL FOR BEN

Denver has never blushed at memorializing its plutocrats, politicians, and parvenus. Boulevard names recall Lindsey's opponents Mayor Robert W. Speer and Governor Henry A. Buchtel. The Denver Landmark Preservation Commission has landmarked and the Colorado

Historical Society maintains the home of William Gray Evans, once the "Napoleon Bill" of local politics. The powerful saw to it that David Moffat, a Goliath among the plutocrats Lindsey fought, had his name put on a great railroad tunnel. Mayor Benjamin F. Stapleton had an airport named for him. Margaret "Unsinkable Molly" Brown's home became a much-visited museum. Lawrence C. Phipps, one of Ben's "bitterest enemies," is remembered at the University of Denver's Phipps Conference Center and at the Denver Museum of Nature and Science's Phipps IMAX Theater, facilities that sprang from Phipps family donations. For a century, Walter Scott Cheesman, another of the nabobs Lindsey skewered, has been blessed, at the Cheesman family's expense, with the city's most beautiful memorial, a Grecian temple in a large park named for Cheesman.

The honors the city has extended to its elite have not often been given to its boat shakers, reformers, and religious and labor leaders. In the Mile High City, ancient grudges die hard, dead gadflies are not deemed good, and those who cannot finance their own memorials often go without.

Captain Silas Soule, who refused to take part in the 1864 Sand Creek Massacre of Cheyenne and Arapahoe Indians, is barely remembered. The once-famous union organizer, William D. "Big Bill" Haywood, buried in honor in Moscow's Red Square, ranks no plaque in Denver where he lived. Edward P. Costigan, John F. Shafroth, and Josephine Roche, towers of reform in the early part of the twentieth century, have been similarly slighted.

Practically no one recalls Ben J. Salmon, whose resistance to the World War I draft won him a penitentiary sentence.[38] Nothing except a modest tombstone at Fairmount Cemetery reminds Denverites of the Reverend Myron Reed, a popular proponent of the social gospel in the 1880s and 1890s, who had the temerity to assert, "[T]he society that permits such deadly parallels as the gorged few and the hungry many cannot last."[39]

For Lindsey there has been, until recently, only a token remembrance, a small bust of the bespectacled judge that Henrietta gave to the Juvenile Court. Historian Phil Goodstein found it in 2003, "broken and stashed in an administrator's office."[40]

Henrietta returned to Denver sometime in the 1940s, bearing a portion of Ben's ashes, which she sprinkled on the site of the old county courthouse near Sixteenth Street and Tremont Place. Even then, the courthouse, torn down in 1933, was vanishing from the city's collective memory. Three years after Lindsey died, former Denver journalist Gene Fowler wrote, "There is no monument to Judge Ben B. Lindsey in the City of Denver. He needs none."[41]

What was true in 1946 became less so as the twentieth century stumbled toward the twenty-first. Like the courthouse where he worked for more than a quarter century, Lindsey faded away. Although featured in a 1965 television drama as part of the "Profiles in Courage" series, his life, diffuse as his dust, was largely forgotten or, at best, scattered in history books.

On March 16, 2009, the Denver City Council retrieved Lindsey's memory from the dustbin of history by naming the city's new courthouse after him and James Flanigan, the first African American to serve as a Denver district judge. At the same time, the city council named the nearby jail after John Simonet, a retired corrections director, and three members of the Van Cise family, including Philip Van Cise, Lindsey's nemesis. Such are the ways of Denver, city of *The Beast*, city of Ben Lindsey.

NOTES

Dated letters to or from Lindsey mentioned in the text with no endnote superscripts given are from the Lindsey Papers, Library of Congress. The author thanks Metropolitan State College of Denver for travel assistance that allowed him to do some research in the Lindsey Papers. Newspapers are often mentioned with their dates in the text, thereby eliminating the need for additional endnotes. In these notes the first (1910) edition of *The Beast* is cited. Page numbers in this University Press of Colorado 2009 reprint of the 1910 edition differ from that edition because of different-sized pages and other factors. The notes use abbreviated citations for books that have full publication information given in the sources section below.

1. *The Denver Post*, September 19, 1909.

2. Ben B. Lindsey, *The Rule of Plutocracy in Colorado: A Retrospect and a Warning* (Denver: Hicks Print House, 1908), 67. In Ben B. Lindsey and Harvey J. O'Higgins's *The Beast* (New York: Doubleday, Page & Company, 1910), 304, Lindsey acknowledged the aid of Ellis Meredith in writing *Plutocracy.* Although Lindsey had 30,000 copies printed, only a few have survived in library collections. In *Plutocracy* and in at least one printing of *The Beast*, Lindsey's name is misspelled as "Lindsay."

3. Upton Sinclair, *Autobiography of Upton Sinclair* (New York: Harcourt, Brace & World, 1962), 148.

4. *The Denver Post*, September 19, 1909.

5. *Rocky Mountain News*, September 19, 1909.

6. *Rocky Mountain News*, September 19, 1909.

7. *The Denver Post*, September 19, 1909.

8. *The Denver Post*, September 19, 1909.

9. Lindsey and O'Higgins, *The Beast*, 22.

10. Lindsey and O'Higgins, *The Beast*, 260–261.

11. Charles Larsen, *The Good Fight: The Life and Times of Ben B. Lindsey* (Chicago: Quadrangle Books, 1972), 14. Larsen learned of Lindsey's father's suicide from Henrietta Lindsey, Lindsey's widow, many years after the judge's death.

12. *Rocky Mountain News*, May 17, 1910.

13. Larsen, *The Good Fight*, 119–120.

14. Lindsey to E. A. Van Valkenburg, September 12, 1913, Lindsey Papers, Library of Congress.

15. Larsen, *The Good Fight*, viii.

16. Typescript of Upton Sinclair speech, May 15, 1914, in Lindsey Papers, Library of Congress.

17. Lindsey to Jane Addams, June 5, 1914, Lindsey Papers, Library of Congress.

18. Benjamin Barr Lindsey and Reuben Borough, *The Dangerous Life* (New York: Horace Liveright, 1931, reprinted in 1974 by Arno Press), 390.

19. Robert A. Goldberg, *Hooded Empire: The Ku Klux Klan in Colorado* (Urbana: University of Illinois Press, 1981), 1, quoting *The Denver Post*, August 8, 1924.

20. Lindsey and Borough, *The Dangerous Life*, 389.

21. Lindsey and Borough, *The Dangerous Life*, 393.

22. Phil Goodstein, in *In the Shadow of the Klan: When the KKK Ruled Denver, 1920–1926* (Denver: New Social Publications, 2006), 420, explains the complexities of counting the votes.

23. Lindsey and Borough, *The Dangerous Life*, 398.

24. Quoted in Larsen, *The Good Fight*, 210.

25. Carl Abbott, Stephen J. Leonard, and Thomas J. Noel, *Colorado: A History of the Centennial State*, 4th ed. (Boulder: University Press of Colorado, 2005), 275.

26. *Rocky Mountain News*, December 11, 1929.

27. *The Denver Post*, December 10, 1929.

28. Larsen, *The Good Fight*, 228.

29. Lindsey and Borough, *The Dangerous Life*, 349–350.

30. Lindsey and Borough, *The Dangerous Life*, 345, 414.

31. Reuben Borough, "The Little Judge," *Colorado Quarterly* (Spring 1968): 379.

32. Larsen, *The Good Fight*, 268–269

33. Samuel Wallace Johnson, *Autobiography* (Denver: Big Mountain Press, 1960), 155.

34. Larsen, *The Good Fight*, 200.

35. William L. Chenery, *So It Seemed* (New York: Harcourt Brace, 1952), 65.

36. Morrison Shafroth, "Recollections in Re Judge Benjamin Barr Lindsey," undated copy of a manuscript sent to Thomas J. Noel, August 10, 1993, by Frank H. Shafroth, Morrison's son.

37. Theodore Roosevelt to Ben Lindsey, September 18, 1913, Lindsey Papers, Library of Congress.

38. Goodstein, *In the Shadow of the Klan*, 428–433.

39. Quoted in Leonard and Noel, *Denver from Mining Camp to Metropolis*, 109.

40. Goodstein, *In the Shadow of the Klan*, 423.

41. Gene Fowler, *A Solo in Tom-Toms* (New York: The Viking Press, 1946), 167.

SOURCES

Lindsey's many accomplishments make him a difficult subject for a short biographical sketch such as the above. It skips or slights parts of his life such as his quixotic 1915 journey on Henry Ford's peace ship, his pacifism that morphed into war support, his post–World War I relief work, his attack on Denver oilman Henry Blackmer for flaunting prohibition laws, his role in reexamining sexual mores, his Hollywood work, and his advocating for the "flaming youth" of the 1920s. Fortunately, those who want to learn more can do so by reading Charles E. Larsen's *The Good Fight: The Life and Times of Ben B. Lindsey* (Chicago: Quadrangle Books, 1972), a first-rate biography that contains a useful bibliography. That book has provided much of the factual information in the above account.

Among Larsen's sources, Frances Anne Huber's detailed 1963 University of Michigan dissertation, "The Progressive Career of Ben B. Lindsey, 1900–1920," is one of the best. Twenty-first-century scholarship of value to Lindsey watchers includes Rebecca L. Davis's " 'Not Marriage at All, but Simple Harlotry': The Companionate Marriage Controversy," *Journal of American History* (March 2008): 1137–1163, and Judith Sealander's *The Failed Century of the Child: Governing America's Young in the Twentieth Century* (Cambridge: Cambridge University Press, 2003), which faults the juvenile court movement for failing to live up to its promises.

Phil Goodstein, who continues Lindsey's fight against the beast, treats the judge and his times in *Robert Speer's Denver, 1904–1920* and in *In the Shadow of the Klan: When the KKK Ruled Denver, 1920–1926* (Denver: New Social Publications, 2004 and 2006). Robert A. Goldberg's splendid *Hooded Empire: The Ku Klux Klan in Colorado* (Urbana: University of Illinois Press, 1981) also provides context and material on Lindsey. Stephen J. Leonard and Thomas J. Noel's *Denver: From Mining Camp to Metropolis* (Niwot: University Press of Colorado, 1990) devotes three chapters to the 1900–1930 period in Denver's history.

Fred Greenbaum's *Fighting Progressive: A Biography of Edward P. Costigan* (Washington, D.C.: Public Affairs Press, 1971), Sybil Downing and Robert T. Smith's *Thomas M. Patterson: Colorado Crusader for Change* (Niwot: University Press of Colorado, 1995), Stephen J. Leonard, Thomas J. Noel, and Donald L. Walker Jr.'s *Honest John Shafroth: A*

Colorado Reformer (Denver: Colorado Historical Society, 2003), and Elinor M. McGinn's *A Wide-Awake Woman: Josephine Roche in the Era of Reform* (Denver: Colorado Historical Society, 2002) all shed light on early twentieth-century reform in Denver and Colorado.

The Lindsey papers, some 95,000 items, are at the Library of Congress. The Colorado Historical Society and the Denver Public Library house small Lindsey collections. Denver Juvenile Court's Web site features biographies of many of the court's judges, including Lindsey, Phillip B. Gilliam, and H. Ted Rubin.

This reprint of *The Beast* on its hundredth anniversary is a welcome addition to the University Press of Colorado's Timberline Books, a collection of important new works and significant classics relating to Colorado.

STEPHEN J. LEONARD
COEDITOR, TIMBERLINE BOOKS

INTRODUCTION

J UDGE LINDSEY IS KNOWN TO THE WORLD at large for
his work in the Juvenile Court of Denver; and, to his little courtroom there, come Children Society agents from all parts of the
states, visitors from England, officers from Germany, and government officials sent from Sweden, Austria, France and Japan to study
his laws and learn his methods. But to himself, to Denver, to his
friends, and—most of all—to his enemies, his famous Juvenile Court
is only an incident, a side issue, a small detail in the man's amazing
career. For years he has been engaged in a fight of which the founding
of his Juvenile Court was only the merest skirmish.

It is a fight that has carried him into politics to find both political parties against him. It has been carried on without the consistent
support of any newspaper, and with now one, now the other, and at
times all the party organs in Denver cartooning and attacking him.
The thieves, the gamblers, the saloon keepers and the prostitutes

have been cheered on against him. There have been times when even the churches have been afraid to aid him. The men of wealth—the heads of the street railway, the telephone company, the gas and electric company, the water company, and most of the other Denver corporations and combinations of finance—have made it their particular ambition and personal aim to beat him down and crush him out of public life. He has fought alone—at times absolutely alone. And he is still fighting!

He has been offered bribes that might buy a millionaire. He has been promised a career in politics, a fortune in law. He has been given the hope of worldly preferments that might seduce the highest ambition. When these have failed to win him, he has been threatened with all the punishments that the most unscrupulous power and the bitterest hate could conceive. To destroy his reputation, false affidavits have been sworn out by fallen women, accusing him of the lowest forms of vice. Attempts have been made to lure him to houses of ill-repute where men were lying in wait to expose him. The vilest stories about him have been circulated in venomous whispers from man to man and woman to woman. Friends have been frightened or bought or driven from him. His life has been threatened. Special laws have been introduced at the State Capitol against him. The Denver Chamber of Commerce has publicly branded him an enemy of the state. At times the very lights in his rooms at the Court House have been cut off—as the last and smallest annoyance of spite—and he has had to go to the corner drugstore at night and buy himself candles to continue his work!

And why? For what has he been fighting? What terrible thing has he sought to attain? Read his story. Here it is, as told by himself, without malice, in a sort of good-humoured indignation, with a smile that is sometimes bitter in spite of a patience that seems beyond words. It is a story that would be appalling if it were not for the fact that through it all he himself moves in the very figure of hope. It is a story that is true not only of Denver but of any other American city in which a Lindsey might appear. It is a story of the fight of one man against the conditions that threaten to make the American democracy a failure in government and a farce in the eyes of the world.

And it is a story of achievement. Without money, without powerful friends, without the dominating qualities of a personal popularity, this one man, in an obscure struggle, has written, upon the statute books of Colorado, laws that have been copied round the world. He has codified probate laws, purged election laws, and instituted a reform in criminal jurisprudence that is as revolutionary in our day as the teachings of Christ were in the "eye-for-an-eye" days of the Jews. The list of reforms he has obtained, charities founded, public improvements instituted and political steals balked, shows nearly a hundred items. He has obtained nothing for himself but the praise and support of some citizens of Denver, and the curse and enmity of others. The Reverend Henry Augustus Buchtel, Chancellor of the Denver University, and ex-Governor of the State of Colorado, in the year 1904, coupled his name with Christ's—no less!—and in the year 1907 called him, through the newspapers, "a nincompoop" and a "fice dog"! Those are the two crowns that have been offered him: a halo and a fool's cap. Which shall it be? To which is he entitled in the eyes of the democracy whose battle he is helping to fight?

Here follows the evidence. The choice shall be your own.

H.J.O'H.

THE
BEAST

THE BEAST

A MONG THE PICTURE PUZZLES of your childhood, there was one that showed a forest of entangled branches, tree trunks, fallen timber and dense underbrush; and the problem was, in that bewildering jumble of lines, to "find the cat." You traced the outline of a tail among the branches; you spied a paw in the crook of a tree limb; you picked out the barrel of the animal's body in the bark of a trunk; an ear pricked up from the underbrush; an eye stared from the bole of a fallen tree. And when, turning the picture on its side, you gathered those clues together in your eye, suddenly you saw—not the housecat you had expected, but the great "cat" of the jungle, crouching there, with such a threatening show of teeth that it almost frightened you into dropping the card. Do you remember that?

Well, there is hidden in our complicated American civilization just such a beast of the jungle. It is not a picture in a picture puzzle.

THE BEAST

It is a fact in a fact puzzle. There is no man among us, in any sort of public business or profession, who has not seen its tail or its paw concealed among the upper branches, or its eyes and ears watching and listening in the lowest underbrush and fallen timber of our life. It is there—waiting. To some it has appeared to be a house cat merely; and it has purred to them very soothingly, no doubt. But some have come upon its claws, and they have been rather more than scratched. And others have found its teeth, and they have been bitten—bitten to the soul. A few, who have watched it and stalked it carefully, know that it is, at the last, very like the dragon in the old fable of Greece, to whom some of the people were daily sacrificed. For it lives upon us. Yes, it lives upon us—upon the best of us as well as the worst—and the daughters of the poor are fed to it no less than the sons of the rich. If you save your life from it, it is at the price of your liberty, of your humanity, of your faith with your fellows, whom you must hand over to it, helpless. And if you attack it——!

I propose to tell, in this story of my own experience, what happens if you attack it. I propose to show the Beast from its tail to its nose-tip, and to show it as it is when it has ceased to purr and bares its teeth. I propose to mark its trail and name its victims, to warn you of where it lurks and how it springs. I do not hope to set you on in any organized assault upon it—for I have learned that this is too much to hope—but I trust that I shall be able to show you where the fight against it is being fought, so that you may at least recognize your own defenders and not be led to cry out against them and desert them—when the Beast turns polecat—and even, at the instigation of treachery, to come behind your champion and stab him in the back!

The Beast in the jungle! How it fights! Any man who truthfully writes the story of his campaigns against it will not write from any motives of vainglory; there is anything but glory to be gained in *that* war. And I do not write in any "holier than thou" attitude of mind, for I understand how I blundered into the hostility, and how the accidents of life and the simplicities of misunderstanding have brought me again and again into collision with the brute. But I write because men have said to me, "You are always crying 'Wolf! Wolf!' when we see no wolf. Show us. We're from Missouri. Don't preach. Tell us the facts." And I am going to tell the facts. They will be "personal." They *must* be personal. I shall have to write about myself, about my friends, about those who consider me their enemy. There is no other way. It is a condition of this whole struggle with the Beast that the man who fights it must come out into the open with his life, conspicuously and with the appearance of a strut—like some sort of blessed little hero-martyr—while it keeps modestly under cover and watches him and bides its time!

CHAPTER I

FINDING THE CAT

I CAME TO DENVER in the spring of 1880, at the age of eleven, as mildly inoffensive a small boy as ever left a farm—undersized and weakly, so that at the age of seventeen I commonly passed as twelve, and so unaccustomed to the sight of buildings that I thought the five-story Windsor Hotel a miracle of height and magnificence. I had been living with my maternal grandfather and aunt on a farm in Jackson, Tennessee, where I had been born; and I had come with my younger brother to join my parents, who had finally decided that Denver was to be their permanent home. The conductors on the trains had taken care of us, because my father was a railroad man, at the head of the telegraph system; and we had been entertained on the way by the stories of an old forty-niner, with a gray moustache, who told us how he had shot buffalo on those prairies where we now saw only antelope. I was not precocious; his stories interested me more than anything else on the journey; and I stared so hard at the old pioneer that I should recognize him now, I believe, if I saw him on the street.

My schooling was not peculiar; there was nothing "holier than thou" in my bringing up. My father, being a Roman Catholic convert from the Episcopalian Church, sent me to Notre Dame, Indiana, to be educated; and there, to be sure, I read the "Lives of the Saints," aspired to *be* a saint, and put pebbles in my small shoes to "mortify the flesh," because I was told that a good priest, Father Hudson—whom I all but worshipped—used to do so. But even at Notre Dame, and much more in Denver, I was homesick for the farm; and at last I was allowed to return to Jackson to be cared for by my Protestant relatives. They sent me to a Baptist school till I was seventeen. And when I was recalled to Denver, because of the failure of my father's health, I went to work to help earn for the household, with no strong attachment for any church and with no recognized membership in any.

I suppose there is no one who does not look back upon his past and wonder what he should have become in life if this or that crucial event had not occurred to set his destiny. It seems to me that if it had not been for the sudden death of my father I, too, might have found our jungle beast a domestic tabby, and have fed it its prey without realizing what I was about. I should have been a lawyer, I know; for I had had that ambition from my earliest boyhood, and I had been confirmed in it by my success in debating at school. (Once, at Notre Dame, I spoke for a full hour in successful defence of the proposition that Colorado was the "greatest state in the Union," and proved at least that I had a lawyer's "wind.") But I should probably have been a lawyer who has learned his pleasant theories of life in the colleges. And on the night that my father died, the crushing realities of poverty put out an awful and compelling hand on me, and my struggle with them began.

I was eighteen years old, the eldest of four children. I had been "writing proofs" in the Denver land office, for claimants who had filed on Government land; and I had saved $150 of my salary before my work there ceased. I found, after my father's death, that this $150 was all we had in the world, and $130 of it went for funeral expenses. His life had been insured for $15,000, and we believed that the premiums had all been paid, but we could not find the last receipt; the agent denied having received the payment; the policy had lapsed on the day before my father's death; and we got nothing. Our furniture had been mortgaged; we were allowed only enough of it to furnish a little house on Santa Fé Avenue; and later we moved to a cottage on lower West Colfax Avenue, in which Negroes have since lived.

I went to work at a salary of $10 a month, in a real estate office— as office boy—and carried a "route" of newspapers in the morning before the office opened, and did janitor work at night when it closed. After a month of that, I got a better place, as office boy, with a mining company, at a salary of $25 a month. And finally, my younger brother found work in a law office and I "swapped jobs" with him—because I wished to study law!

It was the office of Mr. R. D. Thompson, who still practises in Denver; and his example as an incorruptibly honest lawyer has been one of the best and strongest influences of my life.

I had that one ambition—to be a lawyer. Associated with it I seem to have had an unusual curiosity about politics. And where I got either the ambition or the curiosity, I have no idea. My father's mother was a Greenleaf,* and related to the author of "Greenleaf on Evidence," but my father himself had nothing of the legal mind. As a boy, living in Mississippi, he had joined the Confederate army when he was preparing for the University of Virginia, had attained the rank of captain, had become General Forrest's private secretary, and had written—or largely helped to write—General Forrest's autobiography. He was idealistic, enthusiastic, of an inventive genius, with a really remarkable command of English, and an absorbing love of books. My mother's father was a Barr, from the north of Ireland, a Scotch-Irish Presbyterian; her mother was a Woodfalk of Jackson County,

---

* A New England family, to which the poet Whittier was related.

Tennessee, a Methodist. The members of the family were practical, strong-willed, able men and women, but with no bent, that I know of, toward either law or politics.

And yet, one of the most vivid memories of my childhood in Jackson is of attending a political rally with my grandfather and hearing a Civil War veteran declaim against Republicans who "waved the bloody shirt"—a memory so strong that for years afterward I never saw a Republican without expecting to see the gory shirt on his back, and wondering vaguely why he was not in jail. When I came to Denver, where the Republicans were dominant, I felt myself in the land of the enemy. And when I "swapped" myself into Mr. Thompson's office, I was surprised to find that my employer, though a Republican from Pittsburg, was so human that one of the first things he did was to give me a suit of clothes. If there is anything more ridiculously dangerous than to blind a child's mind with such prejudices, I do not know what it is.

However, my own observations of what was going on about me were already opening my eyes. I had read, in the newspapers, of how the Denver Republicans won the elections by fraud—by ballot-box stuffing and what not—and I had followed one "Soapy" Smith on the streets, from precinct to precinct, with his gang of election thieves, and had seen them vote not once but five times openly. I had seen a young man, whom I knew, knocked down and arrested for "raising a disturbance" when he objected to "Soapy" Smith's proceeding; and the policeman who arrested him did it with a smile and a wink. When I came to Mr. Thompson to ask him how he, a Republican, could countenance such things, he assured me that much of what I had been reading and hearing of election frauds was a lie—the mere "whine" of the defeated party—and I saw that he believed what he said. I knew that he was an honest, upright man; and I was puzzled. What puzzled me still more was this: although the ministers in the churches and "prominent citizens" in all walks of life denounced the "election crooks" with the most laudable fervour, the election returns showed that the best people in the churches joined the worst people in the dives to vote the same ticket, and vote it "straight." And I was most of all puzzled to find that when the elections were over, the opposition newspaper ceased its scolding, the voice of ministerial denunciation died away, and the crimes of the election thieves were condoned and forgotten.

I was puzzled. I saw the jungle of vice and party prejudice, but I did not yet see "the Cat." I saw its ears and its eyes there in the underbrush, but I did not know what they were. I thought they were connected with the Republican party.

And then I came upon some more of the brute's anatomy. Members of the Legislature in Denver were accused of fraud in the purchase of state supplies, and—some months later—members of the city government were accused of committing similar frauds with the aid of civic officials and prominent business men. It was proved in court, for example, that bills for $3 had been raised to $300, that $200 had been paid for a bundle of hay worth $8, and $50 for a yard of cheesecloth worth five cents; barrels of ink had been bought for each legislator, though a pint would have sufficed; and an official of the Police Department was found guilty of conniving with a gambler named "Jim" Marshall to rob an express train. I watched the cases in court. I applauded at the meetings of leading citizens who denounced the grafters and passed resolutions in support of the candidates of the opposition party. I waited to see the criminals punished. And they were not punished. Their crimes were not denied. They were publicly denounced by the courts and by the investigating committees, but somehow, for reasons not clear, they all went scot-free, on appeals. Some mysterious power protected them, and I, in the boyish ardour of my ignorance, concluded that they were protected by the Republican "bloody shirt"—and I rushed into that (to me) great confederation of righteousness and all-decent government, the Democratic party.

It would be laughable to me now, if it were not so "sort of sad."

Meanwhile, I was busy about the office, copying letters, running errands, carrying books to and from the court rooms, reading law in the intervals, and at night scrubbing the floors. I was pale, thin, big-headed, with the body of an underfed child, and an ambition that kept me up half the night with Von Holst's "Constitutional Law," Walker's "American Law," or a sheepskin volume of Lawson's "Leading Cases in Equity." I was so mad to save every penny I could earn that instead of buying myself food for luncheon, I ate molasses and gingerbread that all but turned my stomach; and I was so eager to learn my law that I did not take my sleep when I could get it. The result was that I was stupid at my tasks, moody, melancholy, and so sensitive that my employer's natural dissatisfaction with my work put me into agonies of shame and despair of myself. I became, as the boys say, "dopy." I remember that one night, after I had scrubbed the floors of our offices, I took off the old trousers in which I had been working, hung them in a closet, and started home; and it was not until the cold wind struck my bare knees that I realized I was on the street in my shirt. Often, when I was given a brief to work up for Mr. Thompson, I would slave over it until the small hours of the morning and then, to his disgust— and my unspeakable mortification—find that my work was valueless, that I had not seized the fundamental points of the case, or that I had built all my arguments on some misapprehension of the law.

Worse than that, I was unhappy at home. Poverty was fraying us all out. If it was not exactly brutalizing us, it was warping us, breaking our healths and ruining our dispositions. My good mother—married out of a beautiful Southern home where she had lived a life that (as I remembered it) was all horseback rides and Negro servants— had started out bravely in this debasing existence in a shanty, but it was wearing her out. She was passing through a critical period of her life, and she had no care, no comforts. I have often since been ashamed of myself that I did not sympathize with her and understand her, but I was too young to understand, and too miserable myself to sympathize. It seemed to me that my life was not worth living—that every one had lost faith in me—that I should never succeed in the law or anything else—that I had no brains—that I should never do anything but scrub floors and run messages. And after a day that had been more than usually discouraging in the office and an evening of exasperated misery at home, I got a revolver and some cartridges, locked myself in my room, confronted myself desperately in the mirror, put the muzzle of the loaded pistol to my temple, and pulled the trigger.

The hammer snapped sharply on the cartridge; a great wave of horror and revulsion swept over me in a rush of blood to my head, and I dropped the revolver on the floor and threw myself on my bed.

By some miracle the cartridge had not exploded; but the nervous shock of that instant when I felt the trigger yield and the muzzle rap against my forehead with the impact of the hammer—that shock was almost as great as a very bullet in the brain. I realized my folly, my weakness; and I went back to my life with something of a man's determination to crush the circumstances that had almost crushed me.

Why do I tell that? Because there are so many people in the world who believe that poverty is not sensitive, that the ill-fed, overworked boy of the slums is as callous as he seems dull. Because so many people believe that the weak and desperate boy can never be anything but a weak and vicious man. Because I came out of that morbid period of adolescence with a sympathy for children that helped to make possible one of the first courts established in America for the protection as well as the correction of children. Because I was never afterward as afraid of anything as of my own weakness, my own cowardice—so that when the agents of the Beast in the courts and in politics threatened me with all the abominations of their rage if I did not commit moral suicide for *them*, my fear of yielding to them was so great that I attacked them more desperately than ever.

It was about this time, too, that I first saw the teeth and the claws of our metaphorical man-eater. That was during the conflict between Governor Waite and the Fire and Police Board of Denver. He had the appointment and removal of the members of this Board, under the law, and when they refused to close the public gambling houses and otherwise enforce the laws against vice in Denver, he read them out of office. They refused to go, and defied him, with the police at their backs. He threatened to call out the militia and drive them from the City Hall. The whole town was in an uproar.

One night, in the previous summer, I had followed the excited crowds to Coliseum Hall to hear the Governor speak, and I had seen him rise like some old Hebrew prophet, with his long white beard and patriarchal head of hair, and denounce iniquity and political injustice and the oppressions of the predatory rich. He appealed to the Bible in a calm prediction that, if the reign of lawlessness did not cease, in time to come "blood would flow in the land even unto the horses' bridles." (And he earned for himself, thereby, the nickname of "Bloody Bridles" Waite.)

Now it began to appear that his prediction was about to come true; for he called out the militia, and the Board armed the police. My brother was a militiaman, and I kept pace with him as his regiment marched from the Armouries to attack the City Hall. There were riflemen on the towers and in the windows of that building; and on the roofs of the houses for blocks around were sharpshooters and armed gamblers and the defiant agents of the powers who were behind the Police Board in their fight. Gatling guns were rushed through the streets; cannon were trained on the City Hall; the long lines of militia were drawn up before the building; and amid the excited tumult of the mob and the eleventh-hour conferences of the Committee of Public Safety, and the hurry of mounted officers and the marching of troops, we all waited with our hearts in our mouths for the report of the first shot. Suddenly, in the silence that expected the storm, we heard the sound of bugles from the direction of the railroad station, and at the head of another army—a body of Federal soldiers ordered from Fort Logan by President Cleveland, at the frantic call of the Committee of Public Safety—a mounted officer rode between the lines of militia and police, and in the name of the President commanded peace.

The militia withdrew. The crowds dispersed. The police and their partisans put up their guns, and the Beast, still defiant, went back sullenly to cover. Not until the Supreme Court had decided that Governor Waite had the right and the power to unseat the Board—not till then was the City Hall surrendered; and even so, at the next election (the Beast turning polecat), "Bloody Bridles" Waite was defeated after a campaign of lies, ridicule, and abuse, and the men whom he had opposed were returned to office.

I had eyes, but I did not see. I thought the whole quarrel was a personal matter between the Police Board and Governor Waite, who seemed determined merely to show them that *he* was master; and if my young brother had been shot down by a policeman that night, I suppose I should have joined in the curses upon poor old "Bloody Bridles."

However, my prospects in the office had begun to improve. I had had my salary raised, and I had ceased doing janitor work. I had become more of a clerk and less of an office boy. A number of us "kids" had got up a moot court, rented a room to meet in, and finally obtained the use of another room in the old Denver University building, where, in the gaslight, we used to hold "quiz classes" and defend imaginary cases. (That, by the way, was the beginning of the Denver University Law School.) I read my Blackstone, Kent, Parsons—working night and day—and I began really to get some sort of "grasp of the law." Long before I had passed my examinations and been called to the bar, Mr. Thompson would give me demurrers to argue in court; and, having been told that I had only a pretty poor sort of legal mind, I worked twice as hard to make up for my deficiencies. I argued my first case, a damage suit, when I was nineteen. And at last there happened one of those lucky turns common in jury cases, and it set me on my feet.

A man had been held by the law on several counts of obtaining goods under false pretences. He had been tried on the first count by an assistant district attorney, and the jury had acquitted him. He had been tried on the second count by another assistant, who was one of our great criminal lawyers, and the jury had disagreed. There was a debate as to whether it was worth while to try him for a third time, and I proposed that I should take the case, since I had been working on it and thought there was still a chance of convicting him. They let me have my way, and though the evidence in the third charge was the same as before—except as to the person defrauded—the jury, by good luck, found against him. It was the turning point in my struggle. It gave me confidence in myself; and it taught me never to give up.

And now I began to come upon "the Cat" again.

I knew a lad named Smith, whom I considered a victim of malpractice at the hands of a Denver surgeon whose brother was at the head of one of the great smelter companies of Colorado. The boy had suffered a fracture of the thigh-bone, and the surgeon—because of a hasty and ill-considered diagnosis, I believed—had treated him for a bruised hip. The surgeon, when I told him that the boy was entitled to damages, called me a blackmailer—and that was enough. I forced the case to trial.

I had resigned my clerkship and gone into partnership with a fine young fellow whom I shall call Charles Gardener*—though that was not his name—and this was to be our first case. We were opposed by Charles J. Hughes, Jr., the ablest corporation lawyer in the state; and I was puzzled to find the officers of the gas company and a crowd of prominent business men in court when the case was argued on a motion to dismiss it. The judge refused the motion, and for so doing— as he afterward told me himself—he was "cut" in his Club by the men whose presence in the court had puzzled me. After a three weeks' trial, in which we worked night and day for the plaintiff—with X-ray photographs and medical testimony and fractured bones boiled out over night in the medical school where I prepared them—the jury stood eleven to one in our favour, and the case had to be begun all over again. The second time, after another trial of three weeks, the jury "hung" again, but we did not give up. It had been all fun for us— and for the town. The word had gone about the streets: "Go up and see those two kids fighting the corporation heavyweights. It's more fun than a circus." And we were confident that we could win; we knew that we were right.

One evening after dinner, when we were sitting in the dingy little back room on Champa Street that served us as an office, A. M.

---

* This is one of the few fictitious names used in the story. Judge Lindsey wishes it disguised "for old sake's sake."

Stevenson—"Big Steve"—politician and attorney for the Denver City Tramway Company, came shouldering in to see us—a heavy-jowled, heavy-waisted, red-faced bulk of good-humour—looking as if he had just walked out of a political cartoon. "Hello, boys," he said jovially. "How's she going? Making a record for yourselves up in court, eh? Making a record for yourselves. Well!"

He sat down and threw a foot up on the desk and smiled at us, with his inevitable cigarette in his mouth—his ridiculously inadequate cigarette. (When he puffed it, he looked like a fat boy blowing bubbles.) "Wearing yourselves out, eh? Working night and day? Ain't you getting about tired of it?"

"We got eleven to one each time," I said. "We'll win yet."

"Uh-huh. You will, eh?" He laughed amusedly.

"One man stood out against you each time, wasn't there?"

There was.

"Well," he said, "there always will be. You ain't going to get a verdict in this case. You can't. Now I'm a friend of you boys, ain't I? Well, my advice to you is you'd better settle that case. Get something for your work. Don't be a pair of fools. Settle it."

"Why can't we get a verdict?" we asked.

He winked a fat eye. "Jury'll hang. Every time. I'm here to tell you so. Better settle it."[*]

We refused to. What was the use of courts if we could not get justice for this crippled boy? What was the use of practising law if we could not get a verdict on evidence that would convince a blind man? Settle it? Never!

So they went to our client and persuaded the boy to give up.

"Big Steve," attorney for the tramway company! The gas company's officers in court! The business men insulting the judge in his

---

[*] Many of the conversations reported in this volume are given from memory, and they are liable to errors of memory in the use of a word or a turn of expression. But they are not liable to error in substance. They are the unadorned truth, clearly recollected. B.B.L.

Club! The defendant's brother at the head of one of the smelter companies! I began to "connect up" "the Cat."

Gardener and I held a council of war. If it was possible for these men to "hang" juries whenever they chose, there was need of a law to make something less than a unanimous decision by a jury sufficient to give a verdict in civil cases. Colorado needed a "three-fourths jury law." Gardener was a popular young man, a good "mixer," a member of several fraternal orders, a hail-fellow-well-met, and as interested as I was in politics. He had been in the insurance business before he took up law, and he had friends everywhere. Why should he not go into politics?—as he had often spoken of doing.

In the intervals of the Smith suit, we had had a case in which a mother, whose child had been killed by a street car, had been unable to recover damages from the tramway company, because the company claimed, under the law, that her child was worthless alive or dead; and there was need of a statute permitting such as she to recover damages for distress and anguish of mind. We had had another case in which a young factory worker had been injured by the bursting of an emery wheel; and the law held that the boy was guilty of "contributory negligence" because he had continued to work at the wheel after he had found a flaw in it—although he had had no choice except to work at it or leave the factory and find employment elsewhere. There was need of a law giving workmen better protection in such circumstances. Why should not Gardener enter the Legislature and introduce these bills?—which I was eager to draft. Why not, indeed! The state needed them; the people wanted them; the courts were crippled and justice was balked because of the lack of them. Here was an opportunity for worthy ambition to serve the community and help his fellow-man.

That night, with all the high hopes and generous ideals and merciful ignorance of youth, we decided—without knowing what we were about—to go into the jungle and attack the Beast!

THE CAT PURRS

D ENVER WAS THEN, AS IT IS NOW, a beautiful city, built on a slope, between the prairies and mountains, always sunny, cool and clear-skyed, with the very sparkle of happiness in its air; and on the crown of its hill, facing the romantic prospect of the Rockies, the State Capitol raised its dome—as proud as the ambition of a liberty-loving people—the symbol of an aspiration and the expression of its power. That Capitol, I confess, was to me a sort of granite temple erected by the Commonwealth of Colorado to law, to justice, to the ideals of self-government that have made our republic the promised land of all the oppressed of Europe; and I could conceive of no nobler work than to serve those ideals in the assembly halls of that building, with those eternal mountains on the horizon and that sun of freedom overhead. Surely a man may confess so much, without shame, of his youth and his inexperience. . . . It is not merely the gold on the dome of the Capitol that has given it another look to me now.

It was the year 1897. I was about twenty-eight years old, and my partner, Gardener, was three years younger. He was more worldly-wise than I was, even then; for while I had been busy with briefs and court-work, he had been the "business head" of the firm, out among business friends and acquaintances—"mixing," as they say—and through his innumerable connections, here and there, with this man and that fraternity, bringing in the cases that kept us employed. He was a "Silver Republican"; I, a Democrat. But we both knew that if he was to get into politics it must be with the backing of the party "organization" and the endorsement of the party "boss."

The "Silver Republican" boss of the day was a man whom we both admired—George Graham. Everybody admired him. Everybody was fond of him. "Why," they would tell you, "there isn't a man in town who is kinder to his family. He's such a good man in his home! And he's so charitable!" At Christmas time, when free baskets of food were distributed to the poor, George Graham was chairman of the committee for their distribution. He was prominent in the fraternal orders and used his political power to help the needy, the widow and the orphan. He had an engaging manner of fellowship, a personal magnetism, a kindly interest in aspiring young men, a pleasant appearance—smooth and dark in complexion, with a gentle way of smiling. I liked him; and he seemed to discover an affection for both Gardener and me, as we became more intimate with him, in the course of Gardener's progress toward his coveted nomination by the party.

That progress was so rapid and easy that it surprised us. We knew, of course, that we had attracted some public attention and much newspaper notice by our legal battles with "the corporation heavyweights" in our three big cases against the surgeon, the tramway company and the factory owner. But this did not account to us for the ease with which Gardener penetrated to the inner circles of the Boss's court. It did not explain why Graham should come to see us in our office, and call us by our first names. The explanation that we tacitly accepted was one more personal and flattering to us. And when Gardener would come back from a chat with Graham, full of "inside information" about the party's plans—about who was to be nominated for this office at the coming convention, and what chance So-and-so had for that one—the sure proofs (to us) that he was being admitted to the intimate secrets of the party and found worthy of the confidence of those in power—I was as proud of Gardener as only a young man can be of a friend who has all the brilliant qualities that he himself lacks. Gardener was a handsome fellow, well built, always well dressed, self-assured and ambitious; I did not wonder that the politicians admired him and made much of him. I accepted his success as a tribute to those qualities in him that had already attached me to him with an affection rather more than brotherly.

We said nothing to the politicians about our projected bills. Indeed, from the first, my interest in our measures of reform was greater than Gardener's. His desire to be in the Legislature was due to a natural ambition to "get on" in life, to acquire power in the community as well as the wealth and distinction that come with power. Such ambitions were, of course, beyond me; I had none of the qualities that would make them possible; and I could only enjoy them, as it were, by proxy, in Gardener's person. I enjoyed, in the same way, his gradual penetration behind the scenes in politics. I saw, with him, that the party convention, to which we had at first looked as the source of honours, was really only a sort of puppet show of which the Boss held the wires. All the candidates for nomination were selected by Graham in advance—in secret caucus with his ward leaders, executive committeemen and such other "practical" politicians as "Big Steve"—and the convention, with more or less show of independence, did nothing but ratify his choice. When I spoke of canvassing some of the chosen delegates of the convention, Gardener said: "What's the use of talking to those small fry? If we can get the big fellows, we've got the rest. They do what the big ones tell them—and won't do anything they aren't told. You leave it to me." I had only hoped to see him in the Lower House, but he, with his wiser audacity, soon proclaimed himself a candidate for the Senate. "We can get the big thing as easy as the little one," he said. "I'm going to tell Graham it's the Senate or nothing for me." And he got his promise. And when we knew, at last, that his name was really on "the slate" of candidates to be presented to the convention, we were ready to throw up our hats and cheer for ourselves—and for the Boss.

The convention met in September, 1898. There had been a fusion of Silver Republicans, Democrats, and Populists, that year, and the political offices had been apportioned out among the faithful machinemen of these parties. Gardener was nominated by "Big Steve," in a eulogistic speech that was part of the farce; and the convention ratified the nomination with the unanimity of a stage mob. We knew that his election was as sure as sunrise, and I set to work looking up models for my bills with all the enthusiasm of the first reformer.

Meanwhile there was the question of the campaign and of the campaign expenses. Gardener had been assessed $500 by the committee as his share of the legitimate costs of the election, and Boss Graham generously offered to get the money for him "from friends." We were rather inclined to let Graham do so, feeling a certain delicacy about refusing his generosity and being aware, too, that we were not millionaires. But Graham was not the only one who made the offer; for example, Ed. Chase, since head of the gambler's syndicate in Denver, made similar proposals of kindly aid; and we decided, at last, that perhaps it would be well to be quite independent. Our law practice was improving. Doubtless, it would continue to improve now that we were "in right" with the political powers. We put up $250 each and paid the assessment.

The usual business of political rallies, mass meetings and campaign speeches followed in due course, and in November, 1898, Gardener was elected a State Senator on the fusion ticket. I had been busy with my "three-fourths jury" bill, studying the constitution of the State of Colorado, comparing it with those of the other states, and making myself certain that such a law as we proposed was possible. Unlike most of the state constitutions, Colorado's preserved inviolate the right of jury trial in criminal cases only, and therefore it seemed to me that the Legislature had plenary power to regulate it in civil suits. I found that the Supreme Court of the state had so decided in two cases, and I felt very properly elated; there seemed to be nothing to prevent us having a law that should make "hung" juries practically impossible in Colorado and relieve the courts of an abuse that thwarted justice in scores of cases. At the same time I prepared a bill allowing parents to recover damages for "anguish of mind" when a child of theirs was killed in an accident; and, after much study, I worked up an "employer's liability" bill to protect men who were compelled by necessity to work under needlessly dangerous conditions. With these three bills in his pocket, Senator Gardener went up to the Capitol, like another David, and I went joyfully with him to aid and abet.

Happy? I was as happy as if Gardener had been elected President and I was to be his Secretary of State. I was as happy as a man who has found his proper work and knows that it is for the good of his fellows. I would not have changed places that day with any genius of the fine arts who had three masterpieces to unveil to an admiring world.

I did not know, of course—but I was soon to learn—that the Legislature's time was almost wholly taken up with the routine work of government, that most of the bills passed were concerned with appropriations and such necessary details of administration, and that only twenty or thirty bills such as ours—dealing with other matters—could possibly be passed, among the hundreds offered. It was Boss Graham who warned us that we had better concentrate on one measure, if we wished to succeed with any at all, and we decided to put all our strength behind the "three-fourths jury" bill. Since Graham seemed to doubt its constitutionality, I went to the Attorney General for his opinion, and he referred me to his assistant—whom I convinced. I came back with the assistant's decision that the Legislature had power to pass such a law, and Gardener promptly introduced it in the Senate.

It proved at once mildly unpopular, and after a preliminary debate, in which the senators rather laughed at it as visionary and unconstitutional, it was referred to the Attorney General for his opinion. We waited, confidently. To our amazement he reported it unconstitutional, and the very assistant who had given me a favourable opinion before, now conducted the case against it. Nothing daunted, Gardener fought to get it referred to the Supreme Court, under the law; and the Senate sent it there. I got up an elaborate brief, had it printed at our expense, and spent a day in arguing it before the Supreme Court judges. They held that the Court had already twice found the Legislature possessed of plenary powers in such matters, and Gardener brought the bill back into the Senate triumphantly, and got a favourable report from the Judiciary Committee.

By this time, Boss Graham was seriously alarmed. He had warned Gardener that the bill was distasteful to him and to those whom he called his "friends." It was particularly distasteful, it seemed, to the Denver City Tramway Company. And he could promise, he said, that if we dropped the bill, the railway company would see that we got at least four thousand dollars' worth of litigation a year to handle. To both Gardener and myself, flushed with success and roused to the battle, this offer seemed an amusing confession of defeat on the part of the opposition; and we went ahead more gaily than ever.

We were enjoying ourselves. If we had been a pair of chums in college, we could not have had a better time. Whenever I could get away from my court cases and my office work, I rushed up to watch the fight in the Senate, as eagerly as a Freshman hurrying from his studies to see his athletic room-mate carry everything before him in a football game. The whole atmosphere of the Capitol—with its corridors of coloured marble, its vistas of arch and pillar, its burnished metal balustrades, its great staircases—all its majesty of rich grandeur and solidity of power—affected me with an increased respect for the functions of government that were discharged there and for the men who had them to discharge. I felt the reflection of that importance beaming upon myself when I was introduced as "Senator Gardener's law partner, sir"; and I accepted the bows and greetings of lobbyists and legislators with all the pleasure in the world.

When Gardener got our bill up for its final reading in the Senate, I was there to watch, and it tickled me to the heart to see him. He made a fine figure of an orator, the handsomest man in the Senate; and he was not afraid to raise his voice and look as independent and determined as his words. He had given the senators to understand that any one who opposed his bill would have him as an obstinate opponent on every other measure; and the Senate evidently realized that it would be wise to let him have his way. The bill was passed. But it had to go through the Lower House, too, and it was sent there, to be taken care of by its opponents—with the tongue in the cheek, no doubt.

I met Boss Graham in the corridor. "Hello, Ben," he greeted me. "What's the matter with that partner of yours?" I laughed; he looked worried. "Come in here," he said. "I'd like to have a talk with you." He led me into a quiet side room and shut the door. "Now look here," he said. "Did you boys ever stop to think what a boat you'll be in with this law that you're trying to get, if you ever have to defend a corporation in a jury suit? Now they tell me, down at the tramway offices"—the offices of the Denver City Tramway Company—"that they're going to need a lot more legal help. There's every prospect that they'll appoint you boys assistant counsel. But they can't expect to do much, even with you bright boys as counsel, if they have this law against them. You know that all the money there is in law is in corporation business. I don't see what you're fighting for."

I explained, as well as I could, that we were fighting for the bill because we thought it was right—that it was needed. He did not seem to believe me; he objected that this sort of talk was not "practical."

"Well," I ended, "we've made up our minds to put it through. And we're going to try."

"You'll find you're making a mistake, boy," he warned me. "You'll find you're making a mistake."

We laughed over it together—Gardener and I. It was another proof to us that we had our opponents on their knees. We thought we understood Graham's position in the matter; he had made no disguise of the fact that he was intimate and friendly with Mr. William G. Evans—the great "Bill" Evans—head of the tramway company and an acknowledged power in politics. And it was natural to us that Graham should do what he could to induce us to spare his friends. That was all very well, but *we* had made no pledges; *we* were under no obligations to any one except the public whom we served. Gardener was making himself felt, and he intended to continue to make himself felt. He did not intend to stultify himself, even for Graham's good "friends." I, of course, went along with him, rejoicing.

He had another bill in hand (House Bill 235) to raise the tax on large foreign insurance companies so as to help replenish the depleted treasury of the state. Governor Thomas had been appealing for money; the increased tax was conceded to be just, and it would add at least $100,000 in revenue to the public coffers. Gardener handled it well in the Senate, and—though we were indirectly offered a bribe of $8,500 to drop it—he got it passed and returned it to the Lower House. He had two other bills—one our "anguish of mind" provision and the second a bill regulating the telephone companies; but he was not able to move them out of committee. The opposition was silent but solid.

It became my duty to watch the two bills that we had been able to get as far as the House calendar on final passage—to see that they were given their turn for consideration. The jury bill came to the top very soon, but it was passed over, and next day it was on the bottom of the list. This happened more than once. And once it disappeared from the calendar altogether. The Clerk of the House, when I demanded an explanation, said that it was an oversight—a clerical error—and put it back at the foot. I began to suspect jugglery, but I was not yet sure of it.

One day while I was on this sentry duty, a lobbyist who was a member of a fraternal order to which I belonged, came to me with the fraternal greeting and a thousand dollars in bills. "Lindsey," he said, "this is a legal fee for an argument we want you to make before the committee, as a lawyer, against that insurance bill. It's perfectly legitimate. We don't want you to do anything except in a legal way. You know, our other lawyer has made an able argument, showing how the extra tax will come out of the people in increased premiums"—and so on. I refused the money and continued trying to push along the bill. In a few days he came back to me, with a grin. "Too bad you didn't take that money," he said. "There's lots of it going round. But the joke of it is, I got the whole thing fixed up for $250. Watch Cannon." I watched Cannon—Wilbur F. Cannon, a member of the House and a "floor leader" there. He had already voted in favour of the bill. But— to anticipate somewhat the sequence of events—I saw Wilbur F. Cannon, in the confusion and excitement of the closing moments of the session, rush down the aisle toward the Speaker's chair and make a motion concerning the insurance bill—to what effect I could not hear. The motion was put, in the midst of the uproar, and declared carried; and the bill was killed. It was killed so neatly that there is to-day no record of its decease in the official account of the proceedings of the House! Expert treason, bold and skilful!*

Meanwhile, I had been standing by our jury bill. It went up and it went down on the calendar, and at last when it arrived at a hearing it was referred back to the Judiciary Committee with two other anti-corporation bills. The session was drawing toward the day provided by the constitution for its closing, and we could no longer doubt that we were being juggled out of our last chance by the Clerk and the Speaker—who was Mr. William G. Smith, since known as "Tramway Bill."†

"All right," Gardener said. "Not one of Speaker Smith's House bills will get through the Senate until he lets our jury bill get to a vote." He told Speaker Smith what he intended to do, and next day he began to do it.

That afternoon, tired out, I was resting, during a recess of the House, in a chair that stood in a shadowed corner, when the Speaker hurried by heavily, evidently unaware of me, and rang a telephone. I heard him mention the name of "Mr. Evans," in a low, husky voice. I heard, sleepily, not consciously listening; and I did not at first connect

---

* Wilbur F Cannon is now Pure Food Commissioner in Colorado.
† Smith is now tax agent in the tramway offices.

"Mr. Evans" with William G. Evans of the tramway company. But a little later I heard the Speaker say: "Well, unless Gardener can be pulled off, we'll have to let that 'three-fourths' bill out. He's raising hell with a lot of our measures over in the Senate. . . . What? . . . Yes. . . . Well, get at it pretty quick."

Those hoarse, significant words wakened me like the thrill of an electric shock—wakened me to an understanding of the strength of the "special interests" that were opposed to us—and wakened in me, too, the anger of a determination to fight to a finish. The Powers that had "fixed" our juries, were now fixing the Legislature. They had laughed at us in the courts; they were going to laugh at us in the Capitol!

Speaker Smith came lumbering out. He was a heavily built man, with a big jaw. And when he saw me there, confronting him, his face changed from a look of displeased surprise to one of angry contempt—lowering his head like a bull—as if he were saying to himself: "What! That d—— little devil! I'll bet he heard me!" But he did not speak. And neither did I. He went off about whatever business he had in hand, and I caught up my hat and hastened to Gardener to tell him what I had heard.

When the House met again, in committee of the whole, the Speaker, of course, was not in the Chair, and Gardener found him in the lobby. Gardener had agreed with me to say nothing of the telephone conversation, but he threatened Smith that unless our jury bill was "reported out" by the Judiciary Committee and allowed to come to a vote, he would oppose every House bill in the Senate and talk the session to death. Smith fumed and blustered, but Gardener, with the blood in his face, out-blustered and out-fumed him. The Speaker, later in the day, vented some of his spleen by publicly threatening to eject me from the floor of the House as a lobbyist. But he had to allow the bill to come up, and it was finally passed, with very little opposition—for reasons which I was afterward to understand.

It had yet to be signed by the Speaker; and it had to be signed before the close of the session or it could not become a law. I heard rumours that some anti-corporation bills were going to be "lost" by the Chief Clerk, so that they might *not* be signed; and I kept my eye on him. He was a fat-faced, stupid-looking, flabby creature—by name D. H. Dickason—who did not appear capable of doing anything very daring. I saw the chairman of the Enrolling Committee place our bill on Dickason's desk, among those waiting for the Speaker's signature; and—while the House was busy—I withdrew it from the pile and placed it to one side, conspicuously, so that I could see it from a distance.

When the time came for signing—sure enough!—the Clerk was missing, and some bills were missing with him. The House was crowded—floor and galleries—and the whole place went into an uproar at once. Nobody seemed to know which bills were gone; every member who had an anti-corporation bill thought it was his that had been stolen; and they all together broke out into denunciations of the Speaker, the Clerk and every body else whom they thought concerned in the outrage. One man jumped up on his chair and tried to dominate the pandemonium, shouting and waving his hands. The galleries went wild with noisy excitement. Men threatened each other with violence on the floor of the House, cursing and shaking their fists. Others rushed here and there trying to find some trace of the Clerk. The Speaker, breathless from calling for order and pounding with his gavel, had to sit down and let them rage.

At last, from my place by the wall, on the outskirts of the hubbub, I saw the Clerk dragged down the aisle by the collar, bleeding, with a blackened eye, apparently half drunk and evidently frightened into an abject terror. He had stolen a bill introduced by Senator Bucklin, providing that cities could own their own water works and gas works; but the Senator's wife had been watching him; she had followed him to the basement and stopped him as he tried to escape to the street; and it was the Senator now who had him by the neck.

They thrust him back into his chair, got the confusion quieted, and with muttered threats of the penitentiary for him and everybody concerned in the affair, they got back to business again with the desperate haste of men working against time. And our jury bill was signed!

It was signed; and we had won! (At least we thought so.) And I walked out of the crowded glare of the session's close, into an April midnight that was as wide as all eternity and as quiet. It seemed to me that the stars, even in Colorado, had never been brighter; they sparkled in the clear blackness of the sky with a joyful brilliancy. A cool breeze drew down from the mountains as peacefully as the breath in sleep. It was a night to make a man take off his hat and breathe out his last vexation in a sigh.

We had won. What did it matter that the Boss, the Speaker, the Clerk and so many more of these miserable creatures were bought and sold in selfishness? That spring night seemed to answer for it that the truth and beauty of the world were as big above *them* as the heavens that arched so high above the puny dome-light of the Capitol. Had not even we, two "boys"—as they called us—put a just law before them and made them take up the pen and sign it? If we had done so much without even a whisper from the people and scarcely a line from the public press to aid and back us, what would the future not do when we found the help that an aroused community would surely give us? Hope? The whole night was hushed and peaceful with hope. The very houses that I passed—walking home up the tree-lined streets— seemed to me in some way so quiet because they were so sure. All was right with the world. We had won.

CHAPTER III

THE CAT KEEPS ON PURRING

T HE FACT, OF COURSE, was that we had won nothing. Our precious jury law was soon taken to the Supreme Court, on an appeal from a damage suit, and the judges declared it unconstitutional, without any blushing apologies for reversing previous decisions. But this blow did not fall until after an interval of some months; and Gardener and I, resting on our scanty laurels meanwhile, were allowed to reconsider the incidents of the session and count our bruises.

Gardener had had one hard knock, scarcely noticed in the fury and heat of the fight, but now sorely painful. Boss Graham had given him to understand, more or less plainly, that if he intended to continue his career in politics as he had begun it, he need not look for any further support from the Republican machine in Denver. Elections cost money; the money had to come from those who were able to subscribe it; and the Republican machine could not afford to offend such liberal subscribers as Mr. Evans of the tramway company, Mr. Field of the telephone company, Mr. Cheesman of the water company, the insurance magnates and the rest of the "Powers."

I do not know that the ultimatum was expressed even so delicately as this; but it was an ultimatum, and the more Gardener thought of it and talked to me about it, the more disheartened he became. He had one more term to serve in the Senate—and then what? Why then simply extinction—the end of his political career. It was as useless to appeal from the Boss to the convention, in those days, as to turn from a man to ask aid from his shadow. And to go to the people? To ask assistance from the public whom we had tried to serve? We might as well have rushed out into the street, from the decision of the Supreme Court, and called to the passers-by to come in and reverse the rulings of the judges. The people had handed over their political powers to the convention and the Boss as surely as they had delegated their judicial functions to the courts.

What were we to do then? I did not know. My own inclination was simply to fight—not because I saw any prospect of succeeding, but because I enjoyed the "scrap." Fight for the fun of it—fight for exercise—fight for any reason—but fight! We had our law practice to support us. We were not dependent upon politics for our living. We could make reform our hobby and keep the joy of political battle as a sort of recreation for our after-hours.

Gardener shook his head over it, and we went back to our practice. A very interesting development of events began at once to open on us.

Some months earlier, Boss Graham had brought us a case to defend, and he had brought it from the offices of the Denver City Tramway Company. It involved a charge of assault against a streetcar conductor, and nothing more; and we undertook to defend the conductor. But the trial came on during the last days of the legislative session; an evening newspaper was scoring the tramway company viciously in its columns; and we, as attorneys for the defence, shared in the printed abuse of the company.

Here was a situation in which I did not relish finding myself. "Don't worry," Graham said. "They're just blackmailers—trying to hold up the company." "But," I protested, "they'll prejudice the jury against us." "Don't worry," he said. "You can't lose. The jury'll hang." This was even less to my taste. We were not only being set up publicly as co-partners in corruption with the very corporation that we had been attacking, but we were actually being compelled to profit by the jury fixing for which we had assailed the corporation. I could not make up my mind whether this was accidental or malicious; and I went through with the case. It ended in a hung jury. We received $500 from the tramway company.

I objected to Graham that $500 was too much—that we did not charge $500 for such cases. "But," he said, with his suave smile, "you've helped them defeat a civil damage suit that would have taken a lot of the time of one of their leading counsel to defend." I accepted the explanation, though I knew it was not an explanation at all—for it was the hung jury and not we who had won the suit. But our jury law was to be tested before the Supreme Court, on an appeal from a damage suit; and I eased my conscience by telling Graham that if the Court found the law unconstitutional—as he seemed to expect it would—Senator Gardener intended to propose, at the next session, a constitutional amendment permitting the passage of our law.

Then I went to Gardener with my qualms about the whole case and the fee we had received for it. He pooh-poohed my squeamishness. "If they're fools enough to pay us more than the thing's worth," he argued, "that's *their* lookout. The more fools they! If we're going to fight these people, we've got to have money; haven't we? We've got to take every cent we can get. Don't be foolish. You're not practical. You never were. Leave the business end of it to me."

Another case came to us, sent in by another corporation politician, and the defendant was the famous "Jim" Marshall, a well-known gambler and the very same man whom I had seen accused of conspiring with a police captain to rob an express train on the Denver and Rio Grande Railroad. In this case he was involved in a dispute about the lease of a gambling house; and though the city, at the time, was supposed to be "shut down tight" against all gambling, Marshall assured me that this was only a political ruse to deceive the "goody-goodies." It was "on the cards" to open up again very soon, and he wanted the house in readiness.

I learned to like Marshall. He was a goodhearted, fearless man; and in the hands of any other system but that under which we lived, he might have been an invaluable man to the community. We became the best of friends. I learned from him all I wished to know of the connection between the Beast, politics and the gamblers; and what I learned made clear to me the real meaning of the struggle that I had seen between the old Police Board of Denver and "Bloody Bridles" Waite.

We won Marshall's case for him; and without waiting for his bill, he sent us a fee of $1,000. Meanwhile, other corporation cases had been coming in—and bringing large fees. Gardener was jubilant. I became more and more uneasy. These people were not paying us—as I began to see—they were trying to buy us. They were using on us a system which they must have used on hundreds of young men in Denver, before and since—and not only in Denver, but in every city in every state in this Union where Business wishes "special privileges" and debauches the community to obtain them. They were trying to buy us, and they were succeeding. Gardener was becoming cynical. I was, to him, more and more impractical. We discussed it and discussed it—sitting in our offices—(we had taken new ones on Lawrence and Seventeenth Street)—sitting of a Sunday afternoon on the porch of his little home (he was newly married)—walking up and down, of an evening, on the street—or wherever else we happened to have an idle and companionable moment together.

I do not wish to be gossipy; but the situation was typical, and I wish it to be understood. It is easy enough to condemn the man who becomes the tool of the "interests"; and it is common enough to exult in his final disgrace and to congratulate the community on his punishment. But it is better to understand what he had to fight against, to appreciate the overwhelming odds he had against him in the struggle, to pity him, and to save for the men who ruined him the wrath that is wasted, now, upon their victim.

I have written this story, thus far, very ill, if I have not let you see the good there was in Gardener. In our long companionship, he had attached me to him by every admiration that a man has for what is strong and capable. He was ambitious—but is that a crime? He wished to be rich—and who does not? He was eager to take his place as a man of note among his neighbours, to have a career in politics, to be able to enjoy and to have his family enjoy the fruits of that career and the honours of its distinction. Are these the traits of a weakling? Or are they the very qualities that make for the usefulness of a strong man in an honest community? And yet it was even by these qualities that the Beast got him. It is by them that it holds him. It is because of them that he does its work to-day so well.

"Why, Ben," he would say to me, "you know how things are in this town. We can't get a look in on anything if these big fellows don't want to let us. Their men are on the doors everywhere. Look at Graham. They own him, and you know it. And he has the say whether or not I'm ever to get another election to anything! Look at the courts. Those judges get their places through Graham, the same as I do. Look at the hung juries? You don't suppose they have to *buy* those juries, do you? The poor old dubs who wait around, up there, for a job on jury duty know who's who in this town. They want to stand in with the powers. They hang the jury in the hope that some of the big fellows will notice them and give them a soft thing up at the Court House or the Capitol. We're trying to buck up against the whole game. And what do we do it for? For 'the people.' The dear people! To hell with them. A good half of them are in this game themselves. *They* won't help us. They'll turn on us, quick as a cur, as soon as they get the word. And the other half doesn't know and doesn't want to know. They wouldn't believe us if we told them. *They* don't care. All they want is to make a living and keep out of trouble and not be bothered about 'politics.' . . . Our play is to keep quiet and get money and get *known*; and then, when we're Somebody, show these fellows where we're at. Just play the game a while. We can't do anything by raising a kick yet. They'll simply chuck us out and lock the doors."

All this was surely true, and I could not deny it. Nevertheless, I had some sort of vague hope that we should not have to go that way, that perhaps things would turn out better than they seemed. I was impractical, as Gardener said, particularly in money matters. I had started out in my younger days as a grasping little miser, stinting myself for the very necessaries of life, and hoarding up every penny I could get. I had invested my savings in real estate during the Denver land boom; and then values declined; the boom collapsed; and after an agony of worry and apprehension, I lost everything. And I felt relieved. I felt as relieved as if I had wakened up from a nightmare to find a load of terror gone from my mind. With some sort of instinctive fear of financial affairs, I have never since been able to consider them as a wise man should.

As I look back on Gardener's struggle now, I see that it was my own weakness, to some extent, that saved me. I had no more ambition to be rich, and for that reason the bribe that helped to buy Gardener did not properly tempt *me*. I had not his ambition to be prominent in politics; the law satisfied me—as it did not him—and I had gone into politics only to try to improve the laws. I had none of his personal aggressiveness and determination; I was content to drift along, hoping for the best. Yet this very hope was grounded in a silent disinclination to drift into any crookedness; and as Gardener went further and further along the path that was opened up to him by the favour of the "Powers," I found him getting further and further away from me.

There is no need to trace, step by step and incident by incident, the misery of that gradual separation. It went on for months, and it went on in silence. I could not speak of it, for fear of facing the truth about it. Gardener was no hypocrite; that was part of his strength; and I did not wish to hear him say the things I hoped against. But I could not blink the facts for long. They kept coming to me from other people, from friends and acquaintances outside the office; and I saw that Gardener was accepting my silence as a consent to the use of the firm in the service of the "interests." I could not go on accepting their fees. A break between Gardener and me was inevitable. I had to face it.

I faced it alone, in my office, one day that I shall never forget—looking out the window at a sunset that was beautiful on the mountain peaks. Gardener had cried: "Let them say what they like. *Let them call me a 'tool.'* I don't care. I'm going to play the game and play it to win—and there's only one way to do it—and that's to sit in with *them*." I could not answer him. I could only say that I would share in no more corporation fees.

From his point of view he was right; and my own point of view, I knew, was too vague and impractical to argue with him. He had all the evidence, all the tangible proofs, on his side; and I had nothing but a sort of formless hope in the right, a feeling of conscience that I could not voice, a silent reluctance to sell myself even to "gain the whole world." They had taken him up to the mountain top and shown him all the kingdoms of the earth—and he had gone from me as irrevocably as the past in which we had struggled so happily together.

A sunset, at such a moment, is a sad thing to watch. It was carrying away with it all that companionship of youth, all that camaraderie in hope and idealism in which we had lived. It was leaving me with nothing but bitter memories and a failure that almost precluded hope. And yet there burned in the sky a colour of wrath that burned in me too in a hate for the men whom we had fought. Nothing was sacred to them. No one was too low for them. Laws and courts, judges and juries, politicians and gamblers, the Speaker in his Chair and the poor fallen creatures on the street—they debauched them all and bought and sold them all. And the youth who had ideals, who had intellect and ambition—he, too—they must have him. They must have new tools, strong tools, to replace the ones they wore out and cast aside. They had taken Gardener. He had gone. If they had done nothing else, *that* alone would have been enough to make me swear never to forgive them, never to yield to them—to make me resolve to oppose them, to thwart them in whatever small way might be in my small power—to make me fight in any sort of forlorn hope that some time I should see "a new birth of freedom" like a clean day arising upon us, on our city, on our Capitol, on our mountains that I watched there, almost through tears, as they grew more and more sombre with the fall of night.

CHAPTER IV

THE BEAST
IN THE DEMOCRACY

MEANWHILE I HAD THOUGHT I SAW that new birth coming in the rejuvenation of the Democratic party under Bryan, in 1900. I really had thought so. I had learned that the Republican machine represented nothing but the rich corporations of the city and the state; and I naturally concluded that the Democracy, being opposed to that machine, was opposed also to the owners of it. I knew that "Tom" Maloney, then the Democratic boss, was reputed to be in the pay of the gas company, but there was an attempt being made to oust Maloney, and I believed that if he and his henchmen could be gotten rid of, the party would be purged of all uncleanness and we might "raise a standard to which the wise and the honest might repair." Under such a standard, backed by the power of a people's party, we could elect an honest Legislature and pass the anti-corporation laws that the community needed. I took up my hope again. I volunteered my services to the opponents of Maloney.

They were led by Governor Thomas and Boss Speer—Robert W. Speer, who comes into my story, here, to stay. He was then the president of the Fire and Police Board of Denver, and he was recognized already as an astute politician, very smooth and very powerful. He was a man nearly six feet in height, unusually weighty, with a round, clean-shaven face of heavy muscles—with his thin hair trained over his increasing baldness—his skin fresh, his eyes clear, his mouth strong-jawed and firm. He had called a meeting of Governor Thomas's friends in his own real-estate office downtown, one evening, and I attended, sat in a leather chair, joined in the discussion and was appointed "precinct committeeman" of the district in which I lived.

I was in the battle again—if only in the ranks—and I was happy.

My district was a fashionable quarter, on Capitol Hill, where the well-to-do citizens of Denver have built their residences and their coach houses, laid out their rolled lawns and planted their shade trees. It had always been an overwhelmingly Republican district, and I thought I knew why. But I argued that though the rich owners of these houses were naturally of the party of the "interests," their servants would not necessarily be so; and when, in my house-to-house canvass, I was refused admittance at a front door I went to the back one, and talked to the coachman, the cook, the furnace man and the servant girl about the iniquities of Boss Maloney, the crimes of the "interests" and the new hope there was of an honest party of the people to give us just laws and decent government in Denver. (We had female suffrage in Colorado even then, of course.)

I always got a much more respectful hearing in the servants' hall than I did in the parlour. When I got any hearing at all from the master or mistress of the house it was usually a cynical or an indifferent one. I was amazed to find how many people did not vote, and were proud of it—how many would reply, "You can't tell *me* that one party is any better than another; they're all a lot of thieves together"—how many would listen with a "what's-the-use" expression that made me feel I was merely a bore. One curt old doctor, as soon as he heard what I had come for, slammed the door in my face and left me to finish my explanations to his brass name-plate. However, my work was not wasted. At our party's primary, I heard one of my opponents say, "Good heavens! Lindsey's got all the servant girls in the country here." I defeated Maloney's man. And, finally, at the elections, I had the satisfaction of seeing the Republican majority in our district largely reduced.

I do not intend to give here all the tiresome details of the fight between the Maloney faction and the Speer faction. Having rather distinguished myself by my success in the primaries, I was elected a Speer delegate to the local convention, and I helped to pick candidates for the Legislature who should cast their votes for Governor Thomas as United States Senator. I became chairman of the Credential Committee in the Democratic County Convention, and was then made secretary of the delegation to the State Convention. All this gave me considerable prominence and a good deal of influence; but it showed me a near view of more political obliquity than I had expected to see in our party. I found, for example, that the men with whom I was working were thinking only of the spoils of office that would accrue to them if they won. I heard one man, who was a city inspector, say: "My job's only worth $1,500 salary, but I easily make $3,000 on the side"—in graft, of course. In answer to some moral objections to the candidacy of a very corrupt and dissolute man for a place on the ticket, one of the politicians replied: "Oh, you can put any kind of yellow dog on, so long as you have a 'nice man' at the head of the ticket. They'll vote it straight. Don't worry about that." It was all "practical" politics, but it rather soiled my new hope in the people's party. I began to see that the politicians with whom I was working were not so unlike the ones with whom I had fought.

What seemed to puzzle them all was the fact that I showed no ambition to be nominated for any office. They could not understand what I was working for; and I did not tell them. I had worked hard. During the primary contest I did not go home for two weeks, but lived with Speer at a hotel and helped him with those measures of offence and defence that make up the incidents of a factional quarrel.

At the local convention in the Opera House, there had almost been a riot; revolvers had been drawn, and we had had to hold our meeting with our lives in our hands. All this had made my companions very friendly toward me—as such dangers do—and they told me that I was foolish not to look for something from the party in return for the work I had done. They suggested, among other things, that I might become a candidate for the office of District Attorney.

Here was a suggestion that was more than interesting to me. I still had the amateur reformer's idea that the corruption to which I was opposed could be checked and punished if the public guardians of the law would only do their duty; and it seemed to me that the District Attorney was one of the most powerful of those officials. I saw myself administering the office of public prosecutor with a heavy hand, and the prospect gave me a secret joy that made me chuckle. I sounded Boss Speer about the nomination; he said that Governor Thomas had already promised the place to Harry A. Lindsley, a young politician, whose name on the ticket—it was freely said—would ensure a large campaign contribution from one of the Denver public utility corporations. I, of course, had no such support to offer, and the party needed funds. I said no more about the matter.

But I had already spoken of it to Gardener—with whom I was still in nominal partnership—and he had jumped at the idea with an eagerness that was afterward to be explained to me. When I told him what Speer had said, he advised me to disregard it. "Make a fight," he counselled. "I'll help. The thing isn't settled yet. It *can't* be. I'll help."

I have spoken in a previous chapter of Ed. Chase, the gambler, and of his offer to pay Gardener's first election expenses. He was reputed to be a millionaire, and he lived then—as he does now—in considerable luxury on Capitol Hill, and associated with the most reputable business men of the community. He was greatly respected in various quarters, and he had all sorts of good qualities, no doubt; but he made his money out of numerous gambling hells and policy joints which he had conducted for years in Denver under both political parties; and it was understood that he was one of the three men who afterward formed the gambling "trust" of Denver. He was also a stock-holder in several utility corporations, and his influence in politics was well known. There was a law against gambling, of course, and it was spasmodically enforced when public clamour compelled a pretence, at least, of prosecution; but for the most part the gambling was "let alone" with the approval of those business men who believe that this sort of vice helps business by keeping a "wide-open" and attractive town. (They once got up a petition in favour of open public gambling in Denver, on that argument.)

One of Gardener's first moves, in his little campaign to procure me the nomination, was to bring Chase to our office and usher me in to see him. The visit was contrived in a way to make it seem accidental—and perhaps it *was* accidental. At any rate, it was carried off in that jocular and "joshing" tone of serious banter in which a man who is suspected of being squeamish is introduced to a proposal that needs a disguise.

Chase was an elderly man, with gray hair and moustache. He would pass anywhere as a nice, clean "office man," careful of his health and his appearance—as the prosperous owner of a successful dry-goods shop, who was a deacon of his church. He said little. Gardener did the talking.

I knew that Chase was a friend of Boss Speer, a contributor to our campaign fund and a man, therefore, who would have something to say about the candidates who were to be nominated on our ticket. Gardener explained that on account of a crusade which the "reform-ers" had been making against gambling, Chase was particularly interested in the District Attorney's office. And Gardener, as being friendly to both a prospective District Attorney and to the man whom that official would, perhaps, have to prosecute, went on to explain—smiling from one to the other—that Chase did not expect to escape prosecution, that he understood his men would be hauled into court occasionally and fined the limit, and that he would not embarrass me by resenting any such grand-stand plays.

"You know, Ben," Gardener said, "Mr. Chase doesn't want any-thing but what's fair. He doesn't expect to run wide open all the time.

Whenever the District Attorney has to make a demonstration, *he's* willing to pay up. That's understood. You needn't feel worried about that. Need he?"

Chase, it seemed to me, was a little embarrassed. He stroked his moustache, rubbed his chin, nodded when he was appealed to, and relieved his gravity with a half-reluctant smile. I listened, and kept my thoughts to myself.

"They don't want you to do anything crooked, Ben," Gardener laughed. "All they want is fair play. You know gambling can't be stopped as long as men want to gamble. You can handle the thing in a practical way. They'll be reasonable. You needn't be afraid of offending your friends."

I replied, at last, that my nomination was not settled upon, at all—that I had not even made up my own mind about it yet. And I backed out of the interview, at the first opportunity, as unostentatiously as I could.

I understood that Gardener, being now very intimate with Chase, wished to get him to throw his influence for my nomination. A few minutes later, I understood why he was so eager. When Chase had gone, Gardener came to my room in the office, in high feather. Why! with me as District Attorney and himself as counsel for the gamblers, we could make $25,000 a year outside my salary—without the slightest danger of becoming "involved"—and at the same time gain all the credit from the community of enforcing the law and prosecuting the gamblers. No doubt of it. The game had been played in this way, in Denver, before.

I understood the uselessness of arguing with these men. If I replied that I was not in politics "for my pocket" and wished to do what was "straight," they would only give me credit for being either less honest than they were—since I added hypocrisy to guilt—or of being an impractical "goody-goody" who had no business in politics. I had learned, too, the value of keeping my own counsel, if I was to get any of the reforms I wished from the very "practical" men whom conditions had put in power. So I simply told Gardener that I was not District Attorney, and had no prospect of being. I got away from him—feeling rather sick at heart—and dismissed the matter from my mind, with relief. "I didn't understand you, Ben," he told me long after. "And I don't believe you understood yourself." Perhaps not. I was not trying to understand myself. I was trying to find my way through the jungle into which I had walked so gaily.

One thing was certain: I could not maintain even a nominal partnership with Gardener any longer. I should either have to start out in law for myself or take a political office. Boss Speer, when next I met him, said: "Ben, you've got some strong backing for District Attorney. Chase has been up to see me. He says he's *for* you!" I accepted the honour of his support—resolved that if I ever got the office I should play the deuce with some of the gentlemen who had put me in it—but I imagine, from what I have learned since, that all this "strong backing" came from Gardener. Governor Thomas, shortly after, assured me that the nomination had been irrevocably promised to Harry A. Lindsley (who was elected), and I let the matter drop. Gardener said to me, years later, when he had become leading counsel for the head of the gamblers' syndicate: "Chase was saying, only the other day, what a narrow escape we had when we picked you for District Attorney. He said you'd have raised hell with us, sure." And I realize now that I should never have been seriously considered for the place if it had not been for Gardener.

Boss Speer was very apologetic about the way in which I had been "turned down," and he offered me a place as a District Judge. My name was even put on the "slate" that was made up at the caucus. But it was afterward explained to me that the Denver City Tramway Company and the Denver Union Water Company favoured Peter L. Palmer as a candidate for judge, and backed him with the promise of a large campaign contribution; and I was dropped again "for the good of the party." On the ticket that passed the convention my name did not appear at all.

This fact—to the evident surprise of all concerned—did not prevent me from going into the election with as much enthusiasm as ever.

I still had hope that if I maintained my influence in the party, I might use the gratitude of my party friends to slip some of my reform measures through the Legislature. I became a member of the Democratic State Executive Committee and had an opportunity of learning how amazingly high were the legitimate expenses of a campaign. The cost of maintaining watchers and workers at the polls and of paying for carriages and automobiles to bring in voters was incredible; I know that in later campaigns it amounted to $25,000 for the city alone; and this item of cost formed only a small portion of the whole expense, even in the city. I helped to select the members of our finance committee, who had to raise the funds for the campaign; and I learned that these men were selected because of their connection with wealthy corporations. Our chairman, Milton Smith, for example, was attorney for the telephone company and—at times—for the gas company, the brewers, the gamblers and all the rest of that ring. Several other members of the committee were similarly connected. But then, it was pointed out, the director and chief organizer of the Republican campaign, was "Big Steve"!

There was much voluble concern as to which campaign committee would get the largest contributions; and it began to dawn upon me that instead of being a contest of parties, the election was going to be a contest of corporations, through their paid agents, for the control of the machinery of government. The "workers" in the ranks of the fight were working for nothing, apparently, but the promise of this or that picayune "job" under the politicians. The politicians were struggling for nothing, apparently, but the offices and the graft to which they hoped to be elected. The corporations, over them all, were apparently using them all to keep themselves above the laws by owning the sources and the agents of the law. And the people? The "dear people"? In none of the private conversations or secret caucuses of the politicians, do I remember hearing the people mentioned except in the way that the directors of a "wildcat" mining company might speak of the prospective shareholders whom they had yet to induce to buy stock.

That, at least, was the situation as I look back upon it now—as a man having struggled through a bit of tangled underwood looks back upon it from a clearing on a rise of ground. At the time I could not see the forest for the trees. I saw nothing, in the days preceding the election, but the struggles of one or another organization to obtain some partisan advantage by getting this or that party judge and his court to give them an unfair ballot, to complicate it by putting up "tickets" with misleading designations, and to confuse the unfriendly voter in some way or other for the party's benefit. I saw the judges on the bench called into political conferences, in private rooms, to decide these cases in advance. And when I spoke to an old-timer about it, he said: "Don't be too squeamish, young man. This is the way the game is played."

At first it seemed that our party would win both state and county elections. But as the day approached we heard that one band of corporations—led by the local gas company with its Wall Street affiliations—was determined that the Republicans should carry the county. Money began to flow victoriously from the Republican headquarters. Our finance committeemen began to wail that some of the corporations that had promised contributions now refused them. It was as if an army had been deserted, not by its leaders, but by the very government that supplied its pay chest! The United States Marshal, being a Republican official, began to swear in a little army of deputy marshals, composed of all sorts of thugs and Negro rowdies, to do "police duty" at the polls. The Fire and Police Board, being Democratic, swore in special policemen to oppose them; but, on account of the deficit in the payroll, the Board could not compete on equal terms with the Marshal. Then the Democratic organization appealed to the courts, and the Marshal was enjoined by law from interfering with the election. But the Republicans still had the money. They went to the Democratic Sheriff of the county and bought his office for three days for $20,000—according to the confession afterward made—and swore in their outlawed deputy marshals as deputy sheriffs. Thus the Democrats—or rather, the corporations behind them—had the police and the city jail to aid them at the polls; and the Republicans—or the corporations whom they represented—had the Sheriff and the county jail. And the stage was set for riot and murder.

Riot and murder came, with the opening of the polls. I had been at work all night—in charge of Democratic headquarters during the illness of our chairman—and I had lain down in my clothes, exhausted, toward daybreak. I was awakened to receive a telephone report, from one of our watchers, that there was going to be "hell to pay at Twenty-second and Larimer." "These cursed nigger deputy sheriffs," he said, "are butting in here. Our men won't stand for it. It means a shooting. Some one had better hustle down from headquarters and try to settle it."

I hurried downstairs (our headquarters were in the Brown Palace Hotel), called a cab, and ordered the driver to get me to Twenty-second and Larimer as quickly as he could. The streets were quiet and empty in the dingy light of a cold November morning, and we clattered down Eighteenth Street at a noisy gallop. We swung into Larimer Street, in front of the Windsor Hotel—the very hotel that at my first arrival in Denver had seemed so high and so magnificent!—and we had little more than passed it when the driver pulled up with a suddenness that almost shot me from my seat. I flung open the cab door and thrust out my head to see what was the matter. The street was full of excited people who seemed to be scurrying this way and that; and over their heads there hung a thin cloud of smoke, very still in the dead air. As I jumped out and ran toward the polling place, I saw a policeman lying behind a telegraph pole, in a quivering huddle, writhing painfully; a Negro sprawled in blood in the gutter; a little knot of men were supporting a wounded man to a drugstore; the gongs of ambulance and patrol wagons sounded their warnings from a distance; and while men came running up, as I ran, to see what had happened, others quietly made off down the street.

I went over to the Negro. The murder that had been bought and paid for, lay at my feet. His mute eyes were wide open; a puzzled frown puckered his black forehead that was wrinkled like an ape's. He lay there—the broken tool of those same criminals that had used the Clerk of the House whom I had seen bleeding in the Capitol—flung aside now in the gutter, dead, but with this sort of dumb question staring at me from his poor, bestial, bewildered face.

The physical revulsion of the sight nauseated me. When a man touched me on the shoulder I started, with a shudder, as if I had been the author of that horror myself.

"They began it," he said.

They had, indeed, begun it, as I found out when I followed the police and their prisoners to the City Hall station, and got a confession from the Negroes there. And in my indignation against the Republican machine, I accused the Republicans to the reporters, and gloated over the flaring headlines of the "extras" that fixed the guilt of the crime on the Republicans who had sent those irresponsible Negroes to the polls with firearms to "make trouble." But *had* they begun it? Or had it been begun by the men who gave the money to hire them—the heads of the warring corporations who were determined to win that election at the muzzle of the revolver, if need be, so that *they* might be the owners of the hung juries, the paid speakers, the venal clerks, the unjust judges, the free gamblers and all the vice and graft that should keep *them* in power? Yes! The men who had ruined young Gardener had shed that blood. The question on the dead face of that miserable creature in the gutter was theirs to answer. And some day, somewhere, somehow, they *shall* answer—let us hope.

That was my experience in the election of 1900. Those were the lessons I learned from it. Those and one other—of another import—which I have left till the last because it was a lesson of hope, and because, in spite of all, it seems to me there is still ground for hope.

This was it:

Toward the close of September, in the campaign, Theodore Roosevelt, then Governor of New York, came to Denver, and he was challenged by Governor Thomas to defend the position of the Republican party upon certain issues of the contest. Colorado was a free-silver state, almost unanimously, and the game was to make

Roosevelt either embarrass his party or himself by forcing him to handle the free-silver question before an audience that would resent the opinions of an Eastern "gold-bug" however mildly he might put them.

The Opera House was packed with people. Senator Lodge, of Massachusetts, held their attention for a time, but they were impatient to hear "Teddy." He was late. He had not arrived yet. Expectation became noisy, restless, inimical. Presently we heard the low grumble of a crowd shouting in the street. The word was cried about that he was coming. And almost immediately, in a crash of music from the band, he strode down to the footlights and faced the shouting audience.

He looked tired. But without waiting for silence, with his head down as if he were about to charge, he bared his teeth and uttered something unintelligible, in a hoarse voice. The audience roared. He took a long breath, watching them, dogged, determined, filling his lungs; and then—with a sudden gesture that compelled silence—he screamed at them, with all his teeth showing: "We—stand—on a—*gold*—platform!"

It came to them like a blow in the face; and before they could take voice, he added, pounding out the words with his fist: "We stand for the same thing in Colorado that we stand for in New York!"

He got no further. The shout of applause that followed came in a roar of delight from a thousand throats. They cheered him as if he had said the one thing they had been waiting to hear, instead of the very thing that no Republican politician in Denver would have dared to whisper to any single one of them, in the dark, behind a locked door. They cheered him as if they would split their throats. A startled Democratic politician who stood near me cried: "Great G—! He hasn't converted this crowd to the *gold* standard, has he?" (The wisdom of politicians!) They cheered his courage, his truth, his defiance of political hedging, his honesty, his manliness. It was the cheer of pride, of love, of admiration. It was the voice of our people raised to greet those very qualities in a politician which the Beast has tried to crush. It was, to me, the voice of hope.

I went home, that night, resolved never to forget the lesson. Often since, when I have faced the hoot of prejudiced opposition from my own small stage in public life, I have remembered Roosevelt, and filled my lungs again, and cleared my throat for another defiance. For I believe, in *that* way, with *our* people, there is hope.

CHAPTER V

THE BEAST IN
THE COUNTY COURT

W ELL, THE DEMOCRATS CARRIED THE COUNTY
and the state in November, 1900, and our "people's party"
was put in power; but I no longer had any of the illusions
with which I had volunteered in the battle. I had found that most of
my companions in the struggle were not patriots but hired mercenar-
ies, fighting—as our opponents fought—under the black flag of corporation pirates. I had as much hope of getting my reform laws passed
by the machine "bosses" as a man might have of getting a city charter
for a South American town from a party of buccaneers who had taken
the place for pillage. I had drawn up our threatened constitutional
amendment for Gardener, but I knew he would never fight for it; and,
of course, he never did. I was at a standstill, helpless, and not merely
discouraged but convinced that there was nothing I could do.

While I was in this state of mind, I was offered, as a "political
reward," the office of Judge of the County Court, to succeed Judge

R. W. Steele, who had been elected to the Supreme Court and had left the county bench empty. Under the law, the Board of County Commissioners had power to appoint his successor for his unexpired term of nine months. Judge Steele had been one of the heads of the law firm for which I had worked so long as office boy and clerk; and he wished me to succeed him in the county court. The members of the Democratic Executive Committee signed a petition endorsing me for the place. Senator Patterson, with whom I had been associated as counsel in the famous "Tritch Will Case," went before the commissioners without my knowledge and argued my claims. (It has been said that I got Senator Patterson's support as the result of a political "deal," and any one who believes that story is welcome to his credulity. I shall here content myself with denying it flatly. I have disproved it often enough on the platform.) As a result of this political and personal influence on my behalf, the Commissioners appointed me in December, 1900, and I took office in January, 1901.

The Court House of Denver is the usual old stone building, smutted with smoke,* standing in the centre of a city square, with lawns and stone walks and elm trees in which the city sparrows are always noisy. On its front lawn, in the usual decorative fountains, some bronze-coated nymphs and cherubs disport themselves all winter in the memories of a discontinued shower-bath. On the pinnacle of the building's dome there stands the inevitable emblematical figure of Justice, but it has been twice struck by lightning—equally emblematically, no doubt!—so that Justice has lost not only her scales but the arm that upheld them. Here, in the usual dingy court room, with the usual drone of court officials and the usual forensic eloquence of counsel addressing the usual yawns of bored juries, the county court was held. It was then—as it is, now—the busiest court in the state. It had jurisdiction to try election contests and such political lawsuits; it had a varied and general jurisdiction in civil cases in which prop-

---

* It has been "sandblasted" since this was written.

erty to the value of not more than $2,000 was involved—for which reason it was called "the poor man's" and "the people's" court; it was the court of appeal from police magistrates and justices of the peace; it had criminal jurisdiction in all "misdemeanours" and in "felonies" where the accused was under twenty-one years of age; and in addition, it was the probate court for the city and the county. I was just thirty years of age when I took charge of it.

I knew that Judge Steele, whom I succeeded, was an upright and just judge, on whom no party and no corporation had had any "strings." And in taking his place on the bench, I saw myself rising above all the political sculduggery through which I had been struggling so long—to look down on it untempted, with a judge's honour unbesmirched and a mind free to administer justice with clean hands. I forgot that I had been given the place as a "political reward."

I was immediately reminded of it by the expectations of those political "workers" whom the Board of County Commissioners wished me to appoint to offices in my court. They expected to succeed skilled clerks who had been in the service of the court for ten and fifteen years, and they had no qualifications for the places they wished to fill. They assured me that "the Republicans did it," that my party required it of me, and that if I looked to any future in the party I must be loyal now. When I refused to make a single clerk "walk the plank," their indignation was amazing. My friends the "leaders" assured me that I need not expect a renomination to the bench; and the workers assured me that if I ever got a renomination they would "knife" me at the polls. When I pointed out that the court had to be run efficiently, in the interests of the people, they replied: "You'll find out, at the next convention, how much the people care."

Then Mr. Fred. P. Watts, one of the County Commissioners who had voted me into office, came to me with a proposal that I should discharge my obligations to him by appointing him administrator of whatever estates might be involved before the Court; and when I refused this petition also, he promised me that he too would see that I had the proper reward for my ingratitude. (I had to appoint him, later, in one case, in which the litigants demanded it.) And finally, a lawyer-politician—an old friend whom I have not the heart to name—arrived with an incredible proposition that I should use my power as judge to have him appointed—wherever possible—guardian, administrator or referee, as the case might require, in the suits that should come before me; and he in return would divide his fees with me! (He has been my consistent enemy in the legislature ever since my refusal to enter into that abominable conspiracy with him.)

It was with a saddened pride, at last, that I took my place on the bench. I had dropped my partnership with Senator Gardener. I had only nine months of office before me. And already my party had turned against me and my prospects of any future as a judge were as blank as despair.

However, the mills of Justice began to grind; and I was there to see that everything in the hopper passed truly between the stones. Sitting behind a desk that looked as if it had been designed as a wooden sepulchre, I acted as public umpire in will cases that involved interminable petty family quarrels, or in real-estate cases where one long file of witnesses swore to the falseness of the testimony of another file equally long, or in divorce proceedings for non-support, tiresomely formal and undefended usually (probably because they had been pre-arranged), or in involved and technical disputes between landlords and tenants, debtors and creditors, purchasers and agents. Many of the trials were jury trials, and I was no more than a judicial automaton on a dais, obliged to give my decision according to the findings of the jury. Many of the cases involved property of so little value that it would not pay the fees of the empassioned lawyers employed to dispute its ownership; and these cases dragged along for days, till I felt like a man tied to a chair and compelled to listen forever to "a tale told by an idiot, full of sound and fury, signifying nothing."

(I had often admired in some wise old judge the Olympian air of detachment with which he listened to the recital of the human tragedies that were arraigned before him, as if he were above mortality and as indifferent as fate. I understood, now, that it was probably because he had begun young, as the judge of a county court, and been slowly bored to desiccation.)

One winter afternoon, after I had been listening for days to one of these cases—if I remember rightly, it concerned the ownership of some musty old mortgaged furniture that had been stored in a warehouse and was claimed by the mortgagee on the mortgage and by the warehouseman on a storage lien—the Assistant District Attorney interrupted the proceedings to ask me if I would not dispose of a larceny case that would not take two minutes. I was willing. He brought in a boy, whom I shall call "Tony Costello,"* and arraigned him before the court. The Clerk read the indictment; a railroad detective gave his testimony; the boy was accused of stealing coal from the tracks, and he had no defence. Frightened and silent, he stood looking from me to the jury, from the jury to the attorney, and from the attorney back to me—big-eyed and trembling—a helpless infant, trying to follow in our faces what was going on. The case was clear. There was nothing for me to do under the law but to find him guilty and sentence him to a term in the State Reform School. I did it—and prepared to go back to the affair of the second-hand furniture.

There had been sitting at the back of the courtroom an old woman with a shawl on her head, huddled up like a squaw, wooden-faced, and incredibly wrinkled. She waddled down the aisle toward the bench, while papers of commitment were being made out against the boy, and began to talk to the court interpreter in an excited gabble which I did not understand. I signed to the counsel for the warehouseman to proceed with his case; he rose—and he was greeted with the most soul-piercing scream of agony that I ever heard from a human throat. The old woman stood there, clutching her shawl to her breast, her toothless mouth open, her face as contorted as if she were being torn limb from limb, shrieking horribly. She threw her hands up to her head, grasped her poor, thin gray hair, and pulled it, yelling, with protruding eyes,

---

* This name, and those of all other children brought before the court, are disguised in order to protect the families from the consequences of publicity.

like a madwoman. When the bailiff of the court caught hold of her to take her from the room, she broke away from him and ran to the wall and beat her head against it, as if she would batter the court house down on us all and bury our injustice under the ruins. They dragged her out into the hall, but through the closed door I could still hear her shrieking—shrieking terribly. I adjourned the court and retreated to my chambers, very much shaken and unnerved; but I still heard her, in the hall, wailing and sobbing, and every now and then screaming as if her heart was being torn out of her.

I did not know what to do. I thought I had no power, under the law, to do anything but what I *had* done. The boy was guilty. The law required that I should sentence him. The mother might scream herself dumb, but I was unable to help her.

She continued to scream. Two reporters, attracted by the uproar, came to ask me if I could not do something for her. I telephoned the District Attorney and asked him whether I could not change my order against the boy—make it a suspended sentence—and let me look into the case myself. He was doubtful—as I was—about my right to do such a thing, but I accepted the responsibility of the act and he consented to it. After what seemed an hour to me—during which I could still hear the miserable woman wailing—the boy was returned to her and she was quieted.

Then I took the first step toward the founding of the Juvenile Court of Denver. I got an officer who knew Tony, and I went with him, at night, to the boy's home in the Italian quarter of North Denver. I need not describe the miserable conditions in which I found the Costellos living—in two rooms, in a filthy shack, with the father sick in bed, and the whole family struggling against starvation. I talked with Tony, and found him not a criminal, not a bad boy, but merely a boy. He had seen that his father and his mother and the baby were suffering from cold, and he had brought home fuel from the railroad tracks to keep them warm. I gave him a little lecture on the necessity of obeying the laws, and put him "on probation." The mother kissed my hands. The neighbours came in to salute me and to rejoice with the Costellos. I left them. But I carried away with me what must have been something of their view of my court and my absurd handling of their boy; and I began to think over this business of punishing infants as if they were adults and of maiming young lives by trying to make the gristle of their unformed characters carry the weight of our iron laws and heavy penalties.

(Let me add, in parentheses, that I saw, too, in the Costello home, the trail of the Beast. The father was ill of lead-poisoning from working twelve hours a day in a smelter. If society had done its duty by protecting him from the rapacity of his employer—by means of an eight-hour law and an employer's liability law—his son would not have been driven to steal.)

Some days later, when I opened court in the morning, the Clerk told me we had a burglary case to try. I looked about for the burglars. Three small boys, all still in their teens, were arraigned before me, their little freckled faces swollen with tears. They had broken into a barn on Arapahoe Street and had stolen pigeons from a man named Fay. The name startled me. "Fay?" I asked. He was pointed out to me in the court room. I knew him. It was the same man.

It was the same man whose pigeons I had once started out to steal, with three other youngsters, years before, when I was no bigger than the smallest tow-head who stood whimpering before me. I had not had "sand enough" to follow into the barn—it was the same barn—but at the time I had not thought *that* weakness to my credit, and neither had my companions. But "burglary"? It had been mere mischief, an adventure, a boy's way of plagueing old Fay whom we considered the "grouchy" enemy of all boys.

"I don't think these children should be charged with burglary," I said to the Clerk, rather shamefacedly. "Bring them into my chambers."

They came, and I confronted in their small persons the innocent crimes of my own "kid" days. They told me all about their "burglary," their feud with Fay—whom two of the boys accused of having taken *their* pigeons—and their boyish indignation against him for having

THE BEAST

called in the cops in the quarrel. I lectured them—as self-righteously as I could under the circumstances—and discharged them on suspended sentence, with a warning.

I went to the Clerk of the Court, Mr. Hubert L. Shattuck. "This is all wrong," I said. "It's all nonsense—bringing these children in here on criminal charges—to be punished—sentenced to prison—degraded for life!"

"Well, Judge," he explained, "we sometimes get short on our fee accounts, and it helps to increase fees in this office to bring the kids here."

It did. The officers of the court were paid so much for each conviction obtained by the court. They received no regular salaries. When they wished to make up arrears of pay, they rounded up a batch of youngsters and "put them through." The same thing was done in the police court, the court of the justice of the peace, and the criminal court.

It was more than absurd, more than wrong. It was an outrage against childhood, against society, against justice, decency and common sense. I began to search the statutes for the laws in the matter, to frequent the jails in order to see how the children were treated there, to compile statistics of the cost to the county of these trials and the cost to society of this way of making criminals of little children. And the deeper I went into the matter, the more astounded I became.

I found boys in the city jail, in cells reeking with filth and crawling with vermin, waiting trial for some such infantile offences as these I have described. I found boys in the county jail locked up with men of the vilest immorality, listening to obscene stories, subject to the most degrading personal indignities, and taking lessons in a high school of vice with all the receptive eagerness of innocence. I found that the older boys, now almost confirmed in viciousness, had begun their careers as Tony Costello had, or these burglars of the pigeon roost. And I found that many of the hardened criminals were merely the perfect graduates of the system of which I had been a sort of proud superintendent.

It kept me awake at night. It possessed me with a remorseful horror. I went about talking, "agitating," investigating, pestering the jailers, spending my Sundays in the cells among the criminals, trying to draft reform laws and in every way making myself a nuisance to everybody. I put into this work all the balked enthusiasm that my unsuccessful legislative reforms had left me. I could help the children, if I could not help the "grown-ups."

Some of these "grown-ups," whom my activities annoyed, began to say I was "crazy." Our family physician came, on that report, to remonstrate with me. A relative, very much alarmed, asked me to be careful of myself, not to "overdo." And I felt as if I were standing before a burning building, with children crying for help in the flames at the upper windows, while my friends remonstrated: "Be calm. Don't excite yourself so. People will think you're not sane!"

Not sane? Well it depends on what you consider "sane." One very sane thing to do would have been to turn my back on the fire and the children perishing in it, blame the inefficiency of the fire department, shrug a shoulder as if to say: "Well, it's none of my business," and go home to my dinner. I know *that* sort of sanity. I have seen it, many times, myself. But in the transports of my so-called insanity I found a section of the Colorado school law of April 12, 1899, by means of which I could get a ladder up to those doomed children. And this was it:

> "Section 4. Every child . . . who does not attend school . . . or who is in attendance at any school and is vicious, incorrigible or immoral in conduct, or who is an habitual truant from school, or who habitually wanders about the streets during school hours without any lawful occupation or employment, or who habitually wanders about the streets in the night time . . . shall be deemed *a juvenile disorderly person* and be subject to the provisions of this act."

A juvenile disorderly person! Not a criminal to be punished under the criminal law, but a ward of the state, to be corrected by the state as *parens patriae*. The law was a school law, intended only for the disciplining of school children; but it could be construed as I proceeded to construe it. It was not a steel fire-escape built according to the statutory regulations. It was merely a wooden ladder rotting in a back yard. But it would reach the lower stories—and I asked the District Attorney in future to file all his complaints against children under this law, in my court, according to a form which I furnished—and he agreed to do so.

Thus our "juvenile court" was begun informally, anonymously, so to speak, but effectually. It was, as far as I knew, the first juvenile court in America and the simple beginning of a reform that has since gone round the world.[*]

We had still to evolve some system of handling the children. We needed, above all, probation officers; and—proceeding still under the school law—I went to all the school boards, asking for the appointment of truant officers whom I could use in the court. I addressed meetings of schoolteachers, harangued women's clubs, Christian associations, charitable societies and church meetings, boring people with "the problem of the children" wherever I could get leave to speak. All this slowly aroused a public enthusiasm that was to become in time very powerful; it attracted attention to the court and helped me with the parents of delinquent children. It brought in subscriptions from public-spirited men and women to help on the "good work." It prepared for the passage of the necessary laws which I was drafting for the next session of the Legislature. And it led me, finally, as you shall see, into another collision with the Beast.

Meanwhile, however, a more imminent collision was impending.

A reform movement had been started in Denver against the liquor "dives," or "wine rooms," as they were called. There was a law on the statute books forbidding saloons to serve liquor to women, but a great part of the trade of the dives was done with prostitutes, and all the places were fitted up with "cribs" and "private rooms" where young girls could be drugged and ruined and the "white-slave" traffic pro-

---

[*] Chicago is technically entitled to the honour of having founded the first juvenile court so-called—under a law effective in June, 1899, two months after the approval of the law under which I worked.

moted. The wine-room keepers were backed, of course, by the political power of the brewers, and the inmates were used by the System on election day as repeaters, ballot-box stuffers, and poll thugs, as they are in so many of our cities. So, when the reform movement against the "wine-room evil" became so dangerously strong that the members of the Fire and Police Board saw that they would either have to enforce the law or involve the Democratic party in the danger of defeat, a dive keeper named Cronin was put forward in an appeal to the court for protection from the police. He was defended by Milton Smith, who was chairman of our Democratic State Central Committee. From a prosecution in a police magistrate's court, Cronin was brought before District Judge Peter L. Palmer, whose record needs no remark. And Judge Palmer promptly granted an injunction restraining the magistrate and the Fire and Police Board from prosecuting Cronin— grounding his decision on the delicious argument that the "wineroom law" was an infringement of the constitutional rights of women. The ministers who censured him were summoned before him and silenced with threats of fines for contempt of court. Cronin went back to his dive; the Fire and Police Board was rescued from an awkward position; and the wine rooms threw their doors wide open again to seduction.

I was interested in the affair because I had seen how many of the young girls brought before me had been ruined in wine rooms. I had jurisdiction in the case because my court was the court of appeal from the magistrate's court in which the test proceedings against Cronin had been begun. And I went out of my way to bring some friendly pressure to bear on the Deputy City Attorney to get him to file an appeal in my court.

He did it; and before the case was called I was visited in my chambers by another member of our Democratic County Executive Committee, who was also an agent for the brewers' trust. He wished to speak to me about the Cronin matter. "You know, Judge," he said, "there's a liberal element in this town that controls about 10,000 votes. If we offend them in this wine-room business, they'll hook up with the Republicans this fall, and we'll lose the elections. I know you're a good Democrat the same as I am, and I know you don't want to put the party in a hole. I'm interested in you. I want to see you succeed. I want to see you renominated and reelected, and I know you can't do it with this liberal element against you. Can you? Well, now, Judge Palmer has fixed this Cronin case all right. You can leave it with him, as it stands, and no one can say a word against you. It's up to him. If there's any kick from the church people, it's coming to *him*. Let *him* take it." And so on. It was the same ancient mixture of smiles and threats, of promised favours if I "played the game," and of political destruction prophesied if I refused. I was so used to the thing by this time that I was no longer even indignant at it. I thanked my honest friend for his disinterested solicitude about my political welfare, and got rid of him.

The law in the Cronin case was clear. A community, under its police powers, has the right, in the interests of "public health, public morals and public welfare," to forbid women doing anything detrimental to those interests. The wine room was an exercise of the police power. I so held in my decision, and I was sustained by the Supreme Court of Colorado and again by the Supreme Court of the United States when the penniless Cronin, represented by Milton Smith, appealed to those courts. You may wonder where Cronin got the money to carry on such expensive litigation. You would have understood his status in the matter if you had seen the look of reproachful bewilderment that he turned on his counsel when he heard my decision. It was as if he said: "Why, I thought this was only a stall! Where's your pull with this court? What sort of mess are you fellows trying to get me into?"

That was in August, 1901, and the elections were to be held in November. "You're done," the politicians told me. "If you ever get a nomination, you'll be scratched off the ticket by the liberal element. Sure as shooting!"

I did not much care. I had had the satisfaction of getting one heavy whack in on the snout of the Beast, and I went back to my work for the children so as to establish at least a precedent of procedure for my successor to follow. But that work, and my decision in the Cronin case, had brought me to the notice of the "troublesome church element." It would have been poor politics to stand against the sweep of the reform wave in an attempt to prevent my renomination. So I was allowed a place on the Democratic ticket again, and the System prepared quietly to "knife" me and elect my Republican opponent.

At that time I was squeamish about judges "playing politics," and I decided that I should make no speeches and take no active part in the campaign. I had been assessed $1,000 by the finance committee as my contribution to the campaign fund, and an officer of the First National Bank of Denver (in which the court funds were deposited) offered to pay the assessment for me. I was no longer as innocent as I had been in the days of Gardener's first nomination, and I refused the offer and paid the money from my own purse. But it took all I had; I had nothing left even to pay for the printing of a circular letter to the electorate, and I allowed some lawyer friends to pay for that publication—a mistake which I have never made since.

As election day approached it became apparent to every politician that I was hopelessly "out of the running." My Republican opponent was speaking every night—particularly from the bars of saloons—to enthusiastic audiences. I was posted in every "dive" in Denver as the one man on the Democratic ticket who was not "right." Sample ballots were put up, showing how to scratch me. The Democratic workers, to whom I had refused the spoils of office in the County Court, were openly working against me. It was cheerfully predicted at Democratic headquarters that I could not possibly pull through, that I should run "away behind the ticket." After looking over the situation myself, I decided that I had not the shadow of a chance; and I went to bed early, on Election Night, without waiting to hear the returns.

It was not until the following morning, when I came down to breakfast, that I learned, from the newspaper reports, what had happened. The lower wards had "knifed" me unmercifully; but in the upper districts, among the homes, unexpected thousands had rallied to save the "kids' court," and rebuke the "wine-room gang." Instead of running behind my ticket, I had run 8,000 votes ahead of it!

When I saw those headlines, my heart leaped to a beat that almost suffocated me—not only because the result was so unforeseen—such an unheard-of thing for Denver—so startling a shock even to professional politicians, with the ear always to the ground—but because it was to me a warrant of renewed faith in the people, the first sign of an aroused public opinion on which I might rely, the resurrection call to all my dead hopes of reform. It was as if there had come—out of blind darkness—with the flash of a stroke of lightning—the full day! The people were with me! (Even the Denver *Republican*, the paper that had opposed me, later conceded that "Lindsey was honestly elected"—"one officer who did not owe his advancement to illegal votes"—endorsed by "honest Democratic and Republican voters alike!") I gulped my morning coffee as a boy gulps his emotion, with a pain in the throat. I had broken the System. I had sent the Beast to shelter, limping, with its tail between its legs.

(Or rather, I thought I had.) As I walked down to my court that morning, the streets looked cleaner, the air seemed purer, life seemed more than ever good to live. My work was waiting for me, and thousands of good citizens were waiting to help me with it.

CHAPTER VI

THE BEAST
AND THE CHILDREN

M Y WORK WAS CERTAINLY WAITING FOR ME. I had found our Colorado probate law in a muddle. The sections conflicted, and the conflict led to litigation. The cost of administering the estates in the hands of the court was excessive, because the politicians had taken advantage of the conditions to create "jobs" for their henchmen. There was so much red tape that if we wished to sell "real estate" for a ward of the court it took us six months. In short, it was imperative that the law should be codified; and I organized a county judge's association and went to work on it. In the end, we not only simplified and harmonized the statutes, and protected the widows and orphans from legal exploitation, but saved estates in probate $50,000 a year by reducing the court rations of the political "workers."

The fee system needed reformation, and we had to work on laws for that purpose, too; but there is no space here to go in to the details of our struggle with the politicians in the matter. We finally succeeded only in getting a special law that forbade the collection of fees for prosecuting children.

Above all we needed "contributory juvenile delinquency" laws so that we might be able to prosecute parents for neglecting their children, and dive keepers, gamblers and such for tempting and seducing children; we needed laws establishing a juvenile court to which all children should be brought, instead of having them arraigned in the magistrate's court, the county court or the criminal court, haphazard; we had to obtain, for this juvenile court, probation officers with police powers so that we might arrest the wine-room keepers and such, whom the police, for political reasons, were protecting; we needed a detention school, so that children might no longer be put in jail; we had to strengthen the child-labour law and the compulsory school law; we needed trade schools, public playgrounds and public baths. But the Legislature was not to meet for twelve months, and I knew that before we could obtain any of these laws we must arouse a public demand for them. My work during 1902 was all schemed out to that end. And since the evils that we attacked are common to all our American cities, I wish to give the story of our fight in some detail.

Those politicians in Denver who love darkness and gum shoes are never tired of screaming from their burrows that I am a "grandstander." This is to them an epithet of opprobrium, you understand. They apply it to Roosevelt, La Follette, Folk, Jerome, Hughes and every other politician who has raised the window and shouted "Burglars!" when he heard the centre-bit in the night. It was in the year 1902 that I was first branded "a grand-stander." Ineffaceable stigma! I appealed to the people to help me obtain laws for the people. I even did *that!*

I appealed to them directly and indirectly, from the platform whenever I could get any of them before a platform, and through the newspapers whenever a reporter gave me an interview or an editor allowed me a column for an article. And pursuing the same policy

I even used my place in the county court to arouse public opinion, and did it with a "sensational" denunciation that was flagrant "grandstanding" of the most deliberate sort.

It happened in this way: I found on my return to the bench that the law against the wine rooms was not being enforced. I found that the gambling hells were all open. I made the rounds of them at night, unrecognized, and saw boys in knickerbockers at tables evidently reserved for their use. I saw indescribable things in the wine rooms and the dance halls connected with them, where young girls from laundries, factories, hotels and restaurants were being debauched. (For example, three girls who had been enticed into a saloon were discovered next day in the cellar of the building, by a woman passing on the street, who heard their groans; they were lying there stark naked, horribly ill and praying for death; and the policeman on the beat, when he was appealed to, refused to arrest the dive keeper.)

Poor mothers appealed to my court to recover from the gamblers the money lost by their young sons. Employers prosecuted, before me, unfortunate boys who had stolen to make good their losses at the gaming tables. Even the newsboys were being encouraged to play "policy" with their pitiably small earnings. And when I presented to the Assistant District Attorney the evidence against the gamblers taken publicly in my court, he confessed—confidentially—that his chief, District Attorney Lindsley, would not prosecute, because that was "the policy of the administration."

I went to the District Attorney and demanded, "Why don't you arrest the dive keepers?" He replied that this was the duty of the police and that the Police Board refused to act. I wrote to the Chief of Police and he replied that he had given my letter to the president of the Board—Mr. Frank Adams.

Mr. Frank Adams was not only president of the Police Board; he was president, also, of the ice trust that supplied brewers, saloon keepers and wine-room men with ice. He was a machine politician, with two brothers in the game; and he played the game "for all there was in it."

My letter to the Chief brought Frank Adams to my chambers to see me, and I made a personal appeal to him, on behalf of the children, with my hand on his shoulder, looking him in the face. I told him of what I had seen, of how the young girls and boys were being sacrificed; and he promised, and repeated his promise, that he would see that the laws were enforced and the children protected. But he did not keep his word. I saw as much, with my own eyes, in a personal investigation; and the officers of my court confirmed it. I sent for the Chief of Police, showed him affidavits furnished by Mr. E. K. Whitehead, the secretary of the Humane Society, exposing the conditions, and accused the Police Board and himself of bad faith.

He replied: "You're right. Things are just as you say, but I'm not going to be held responsible any longer. It's the policy of the administration. They think they need the support of these people to carry the next elections. Your kick must be against the Board and not against me."

This was corroborated by what I had heard from a dive keeper whom I had sentenced in my court. "Judge," he had said, "I don't blame you, but I do blame that Police Board. Their man came to me collecting for the chairman of the party committee, and I put up $500, on the promise that the police wouldn't interfere with my saloon. Now he says you're kicking up a fuss and he can't protect me here." It was corroborated later by Frank Adams himself, when he tried to persuade me not to interfere judicially with the Police Board's right to appoint licence inspectors, because, he said, "We've got to keep these dive keepers in line." It was the System again; the System was making money from the debauching of young girls, and the Police Board was acting as toll keeper on this public road to prostitution.

I wrote a note to the members of the Board inviting them to my court one Saturday morning, in May, got the newspaper reporters to come, and then took my place on the bench and publicly accused the astonished commissioners of neglecting their duties, of knowingly permitting the dives to ruin children, and of being personally responsible for much of the appalling immorality that came before my court.

I addressed myself to them, but it was to the public ear that I was speaking. I described the cases that had come under my own eyes and named the dives in which they had originated. For the public ear again, I threatened that if the Board did not stop this traffic in the debauchery of little children, I should find means of obtaining power whereby our court could stop it. In short, I "grand-standed"—with a megaphone.

The newspapers were the megaphone. They printed, on the front pages, "scare-head" accounts of that scene in the court room, with portraits of the police commissioners and cartoons of them "sweating" under the denunciations of the court. The ministers took up the shout and repeated from their pulpits the facts I had given and the charges I had made. There was no withstanding the storm. The worst of the dives put up their shutters forthwith, and before they dared open again we had obtained from the Legislature the "contributory delinquency" laws and the police powers for probation officers that put the protection of the children in our hands. The System still has in Denver its tollgates for the men and women who go "the primrose path to the everlasting bonfire," but at least it no longer levies on the helpless boys and girls whom it once dragged forcibly to physical and moral ruin.

Meanwhile, we had been carrying on, also, our campaign against the jail, with the ultimate purpose of obtaining a detention home-school for children. I had found conditions in the jails almost as bad as they were in the dives. Boys repeated to me the obscene stories they had heard there, from the older prisoners, and described the abominable pollutions that had been committed on their little bodies. I learned from a boy sixteen years old, a confirmed criminal, that he had been first imprisoned when he was ten and that he had learned in jail how to crack safes and had practised that art successfully when he was fifteen; he told of it with pride, and with an admiration of the man who had taught him. He said it was his ambition now to kill a policeman whom he hated, and he had taken as his model in life a young outlaw named Harry Tracy whose exploits had been reported in the newspapers. I found that the boys were guilty of indecent practices among themselves and that, being confined in the matron's quarters, they had broken off the plaster of the wall that separated them from the women's room; and the girls there—it is unmentionable. Schoolboys they were. And when they were released, they went back to school, with the evil lessons they had learned, and taught them to their companions, spreading the plague, and infecting hundreds of young lives with the deadly virus of a physical vice.

In addition to all this I found that some of the police were guilty of cruelties to the boys, used language to them that is unreportable, and unconsciously taught the boys to hate the law and look upon us all as their enemies. Several boys complained to me that they had been beaten by the jailer, and I found on investigation that they had; the welts and bruises on their bodies showed it; and prisoners who had seen them beaten testified to it. One morning a boy, released from jail where he had been locked up on a suspicion that proved false, came running into my chambers in hysterics, with the most awful look of horror on his face, and poured out to me with sobs and frightened shudderings, the story of how the police had cursed and abused him, and of how the vagrants and criminals in the "bull pen," where he had been thrown, had spat upon him and maltreated him. I kept going to the Chief of Police with these complaints, and to Frank Adams, the president of the Police Board. And they kept replying that the boys were lying to me, and that I was "going batty" on the "kid question" and encouraging the "little devils" to resist the police.

Things went on in this way until our juvenile bills came before the Legislature, and then the opposition of the Police Board and the System came to a head under Senator "Billy" Adams, a brother of Frank Adams, the president of the Police Board. Nothing was done openly. The Board, of course, objected to allowing our probation officers police powers, chiefly because we could then prevent the wine-room keepers from getting "protection" and paying for it; but such a reason for opposition could not be acknowledged. Instead, the bills were fought secretly in the committees and kept from a vote in the House by means of the same jugglery on the calendar that I had seen used before, on our "three-fourths jury" bill. After consulting with a friendly newspaper reporter named Harry Wilbur, of the *Rocky Mountain News*, I decided to "grandstand" again. Wilbur had been a police court reporter and knew conditions in the jails. I gave him an interview in which I described some of the cases I had seen and investigated, and I gave him a free hand to add any other "horrible an' revoltin' details" that he knew to be true.

The result was an article that took even my breath away when I read it next day on the front page of the newspaper. It was the talk of the town. It was certainly the talk of the Police Board; and Mr. Frank Adams talked to the reporters in a high voice, indiscreetly. He declared that the boys were liars, that I was "crazy," and that conditions in the jails were as good as they could be. This reply was exactly what we wished. I demanded an investigation. The Board professed to be willing, but set no date. We promptly set one *for* them—the following Thursday at two o'clock in my chambers at the Court House— and I invited to the hearing Governor Peabody, Mayor Wright, fifteen prominent ministers in the city, the Police Board and some members of the City Council.

On Thursday morning—to my horror—I learned from a friendly Deputy Sheriff that the subpoenas I had ordered sent to a number of boys whom I knew as jail victims had not been served. I had no witnesses. And in three hours the hearing was to begin. I appealed to the Deputy Sheriff to help me. He admitted that he could not get the boys in less than two days. "Well then," I said, "for heaven's sake, get me Mickey. " And Mickey? Well, Mickey was known to fame as "the worst kid in town." As such, his portrait had been printed in the newspapers—posed with his shine-box over his shoulder, a cigarette in the corner of his grin, his thumbs under his suspenders at the shoulders, his feet crossed in an attitude of nonchalant youthful deviltry. He had been brought before me more than once on charges of truancy, and I had been using him in an attempt to organize a newsboys' association under the supervision of the court. Moreover, he had been one of the boys who had been beaten by the jailer, and I knew he would be grateful to me for defending him.

It was midday before the Sheriff brought him to me. "Mickey," I said, "I'm in trouble, and you've got to help me out of it. You know I helped *you*."

"Betcher life yuh did, Judge," he said. "I'm wit' yuh. W'at d' yuh want?"

I told him what I wanted—every boy that he could get, who had been in jail. "And they've got to be in this room by two o'clock. Can you do it?"

Mickey threw out his dirty little hand. "Sure I kin. Don't yuh worry, Judge. Get me a wheel—dhat's all."

I hurried out with him and got him a bicycle, and he flew off down Sixteenth Street on it, his legs so short that his feet could only follow the pedals half way round. I went back to my chambers to wait.

I trusted Mickey. He was the brightest street gamin that our court ever knew. Once we organized a baseball nine, with Mickey as captain, in his quarter of the town where the Irish boys were continually at war in the streets with the Jewish children of the district. We gave them uniforms and bats and balls, on condition that they stop smoking cigarettes and fighting. His nine became the "champines" of the town among boys of their age; and one day in court I congratulated Mickey on his victories. "Aw well, Judge," he said, "yuh see it's dhis way: half o' dhese kids is Irish an' half o' dhem 's Jews. An' yuh know when dh' Irish an' dhe Jews get togedher dhey kin lick anyt'ing dhat comes down dhe pike!" "How can that be," I asked him, "when there are nine boys in a baseball team? There must be more of one than the other." "No, dhere ain't, neidher," he said. "Dhe pitcher's an Irish Jew an' dhe best kid in dhe bunch. Come here, Greeny." "Greeny" was a Greenstein and he was red-headed. If he was not an Irish Jew I don't know what he could have been!

Anyway, I knew that if Mickey could not get the boys for me, no one could. I waited. As two o'clock approached, the ministers began to come into my room, one by one, and take seats in readiness. Mr. Wilson of the Police Board arrived to represent his fellow-commissioners. The Deputy District Attorney came, the president of the upper branch of the City Council came, Mayor Wright came, and even Governor Peabody came—but no boys! I felt like a man who had ordered a big dinner in a strange restaurant for a party of friends, and then found that he had not brought his purse. . . . I was just about to begin my apologies when I heard an excited patter of small feet on the stairs and the shuffle and crowding of Mickey's cohorts outside in the hall. I threw open the door. "I got 'em, Judge," Mickey cried.

He had them—to the number of about twenty. I shook him by the shoulder, speechless with relief. "I tol' yuh we'd stan' by yuh, Judge," he grinned.

He had the worst lot of little jailbirds that ever saw the inside of a county court, and he pointed out the gem of his collection proudly— "Skinny" a lad in his teens, who had been in jail twenty-two times! "All right, boys," I told them, "I don't know you all, but I'll take Mickey's word for you. You've all been in jail and you know what you do there—all the dirty things you hear and see and do yourselves. I want you to tell some gentlemen in here about it. Don't be scared. They're your friends the same as I am. The cops say you've been lying to me about the way things are down in the jails there, and I want you to tell the truth. Nothing but the truth, now. Mickey, you pick them out and send them in one by one—your best witnesses first."

I went back to my chambers. "Gentlemen," I said, "we're ready."

I sat down at the big table with the Governor at my right, the Mayor at my left and the president of the Board of Supervisors and Police Commissioner Wilson at either end of the table. The ministers seated themselves in the chairs about the room. (We allowed no newspaper reporters in, because I knew what sort of vile and unprintable testimony was coming.) Mickey sent in his first witness.

One by one, as the boys came, I impressed upon them the necessity of telling the truth, encouraged them to talk, and tried to put them at their ease. I started each by asking him how often he had been in jail, what he had seen there, and so forth. Then I sat back and let him tell his story.

And the things they told would raise your hair. I saw the blushes rise to the foreheads of some of the ministers at the first details. As we went on, the perspiration stood on their faces. Some sat pale, staring appalled at these freckled youngsters from whose little lips, in a sort of infantile eagerness to tell all they knew, there came stories of bestiality that were the more horrible because they were so innocently, so boldly, given. It was enough to make a man weep; and indeed tears of compassionate shame came to the eyes of more than one father there, as he listened. One boy broke down and cried when he told of the vile indecencies that had been committed upon him by the older criminals; and I saw the muscles working in the clenched jaws of some of our "investigating committee"—saw them swallowing the lump in the throat—saw them looking down at the floor blinkingly, afraid of losing their self-control. The Police Commissioner made the mistake of cross-examining the first boy, but the frank answers he got only exposed worse matters. The boys came and came, till at last, a Catholic priest, Father O'Ryan, cried out: "My God! I have had enough!" Governor Peabody said hoarsely: "I never knew there was such immorality *in the world!*" Some one else put in, "It's awful— awful!" in a half groan.

"Gentlemen," I said, "there have been over two thousand Denver boys put through those jails and those conditions, in the last five years. Do you think it should go on any longer?"

Governor Peabody rose. "No," he said; "no. Never in my life have I heard of so much rot—corruption—vileness—as I've heard to-day from the mouths of these babies. I want to tell you that nothing I can do in my administration can be of more importance—nothing I can do will I do more gladly than sign those bills that Judge Lindsey is trying to get through the Legislature to do away with these terrible conditions. And if," he said, turning to the Police Commissioner, "Judge Lindsey is *'crazy,'* I want my name written under his, among the *crazy* people. And if any one says these boys are 'liars,' that man is a liar himself!"

Phew! The "committee of investigation" dissolved, the boys trooped away noisily, and the ministers went back to their pulpits to voice the horror that had kept them silent in my small chamber of horrors for two hours. Their sermons went into the newspapers under large black headlines; and by the end of the next week our juvenile court bills were passed by the Legislature and made law in Colorado.

While public indignation was still steaming we got a grant from the City Council for our Detention School, and then we followed up with a demand for public playgrounds and public baths. Neither came easily. It took us two years of almost continuous "agitation" in the newspapers, at council and committee meetings and from the public platform. We had to found a juvenile improvement association, collect statistics pertinent to the matter, get estimates of the probable cost of the improvements and so forth. Mr. W. M. Downing, a member of the Park Board, finally carried the day with his associates and got a grant for the playgrounds, but the public bath was still lacking. For a time the Board of County Commissioners allowed us to fit up a sort of bathhouse for court children in the basement of the Court Building, but this aid was withdrawn when I antagonized the Board in another matter. Finally I turned the Court House fountains over to the street gamin—on condition that they wore swimming trunks—and protected them when they ran, dripping, into my court room from the pursuit of the indignant "cops." It seemed to me that if the citizens of Denver could afford a perpetual shower bath to a few bronze painted cherubs in a fountain, they could afford it to these more sensitive and grateful cherubs of flesh and blood, who were coated with dust and dirt. The council finally saw the matter from the same point of view, and the free baths were established.

Do I boast? By no means—although here is the only opportunity I shall have to boast throughout this story of the war with the Beast. I do not feel like boasting; for while we were winning in the fight for the children, I struck the trail of the Beast in a wholly unexpected quarter, followed it up blindly and stumbled into a struggle that showed me for the first time how the brute could defend itself. It had been merely dodging me and growling at me heretofore. Now it fell upon me tooth and claw; and the fact that I have any public life or reputation left to me at all is due to the lucky chance that is only short of being a miracle.

CHAPTER VII

THE BEAST, GRAFT AND BUSINESS

ONE SATURDAY MORNING in the early part of May, 1902—while we were still in the midst of our fight against the wine rooms and against the jail—I saw a package of ledger sheets lying on a chair in the office of Mr. Thos. L. Bonfils, who was then Clerk of my court, and on top of the package there was a bill. I picked it up, absent-mindedly. It was from the Smith-Brooks Printing Company, who held the county contract for such supplies. It read: "To 1,000 sheets of paper, $280."

Twenty-eight cents a sheet!

"What?" I asked the Clerk. "Are we paying twenty-eight cents a sheet for ledger paper?"

He replied: "I don't know. The bills never come here. They go to the Commissioners. That one must have been left by mistake."

"Well," I said, puzzled, "it seems funny! Twenty-eight cents a sheet. Go down to Smith-Brooks for me and ask if this bill's right."

Court had adjourned. I went into my chambers and took up my
work there—until the Clerk came back from Smith-Brooks with the
explanation that the bill should have been delivered to the Clerk of the
Board of County Commissioners. To my inquiry about the correct-
ness of the price charged, they returned the courteous reply: "That's
none of your business!"

It seemed to me that since the bill was charged against our court,
it *was* somewhat our business, and I felt a desire to know how many
bills of this sort we were being charged with. I sent a highly disin-
genuous message to the Clerk of the County Board, telling him that
I thought he was mixing up our accounts with those of some other
court, and charging us with supplies that we had not received; and I
asked him to send us our bills, to let us see them. At five o'clock that
afternoon I received a large bundle of them. One hasty glance showed
me what I had stumbled upon.

Graft! Petty graft! And not so very petty, either. We were being
charged $6 each for letter files that, I knew, were not worth more than
forty cents. Letter paper furnished for my use was costing the county
$36 a thousand sheets and I was sure that it was not worth more than
$4 a thousand. On every item in those bills the county was being
charged from ten to twenty times the ordinary market price of the
goods. I could scarcely believe my eyes. I did not believe them until I
had called into my chambers a wholesale printer whom I knew; and he
confirmed my suspicions, reluctantly, and only after I had promised
not to involve him in the affair.

I was now convinced that the county was being robbed, but I was
not convinced that the Commissioners were aware of the robbery. So,
that afternoon, I wrote a letter to the chairman of the Board asking him whether the Commissioners knew what was being paid for
these supplies, and what should have been paid for them. I received no
answer. I waited, hoping to hear ultimately that during his silence he
had been honestly looking into the matter. I waited ten days. Then I
wrote again, telling him what I had discovered and asking him what
it meant.

This brought Mr. Fred Watts, a member of the Board, to ask my stenographer: "What the devil's the matter with Ben? Hasn't he got any gratitude? Ask him what the hell he means." It brought also a number of political friends with the same question. One of them said: "Judge, those fellows may be guilty, and I believe they are, but it's not your place to show them up. You were appointed to your office by these men originally, and you ought to stand by your friends." I went to a fellow-judge and told him what I had discovered. He replied: "I don't want to know about it. I don't want to be in any way responsible. You had better let the whole thing alone. You know what politics *are* in this town. It's the District Attorney's place to investigate—not yours." I did not believe that District Attorney Lindsley would investigate, except under pressure, and I asked this judge if he would join me in demanding that Lindsley *should* investigate. He replied: "No, no. I'll have nothing to do with it." Other judges made similar replies. A county official said: "Lindsey, those men appointed me to my office here, and I don't give a d—— if they steal the county blind. It will ruin you, if you have anything to do with it. Keep out of it if you want to have any future in politics!"

I went on with my court work, carrying this guilty secret in my mind; and it was as heavy as remorse. I kept coming back to it, examining and reexamining the bills, and comparing them with the prices that I got from other stationers from time to time. And the more I thought of it, the worse it seemed. Finally I wrote a peremptory letter to the Commissioners threatening them that if they did not do something in the matter I should move for an investigation myself.

My previous letters had been merely polite raps on a locked door. This last one had the effect of threatening to burst in with a sledge hammer. Tom Phillips,* the chairman of the Board, rushed out of his silence to assure me of his own innocence and accuse two other members, Fred Watts and Frank Bishop. They promptly followed with

---

* Phillips is now head of the Street Sprinkling Department in Denver.

messages accusing Phillips of grafting on bridge contracts, and demanding an investigation into the bridge contracts if there was to be one into the stationery supplies. Through Phillips, I got access to the county files, had copies made of all the stationery bills I could find, and appointed an investigating committee on my own responsibility to draw up a report—a committee consisting of a wholesale stationer, a lawyer, and the Clerk of our court. Their investigation showed that during the sixteen months previous to April, 1902, the county, on the bills that we had obtained, had paid Smith-Brooks about $40,000 more than the supplies were worth.

What was worse, we found that the county specifications for the contract were worded in such a way that honest bids under them were impossible. For example, Smith-Brooks would offer to sell a 26-page index for $12, and a 52-page index for $1. No one could afford to sell a 52-page index, as specified, for $1; and, of course, none was ordered from Smith-Brooks at that figure. The county always bought the smaller index for twelve times the cost of the larger one. But if a printer who did not "stand in" with the Commissioners had made such a bid, the Board could have put him into bankruptcy. Paper, envelopes, court blanks and all other stationery supplies were bought in the same way. It was clearly a contract of disguised fraud arranged and carried out by both Smith-Brooks and the County Board.

I give all these tiresome details, because of what followed. And the reason for what followed was at the time not clear to me. I was in the jungle again—a jungle of petty graft and public robbery, assailed on all sides by political animosities, little spites, threats and insults. And in the tangle of intricate intrigue, distracted by buffets from all sides, in despair of honesty in any quarter, I could no more than struggle blindly ahead, bewildered and half dazed.

In order that what followed may not be as bewildering in the recital as it was in the fact, let me explain that the County Commissioners were valuable to the utility corporations in two ways: they claimed and exercised power, under the law, to raise or lower assessments, and to equalize and rebate taxes; and they appointed the "judges of elec-

THE BEAST, GRAFT AND BUSINESS

tions" who were supposed to guard the ballot boxes from fraudulent votes. They had reduced the assessment of the Denver Union Water Company from $1,000,000 to $300,000—the water company whose property was recently valued by its own appraisers at $14,400,000. In the years 1901 and 1902 the Denver Union Water Company and the Denver City Tramway Company had had their taxes rebated nearly $200,000 by these Commissioners whom I was accusing. By an illegal legal proceeding they remitted fines imposed by the courts on dive keepers who were "in right" with the System. (See case Supreme Court of Colorado 5662, Taylor *vs.* Kelleher, reported 97 Pacific, 353.) Many election judges whom they appointed were notorious crooks. The Board, in fact, was a vital and sensitive part of the Beast, situated midway in the barrel of its body, where the man who attacked it came within reach of all its fore and hind claws.

The hind claws reached for me first. I began to receive perfumed notes from unknown young women, inviting me to meet them at various places downtown. Not having been accustomed to receive such billets-doux, I thought some practical joker among my friends was making game of me; and I merely filed the letters with the court correspondence, and did not answer them. Then one "Len" Rogers, whom I knew as a member of the Democratic Club, and an election crook, came to me one evening, with a verbal invitation of a similar sort from a young woman who, he assured me, was " crazy" about me. I had no overwhelming desire to meet any of "Len" Rogers's young ladies, but I did not tell him so. I said I was busy. He was not discouraged. He came back again another night with a more pressing invitation. I became curious. Where did the young lady live? He named a section of Curtis Street where there were a number of houses of ill-repute; and I found out, afterward—from a friendly newspaper reporter who heard the story, as reporters do—that several members of "the gang" were waiting for me, in the house, to expose me as a libertine if I came there. (I wonder how often the Beast has succeeded in this little game? Did you ever notice how many reformers are nipped in the beginning of a career by a timely scandal?)

Having failed to catch me in that way, an investigation of my private life was started. Fortunately I had no private life worth investigating. My life—what there was of it—had all been public; and I had been too poor and too busy to get into mischief. The sleuthing gave me an uncomfortable feeling of being watched and hunted, but nothing "eventuated," as the newspapers say. After that came threats—vague threats of public dishonour—the end of my political career! Childish threats and childish persecutions. The engineer of the Court House would cut off the electric light in my chambers at night when I was working with our "investigating committee"; and our investigation was actually carried on by the light of candles that we bought at the corner drugstore. The janitor refused to clean our offices until the closets became so unsanitary that we had to appeal to the Board of Health. I became a sort of outcast among the county officials, and no one would speak to me in the corridors. As I went to my court room, men would mutter, for me to hear: "There's the perjured little ——!" I found myself avoided on the streets and shunned on the cars; and friends came to me with scandalous stories that were being circulated about me downtown. For the first time in my life I thanked my lucky stars that I was not married. I began to feel as if I were living in a nightmare. It is impossible to convey the effect of it—but it *was* effective. Oh, the Beast knows how to fight!

It was effective and it was not; for besides getting on my nerves it got on my temper. I pushed on the work of investigation, resolved to reply to the covert attacks on me by a public exposure that should at least let in the light upon the struggle. At once all my old friends in the Democracy flocked to me, pleading with me not to ruin the party's chances in the next election by publishing the scandal. Mr. John T. Bottom, then attorney for the Commissioners, made the same plea. "After the elections, Judge," he promised, "we'll bring suit and recover the money." He begged me to spare "the boys," and not be an "ingrate." He quoted lines from "Julius Caesar" about the ambition that climbs a ladder and then scorns the "base degrees" by which it ascended. He came with two of the guilty Commissioners, Fred Watts and Frank Bishop, to my chambers, and I had to face their appeals not to ruin them and disgrace their families. (Bishop was then a candidate for Governor, and I had always thought a good deal of him.) They reminded me that they had made me County Judge in the first place. That took me on the raw. I said: "It was not *your* office. It belongs to the people. I am serving *them*, not you. Do you think because you used your public trust to appoint me a judge that I must let you steal? Besides, I wrote you letters, friendly letters, about these outrageous bills a month ago, and you did nothing. That contract with Smith-Brooks is still in force. Supplies are being delivered to my court, for which I am responsible, at outrageous prices. You have acted like a lot of thieves and grafters—and you keep it up—and you want me to protect you in it. I won't do it. I'm going to make my report public. If this stealing is to go on, it must go on in public. I refuse to protect it and be a silent party in it. I'll publish my report."

It was published in the Democratic paper, *The Rocky Mountain News*, on June 11, 1902.

You think, perhaps, that it made a great stir. And it did. But if you think that the Commissioners were immediately indicted and condemned, you are as simple as I was. They were first allowed to appoint an investigating committee of two men friendly to them; and I—after a public protest—was allowed to appoint a third member, the printer who had been on my first committee. Their investigation was a farce, but it had one serious aspect for me. The business men who had given me the price lists, etc., on which we had founded our first report—men who had said to me that the Commissioners were "thieves" and the Smith-Brooks Company were "thieves"—went to the witness stand before this white-washing committee and testified for Smith-Brooks and for the Commissioners. They could not "afford" to hurt their business, they confessed to me. One stationer whom I knew as an honest man and a prominent church member, said to me: "What! Do you expect me to go on the witness stand and tell what I told *you*? Never. I do business with the county. It'd ruin me." I found that he had a "sub-contract" with the principal contractor for supplies, and when he appeared in court, it was as advisor to the grafters. (The Beast is to the business man what the "Black Hand" is to the Mulberry Street banker.)

I was not allowed to appear before this committee, although I offered to testify; and at the conclusion of the "investigation" the two friends of the Commissioners made a report exonerating them. This, however, did not stay the public clamour. The *News* kept insisting that the District Attorney, Harry A. Lindsley, must prosecute. It became evident that he must either do so or ruin himself in the public estimation. And in July the three Commissioners were charged with a misdemeanour instead of a felony—under a statute that provided, as the extreme penalty of guilt, a fine of $300 and dismissal from office— and the Commissioners were about to go out of office, in any case.

It was nearly a year before we could get them brought to trial, and in the meantime—October and November, 1908—Mr. Charles J. Hughes, Jr., attorney for the tramway company, assisted by the company's agent, William G. Smith (whom I had known as Speaker of the House of Representatives) obtained from the accused Commissioners a rebate of $70,000 on back taxes owed by the tramway company. Judge Peter L. Palmer dismissed the injunction proceedings that had been begun by the Municipal League, to prevent the granting of the rebate. And John T. Bottom, attorney for the Commissioners, favoured and argued for the rebate. "Is it possible," the Denver *Post* asked editorially, "that the fact that Charles J. Hughes, Jr., is also attorney for the Commissioners in the criminal cases brought against them in connection with the county printing steals has had anything to do with the Board's action in this matter of tax compromise with the tramway?" It had seemed to me that it *was* faintly possible; and the possibility became less faint with every day that followed.

The elections had come on. I was interested in the contest for various reasons, but I was as carefully shunned by politicians as if it had been I, and not the Commissioners, who was accused of crime. A friend who was a member of the Democratic Executive Committee went so far as to invite me to a meeting of the committee with the ward leaders and such—being able, under the rules, to invite one initiated guest to the council—but he did it only after I had pledged myself not to say who invited me. I went. And heavens! What a reception!

The meeting was held in the Windsor Hotel, in a long and narrow back room that had been stripped of everything but chairs, ranged along the walls for the "leaders," and a small table for the chairman and his secretary. Bill Davoren* presided—the redoubtable Bill—with his small head broadly based on his pink jowls. The "interests" never had a more faithful trencherman than "Bill." The grafting Commissioners were conspicuous to his left. The District Attorney, Harry A. Lindsley, was equally conspicuous to his right. Along the walls a galaxy of "the gang" was seated, somewhat in the order of importance. I slid into a chair near the door, scowled at, snubbed and carefully avoided even by those who, I knew, were not unfriendly to me. I was a political leper among clean men.

As soon as proceedings began, Harry Lindsley made a motion that no one should be allowed to address the meeting except members of the executive committee, unless called upon by the chairman. After some significant glances in my direction, the motion was carried. I did not speak—except once. That was to remark, to a man next me, that one of the candidates named for an office was "a good man for the place." I was overheard. My commendation was passed along the line; and the name of the candidate was promptly crossed off the slate! ("Hell!" a friend of his said to me, "what did you say that for?" I apologized.)

I had been warned not to "start the commissioner business." "You know," my friend had told me, "we've got to get our election judges appointed, and Tom Phillips says if we don't stand by him and the other Commissioners, they'll appoint men that'll knife us at the polls." But the air was full of "the commissioner business." The *News* was charging that the "grafters' ring" was in control of the party. There was a popular demand for their repudiation. And some one at

---

* Davoren is now president of the Denver Fire and Police Board.

this executive meeting proposed a plank in the Democratic platform declaring, mildly, for honesty in public office and an investigation of any alleged dishonesty.

Tom Phillips, in an angry outburst, maintained that this plank was a reflection on the Commissioners. "We won't stand for it," he said. "We won't stand for it." And in a confused and somewhat befuddled harangue, he threatened that if the plank was inserted he would do what he would do.

"Dear people," behold your politicians! They did not dare declare for any investigations of honesty in public office. Mr. Chas. J. Hughes, Jr.,—who is now United States Senator from Colorado, and was then attorney for the tramway company—Chas. J. Hughes, the cleverest corporation lawyer at the Colorado bar, wealthy, honoured, brainy, and distinguished—Chas. J. Hughes rose to oppose the resolution, in a ringing and eloquent speech. Had not these Commissioners served their party and their county faithfully for many years? Should the party turn upon them now? They had not been tried. They had not been found guilty. No, no. No declaration for any investigations of honesty in public office for Mr. Chas. J. Hughes. And after some satirical shafts directed toward the obscure corner in which I sat, he concluded a corporation attorney's defence of a corporation's tools in office, with an appeal that carried the day.

The plank was voted down. I do not remember that any "leader" at the caucus except ex-Governor Thomas, said even a mild word in defence of honesty and in support of an investigation.

At the party convention, next day, I appeared by proxy—I was not a delegate—to make a speech in support of this declaration for "honesty in public office" (with no names mentioned), which Mr. Ed. Keating of the *Rocky Mountain News* was to propose. The chairman of the convention was the attorney for Smith-Brooks! John T. Bottom, attorney for the Commissioners, met me on the floor and threatened that if I opened my mouth I should be accused before the convention of something awful, something damning, something, however, unspecified! I told him to go ahead and be as awful as he chose.

Keating proposed the resolution, and I tried to speak to it, but we were howled down with contempt and anger, curses and execrations. We were treated as if we had been a pair of rowdies who had interrupted, with profanity and an unclean presence, a meeting in a church. I shall never forget the angry indignation in the eyes of some of the delegates about me.

I began to ask myself: "What have I done? Am I really the sort of despicable hound that I seem to appear to these fellow-Democrats?" I actually began to wonder whether I might not be some sort of political renegade, incapable of appreciating my own treason. And yet, some way, I could not see that I was!

When Bryan came to town, a great mass-meeting was held for him; and all the county judges—excepting myself—and all the county officials—*including* the three grafting Commissioners—were invited to sit on the platform behind him. I squeezed into the crowded hall and watched the Commissioners, on the stage, lead the rip-roaring applause that greeted Mr. Bryan's fervid defence of the people and the people's rights. I knew, of course, that the officials would return next day to the Court House, and send an order for supplies to a "prominent business man" that would read something like this: "One dozen letter files, $78" (value $4.80); "one thousand sheets of ruled paper, $280" (value $10); "fifty index books, $600" (value $30). And when Roosevelt came to town, the "prominent business man" (being a Republican) would cheer Roosevelt as wildly as the Commissioners cheered Bryan. And the people's rights would be safe. Quite safe.

Do not imagine that I am cynical. I am not attacking men. I am attacking the conditions that debauch men. I am not attacking these victims of the Beast and the System; I am trying to show the power of the Beast and the effects of the System. "Judge," Tom Phillips once said to me, "if these big guys, who put up the money to elect us, expect us to help their big graft of hundreds of thousands in rebates of taxes to their corporations, why shouldn't we get a little on the side?" "And, Judge," the prominent business man pleaded, "I've got to do business with these people. They can ruin me in a week if they want to.

I can't afford to quarrel with my bread and butter." "And, Judge," a beady-eyed little crook said to me one day in my chambers, "I read the papers. I know what's goin' on in this burg. What do you want to jump on *me* fer? I ain't swipin' the way those fullahs is."

Long before the Commissioners came up for trial I knew that it was I who was to be tried, not they. They were to be acquitted, vindicated, and I was to be "put in a hole." The sheriff was friendly to the "accused." The jury was made up of their friends and of men with whom they did business. The judge was brought in from Pueblo County, where the Colorado Fuel and Iron Company controlled the political machine, and he had aspirations. Cass Herrington, counsel for the Colorado Fuel and Iron Company, acted as a sort of silent attorney for the defence. Charles J. Hughes, Jr., attorney for the corporations, was the chief counsel, and when he got me in the witness box what a time he had, to be sure! District Attorney Lindsley refused to appear in court against the grafters, but I had a friend in his office, a deputy attorney, George Allen Smith, and for his attempt to convict the grafters he was forced later to resign his place. The strain of the trial and of the persecutions that accompanied it, wore me out. I was ill. I heard on all sides that the Commissioners were to be acquitted and that I was to be prosecuted for perjury. I heard it from men in the District Attorney's office, from newspaper reporters, from county officials. I overheard men talking of it in the corridors. I saw it in the exulting eyes of enemies in my court room. And when, on the morning that the verdict was returned, the old bailiff of my court came running up to the bench where I sat hearing cases in a sick despondence, I nearly fainted in my chair when he whispered: "They've found 'em guilty!"

How! How did it happen? Why, one of the jurors argued: "Boys, these fellows are only charged with a misdemeanour. The worst they can get is a little fine. But if we acquit them on this charge and another District Attorney gets into office, he may charge them with a felony and get them sent to the penitentiary." And the friendly jury found them guilty of a misdemeanour to save them from a worse fate!

"Judge," that juror said to me afterward, "no one'll ever get me into any graft investigations again. I was blamed for that verdict by the other fellows when the grafters went after them for it, and I tell you I've lost thousands of dollars in my business by it. And d—— them, I did it as a favour to them—to save them from the pen!"

The Commissioners were furious. The District Attorney was scared white. And the judge—Judge Voorhees, of Pueblo—well, here is part of his speech, from the newspapers of August 18, 1903:

"In passing sentence, this statute, while it is penal in its nature, as I look at it, does not brand these gentlemen as being criminals. I don't think the evidence in this case warrants any such conclusion." He believed "these defendants to be honourable gentlemen." He did not ask them as ordinary criminals to "step up to be sentenced," but merely gave them "an opportunity, if any of them have anything to say," to say it before he passed sentence. And his sentence was a fine of ten dollars each!

Do you blame the judge? Do you blame the jury, the District Attorney, the court officials, or even the accused? Why should you? Would you blame the girl who was ruined in the wine room or the dive keeper who was ruined to ruin her? Would you blame the boys who were polluted in the jails? No! They were the victims, not the authors, of their infamy. If you must blame some one, blame those heads of lawless public-service corporations in Colorado who corrupt judges, juries, legislators, public officials, political workers, gamblers, dive keepers, and prostitutes, so that *they* and their corporations may be safe above the law and in power to loot the people. *They* are the men. To them accrues the profit of this debauchery. Let them bear its shame.

Benjamin Barr Lindsey is most famous for establishing one of the nation's first juvenile courts. Through Lindsey's popular writings and lectures, the Denver court became a model for juvenile justice in the United States. (Courtesy of Colorado Historical Society.)

At five feet five and ninety-eight pounds, the judge stood not much taller than many of the young lawbreakers he strove to rehabilitate. (Ca. 1905 photo by Harry H. Buchwalter, courtesy of Colorado Historical Society.)

THIRTEENTH YEAR   DENVER, COLORADO, TUESDAY, OCTOBER 4, 1904.—16 PAGES.

CAN BEN LINDSEY'S LABOR of LOVE be DESTROYED by the TIGER of POLITICAL REVENGE?

As an advocate for cleaning up Denver politics, Lindsey described the Democratic machine as a paw of the beast. The beast, as shown in this October 4, 1904, *Denver Post* cartoon, struck back. (Courtesy of Denver Public Library.)

Ben Lindsey posed, probably in his Denver home at 1343 Ogden Street, with his adopted daughter, Benetta. (Ca. 1930 photo by Harry Rhoads, courtesy of Denver Public Library.)

Judge Lindsey with some of his friends. (Photo from the 1910 Doubleday edition.)

Lindsey's genius for publicity led to roles in Hollywood movies such as the 1920s *Judge Ben B. Lindsey's Juvenile Court*. Billed as the "Greatest Picture of Modern Times," the film drew Denver kids to the Paris Theater at 1751 Curtis Street. In the silent film *The Soul of Youth*, Lindsey played himself. (Courtesy of Denver Public Library.)

Facing page: After Ben Lindsey's removal from the Juvenile Court in 1927 following a contested election against a Ku Klux Klan opponent, he burned the records of young offenders. He feared that these confidential documents would fall into the slimy hands of the KKK. (Courtesy of Denver Public Library.)

At the Arapahoe County Courthouse, at Sixteenth Street and Court Place, Judge Ben Lindsey presided over the Juvenile Court. After construction of the new City and County Building, the old landmark was put up for sale and demolished in 1933. Following Lindsey's death in 1943, his widow, Henrietta, scattered his ashes on the courthouse site. In 2009 Denver named its new courthouse in honor of the city's most famous jurist. (Courtesy of Denver Public Library.)

CHAPTER VIII

AT WORK WITH
THE CHILDREN

Through these two years of quarrelling and crusading, our court work for the children was going on very happily. It was a recreation for us all, and it kept me full of hope—for it was successful. We were getting the most unexpected results. We were learning something new every day. We were deducing, from what we learned, theories to be tested in daily practice, and then devising court methods by which to apply the theories that proved correct. It had all the fascination of scientific research, of practical invention, and of a work of charity combined. It was a succession of surprises and a continual joy.

I had begun merely with a sympathy for children and a conviction that our laws against crime were as inapplicable to children as they would be to idiots. I soon realized that not only our laws but our whole system of criminal procedure was wrong. It was based upon fear; and fear, with children, as with their elders, is the father of lies. I found that when a boy was brought before me, I could do nothing with him until I had taken the fear out of his heart; but once I had gotten rid of that fear, I found—to my own amazement—that I could do anything with him. I could do things that seemed miraculous, especially to the police, who seldom tried anything but abuse and curses, and the more or less refined brutalities of the "sweat box" and the "third degree." I learned that instead of fear we must use sympathy, but without cant, without hypocrisy, and without sentimentalism. We must first convince the boy that we were his friends but the determined enemies of his misdeeds; that we wished to help him to do right, but could do nothing for him if he persisted in doing wrong. We had to encourage him to confess his wrongdoing, teach him wherein it had been wrongdoing, and strengthen him to do right thereafter.

I found—what so many others have found—that children are neither good nor bad, but either strong or weak. They are naturally neither moral nor immoral—but merely unmoral. They are little savages, living in a civilized society that has not yet civilized them, often at war with it, frequently punished by it, and always secretly in rebellion against it, until the influences of the home, the school and the church gradually overcome their natural savagery and make them moral and responsible members of society. The mistake of the criminal law had been to punish these little savages as if they had been civilized, and by so doing, in nine cases out of ten, make them criminal savages. Our work, we found, was to aid the civilizing forces—the home, the school, and the church—and to protect society by making the children good members of society instead of punishing them for being irresponsible ones. If we failed, and the child proved incorrigible, the criminal law could then be invoked. But the infrequency with which we failed was one of the surprises of the work.

Take, for example, the case of Lee Martin and his "River Front Gang." He was a boy burglar, a sneak thief, a pickpocket, a jail breaker, and a tramp; and his "gang" was known to the newspapers as the most desperate band of young criminals in Denver. Lee Martin and another member of the gang, named Jack Heimel, were one night caught in a drugstore into which they had broken; and when I went to see them in jail, I found them strapped to the benches in their cells, bruised and battered from an interview with the police, in which they had been punished for refusing to "snitch" (tell) on their fellow-members of the gang. This was before the passage of our juvenile court laws and I wished to have an opportunity to try what I could do with these two boys. The police did not wish me to have them.

I told the boys that I intended to try to help them, and they sneered at me. I told them that I thought they had not been given "a square deal"—which was true—but they did not respond. I used what tact and sympathy I could to draw them out and get their side of the story of their war with society, but it took me something like a month of frequent visits to get them to trust me and to believe that I wished to help them. In the end I was successful. I got their story—a story too long to repeat here; but it proved to me that the boys had been as much sinned against as sinning. They had begun as irresponsible little savages, and they had been made desperate young criminals. Their parents had failed to civilize them, and the school and the church had never had an opportunity to try. I resolved to see if it was too late to begin.

The police captain assured me that it was. "You can't 'baby' Lee Martin," he said. "He's been in jail thirteen times, and it hasn't done him any good."

"Well, I'd like to see what we can do," I replied. "If we fail, we'll still have twelve times the best of the jail. It has cost this city, in officers' fees alone, over a thousand dollars to make a criminal of him. Let us see how much it will cost to turn him into an honest boy."

The officer reeled off a long list of Martin's offences, and I retorted by showing a typewritten record of them, twice as long. "How in the world did you get 'em, Judge?" he said. "We couldn't *sweat* 'em out of him."

After a week of such argument, we got the case referred to our court. The boys were tried; and, of course, their guilt was clear. I sent them back to the jail under suspended sentence, and thought the matter over.

One night I had them brought to my chambers under guard, and after a talk with Heimel I sent him and the guard away, and concentrated on Martin. I decided to put my influence over him to the test. I told him of the fight I was making for him, showed him how I had been spending all my spare time "trying to straighten things out" for him and Heimel, and warned him that the police did not believe I could succeed. "Now, Lee," I said, "you can run away if you want to, and prove me a liar to the cops. But I want to help you, and I want you to stand by me. I want you to trust me, and I want you to go back to the jail there, and let me do the best I can."

He went. And he went alone—unguarded.

Then I put him and Heimel on probation, and in a few days they came to see me and brought "Red" Mike and Tommie Green, of the "River Front Gang." I talked to them about their offences against the law, and told them I wanted to help them do what was right and live honest lives, unpersecuted by the police; and I praised Martin for his moral strength in going back to the jail alone. Before they left me, "Red" and Tommie had "snitched" on themselves, and I had two new probationers. One by one the others followed, until I had all seven members of the gang on my list, all confessed wrongdoers pledged to give up crime and make an honest effort to be "straight." Six of the seven are to-day honest young workmen; Lee Martin failed, after a long and plucky fight, and is now in the penitentiary. "The River Front Gang," to my knowledge, has been responsible for the reformation of thirty boys in Denver; and Lee Martin, in his time, did more to discourage crime than any policeman in the city.

For example: one day a boy—whom I knew—stole a pocketbook from a woman in a department store. I told Lee that something ought to be done for that boy, and Lee brought him to me—from a cheap theatre where he had been "treating the gang." We worked on him together, and we straightened him up. He has since become a trusted employee in the very store in which he stole the pocketbook.

In another instance, I sent Lee after a boy, arrested for stealing a watch, who had sawed his way out of jail and had not been recaptured by the police. Lee got him—in El Paso—and brought him to me. After a talk with him, I gave him a twenty-dollar bill and sent him, alone, unshadowed, to redeem the watch, which he had pawned for $3. He returned with the watch and the $17 change. Then I persuaded him to return the watch to the man from whom he had stolen it, and, of course, the prosecution against him was dropped. We have never since had a complaint against that boy, although he had been one of the worst boy thieves in the city.

I could relate cases of this sort interminably. I *have* related them, in newspaper interviews, in magazine articles, and from the public platform. And I find that many people have misunderstood me and have accepted my statements as evidence that I have some sort of hypnotic power over boys and can make them do things contrary to their natures. I can not. I do nothing that any man or woman cannot do by the same method. It is the method that works the miracle—although, of course, no one in his senses will claim that the method never fails, that there are *no* cases in which force and punishment have to be used.

Another lesson about boys I learned from little "Mickey"—when I was investigating his charge that the jailer had beaten him. The jailer said: "Some o' those kids broke a window in there, and when I asked Mickey who it was he said he didn't know. O' course he knew. D' you think I'm goin' to have kids lie to me?" A police commissioner who was present turned to Mickey: "Mickey," he said, "why did you lie?" Mickey faced us, in his rags. "Say," he asked, "do yuh t'ink a fullah ought to snitch on a kid?" And the way he asked it made me ashamed of myself. Here was a quality of loyalty that we should be fostering in him instead of trying to crush out of him. It was the beginning, in the boy, of that feeling of responsibility to his fellows on which society is founded. Thereafter no child brought before our court was ever urged to turn state's evidence against his partners in crime—much less rewarded for doing so, or punished for refusing to do so. Each was encouraged to "snitch" on himself, and himself only.

THE BEAST

Still another lesson I learned from an inveterate little runaway named Harry. After several attempts to reform him, I sentenced him to the Industrial School in Golden; and this being before the days of the Detention School, he was returned to the jail until a sheriff could "take him up." That night the jailer telephoned me that Harry was in hysterics, screaming in his cell and calling wildly to me to help him. "You'd better come down, Judge," the jailer said, "an' see if you can get him quiet." I went to the jail. Inside, the steel doors were opened and the steel bolts withdrawn, one by one, with a portentous clanking and grating. It was as if we were about to penetrate to some awful dungeon in which a murderous giant was penned—so formidable were the iron obstacles that were swung back before us and clashed shut on our heels. And when I reached, at the end of a guarded corridor, the barred door of Harry's cell, there, in the dim glow of a light overhead, the boy lay asleep on the floor, his round little legs drawn up, his head pillowed on his tiny arm, his baby face pale under the prison lamp. The sight was so pitifully ridiculous that I choked up at it. It seemed such a folly—such a cruel folly—to lock up a child in such a place of lonely terror.

The jailer opened the cell door for me, and I began to raise the boy to put him on his prison "stretcher." His head fell back over my arm, like an infant's. He woke with a start and clutched me, in a return of the hysterical fear that had been mercifully forgotten in sleep. And then, when he recognized me, "Judge," he pleaded, "Judge. Gi' me another chance. I'll be good. Judge! Just once—once more. Judge!" I had to sit down beside him on the floor and try to reassure him.

I tried to be stern with him. I told him that I had trusted him and trusted him again and again; and he had failed me every time. I explained that we were sending him to the Industrial School for his own good, to make a "strong" boy of him; that he was "weak," untrustworthy. "I can *help* you, Harry," I said. "But you've got to carry yourself. If I let boys go when they do bad things, I'll lose my job. The people'll get another judge, in my place, to punish boys, if *I* don't do it. I can't let you go."

We went over it and over it; and at last I thought I had him feeling more resigned and cheerful, and I got up to leave him. But when I turned to the door, he fell on his knees before me and stretching out his little arms to me, his face distorted with tears, he cried: "Judge! Judge! If you let me go, *I'll never get you into trouble again!*"

I had him! It was the voice of loyalty. "Mac," I said to the jailer, "this boy goes with me. I'll write an order for his release."

I took him to his home that night, but his mother did not wish to have him back. Her husband had deserted her; she worked all day in a hotel kitchen; she could not take proper care of her boy, and she was afraid that he would be killed on some of his long "bumming" trips in the freight cars. But she finally consented to give him another trial; and this time he "stuck." "Judge," she told me long afterward, "I asked Harry, the other day, how it was he was so good for *you*, when he wouldn't do it for me or the policeman. And he says: 'Well, maw, you see if I gets bad agin, the Judge he'll lose his job. I've got to stay with him, 'cause he stayed with me.'" I have used that appeal to loyalty hundreds of times since, in our work with the boys, and it is almost infallibly successful.

I saw, too, from Harry's case, that if we were to reform children we must help parents who were unable to keep a close watch on their children. And nowadays if one of our probationers fails to arrive at school, the teacher is required to telephone the Juvenile Court immediately, and a probation officer starts out at once to find the delinquent. Every two weeks, on "report day," the probationers must bring us reports on their behaviour from the school, the home and the neighbourhood; and by praising those who have good reports and censuring those who have bad ones, we are not only able to prevent wrongdoing but to encourage right-doing. We impress on the children the need of doing right because it is right, because it "hurts to do wrong," because only "weak kids" do wrong—*not* because wrong is punished; for *that* teaching, I believe, is the great error of our ethics. The fear of punishment, I find, makes weak children liars and hypocrites, and, with strong ones, it adds to the enticement of evil all the proverbial sweetness of forbidden fruit.

During the first two years of our work, 554 children were put on probation; only 31 were ever returned to the court again, and of these 31 a number were returned and sent to Golden because of the hopelessness of reforming them in their squalid homes.

One evening a probationer brought four boys to my chambers with the announcement that they wished to "snitch" on themselves. They had been stealing bicycles—making a regular practice of it— and they had five such thefts to their discredit. I investigated their story and found it to be true. The police had a complete record of the thefts, and I tried—and got the boys to try—to recover the wheels, but we could not; they had been sold and resold and quite lost track of. A police officer, with whom I consulted, insisted that the boys should be arrested and sentenced to jail; and while I listened to him it dawned upon me what the difference was between the criminal procedure and the methods of our court. "Officer," I said, "you are trying to save bicycles. I am trying to save boys. The boys are more important than the bicycles. And if we can save the boys we can save bicycles in the future that we could not save in the past." I put the boys on probation, with the understanding that if they did not live up to their new resolve to be honest, I should be allowed to use their confessions against them. Not one of them failed me. The court helped them to get work and they are honest and useful members of society to-day.

In one year 201 boys came in this way to our court, voluntarily, and confessed their wrongdoing, and promised to "cut it out."

One evening, after I had adjourned court and the room had emptied, I saw a youngster sitting in a chair by the rear wall, apparently forgotten by his parents. He was no bigger than a baby. I sent the bailiff to ask him if he knew his name or his address. He came up to the bench—to my chair on the platform—and hiding his face against my shoulder he began to cry. He had been "swipin' things," he said, and wanted to "cut it out." And would I give him a chance—as I had another boy he knew? We gave him a chance. He reported regularly, for more than a year, and proved to be an honest, sturdy boy. Another boy who came to my chambers with a similar confession was so small that I said to him, "You're a mighty little boy. How did you find your way down here?" "Well," he replied, "most every kid I seed knew the way." I found that nearly all these boys were members of neighbourhood "gangs," that some member of the gang had been in court, had gone back to the gang with the lessons we had tried to teach him and had used his influence to send the other boys to us. We began to reach for this gang spirit and to turn it to our uses instead of against us; and we succeeded there, too, in time. I could relate scores of stories that came to us of how the gangs threatened to "beat up" some young delinquent if he did not play "square with the Judge." We taught the boys who had been doing wrong that they should try to "overcome the evil" they had done, by now doing something good; and they practised that doctrine by persuading their companions to desist from some mischief they had planned.

I even had a little newsboy come to me with the assurance that if I wanted the "street kids" to stop "shooting craps," I need only go down and tell them so. "Dhere ain't a kid in dhe whole push," he said, "dhat won't go down the line wit' yuh, Judge. Dhe cops can't make 'em stop craps, but I bet dhey'd do it fer *you*." I did not try it. I did not believe that I could permanently stop street boys shooting craps; it is as natural for them to gamble as for schoolboys to play marbles. But I rejoiced in the loyalty, the spirit of cooperation, shown by these street gamins. Therein lies the success of the Juvenile Court.

In the days before we got our Detention School any boy sentenced to the Industrial School at Golden had to be returned to the jail to wait until a deputy sheriff could "take him up." I found that the deputies were keeping the boys in jail until there were several under sentence, and then making one trip and charging the county mileage on each boy. Petty graft again! And conditions in the jail were as I have already described them.

I tried to make the deputies take the boys separately, immediately after sentence; but I did not succeed. The grafters were protected by the politicians, and I was powerless. "Very well," I said, "I'll see whether I cannot send these boys to Golden alone, without any guard, and cut out your fees entirely." And I succeeded.

I took each boy into my chambers and told him that I wanted him to go to Golden. "Now," I would say, "if you think I'm making a mistake in trying to save you—if you think you're not worth saving— don't go. Run away, if you feel that way about it. I can't help you if you don't want to help yourself. You've been a weak boy. You've been doing bad things. I want you to be a strong boy and do what's right. We don't send boys to Golden to punish them. We do it to help them. They give you a square deal out there—teach you a trade so you can earn an honest living and look anybody in the face. I'm not going to bring a deputy in here and handcuff you and have you taken away like *that*. Here are your commitment papers. Go yourself and go alone— or don't go at all if you don't think I'm trying to help you and sending you there for your own good." And invariably, the boy went. In eight years, out of 507 cases, I had only five failures. One of these was a boy who thought he was being followed and who ran away instinctively "to beat the game." Another was a boy who confessed that he couldn't "make it," because the route to Golden led him past his old "stamping grounds"; and when I gave him tickets over another route, he made the trip successfully. A third was an hysterical youngster who got as far as the railroad station with an older lad, but broke down there and could not go on. None of the failures were outright; and none of the boys were lost. (During these eight years, the police, I was told, lost forty-two "breakaways" who were never recovered.) And we saved the county several thousand dollars in mileage fees.

One boy, whom the police considered the worst little runaway in town, took his papers and delivered himself at Golden while the police waited, with expectant grins, to hear that he had made off; and those police were so sure he would fail me that they had two reporters "tipped off" to watch the case and write it up. I have had a young burglar, on trial, escape from the court room and evade the police— only to come to my house at midnight and surrender himself to me, because his gang had told him that I would "be square" with him if he was "square" with me. And not only children have gone alone to jail. Grown men whom I have found guilty of "contributory delinquency" have done the same thing, satisfied that they had broken the laws and should bear the penalty.

This achievement of our Juvenile Court has attracted more attention than anything else we have done; and yet it is not an isolated act; it is merely one of the results of the method. The criminal law is founded on vengeance. It treats all criminals as born criminals, incorrigible and unforgivable. It is designed to save property, not to save men; and it does neither: it makes more criminals than it crushes. I believe that the methods of our Juvenile Court could be applied to half the criminal cases on our calendars. The majority of our criminals are not born, but made—and ill-made. They can be re-made as easily as the "River Front Gang" was re-made if we would use the methods of Christianity on them and not those of a sort of fiendish paganism that exacts "an eye for an eye," and exacts it in a spirit of vengeance.

Does this read as if I were "crazy"? Do not think so. It is a conclusion based upon years of thoughtful experience. I have obtained a law in Colorado—the first of its kind in the history of jurisprudence, if that be anything against it!—by which an adult accused of crime can be tried as our children are tried and aided and corrected by the state as *parens patriae*, just as our children are aided and corrected. And I am willing to stake my faith on it that if our courts and our prisons ever learn how to work under such a law, you will see not only children but grown men and women going from the court rooms with their commitment papers in their hands and knocking on the gates of the prisons to be admitted. Crazy? When I first told one of our deputy sheriffs that in future I should send boys to Golden without him, he said to my clerk: "Well, I've always heard Lindsey was crazy, but I never believed it till to-day!" And when a hardened young criminal went, from my court, 850 miles to the Buena Vista reformatory alone, and presented himself at the gates of the prison, "the sentry" (as I was afterward told) "almost fell off the walls." Crazy? Do you know that over half the inmates of reformatories, jails and prisons in this country are under twenty-five years of age? (Some authorities say under twenty-three.) Do you know that an English prison commission not long ago reported to Parliament that the age of sixteen to twenty was the essentially criminal age? Do you know that the Earl of Shaftesbury after much study declared that not two out of any hundred criminals in London had formed the habits that led to criminality after the twentieth year? I may be very crazy and yet not be as crazy as the people who in the face of these facts believe that the criminal methods of our civilization are anything but a gigantic crime and a stupendous folly. Some day our descendants will read of our methods of handling criminals as we now read of how our ancestors imprisoned the insane in chains and used the methods of a Siberian jailer on the inmates of the madhouse! Never doubt it. Under our civil laws to-day Masters of Discipline could be appointed—as Masters in Chancery are appointed—to aid and correct delinquents, especially young delinquents, in our cities; to allow them to repent and make reparation—as they cannot under our criminal procedure; to help them rise from immorality and clean their hands of crime—as no judge can help them now, without being guilty of "compounding a felony." That will come, some day. If not in *our* day, then so much the worse for us!

I cannot conclude this chapter without adding the final lesson I learned in our work with the children—the lesson that leads me back again into the quarrel with the Beast. It is this: criminals are born *and* criminals are bred, but the conditions of which they are born and under which they are bred in Denver are the same conditions that debauch our Legislature, our judiciary, our press, our business life, and our poor. I found no "problem of the children" that was not also the problem of their parents. The young bud was blighted by the same corruption that infected the twig, killed the branch and ate out the heart of the trunk. The rule of the plutocracy in Denver was the cause of three-quarters of the crime in Denver. The dependent and delinquent children who came into my court came almost wholly from the homes of dependent and delinquent parents who were made such by the hopeless economic conditions of their lives; and those conditions were made hopeless by the remorseless tyranny of wealthy men who used their lawless power to enslave and brutalize and kill their workmen. Legislatures, corrupted by corporate wealth, refused to pass the eight-hour law that would give the child's home a parent able to fulfil his parental duties—refused to pass the employer's liability law that would save the widows from starvation and the children from the streets—refused to pass even a "three-fourths jury" law that would allow the poor victim of corporate greed to obtain a little pittance of justice in the courts. The saloons, protected by the political power of the corporations, debauched the parents and destroyed the homes of our children, and the protected gambler hunted and preyed with the protected saloon. I could not do my duty toward the children without attacking the conditions that deformed the lives of the children. And when I tried to do *this*—as you shall see—the Beast replied: "Then you shall not be allowed to save even the little children."

CHAPTER IX

THE BEAST AND THE BALLOT

THESE DAYS OF 1902, 1903 and 1904 were the heydays of our Juvenile Court, and I should like to dwell upon them fondly— as the song says—because of what ensued. Our campaigns against the wine rooms, the jails, and the grafting Commissioners had made the court as popular as a prizefighter, and the newspapers kept it constantly in the public eye. The Denver Chamber of Commerce—(let me boast of it!)—invited me to luncheon, gave a reception in my honour, and praised me to the last blush. (This is the same Chamber that has since branded me an enemy of the state.) Philanthropic men and women assisted our Juvenile Improvement Association, helped with our charity benefits, and contributed to the Fresh Air Fund, the summer camp, the day nursery, and other branches of our work, with all the delighted eagerness of Lady Bountiful herself. (At a recent "benefit" given in the aid of the Juvenile Court by Miss Olga Nethersole there were not two hundred persons in the whole house; and "Society" was conspicuously elsewhere.) Mr. Walter S. Cheesman, president of the water company, was at the head of our Association, and if we needed money we had only to ask for it. (This is the same Walter S. Cheesman who afterward lent a vacant lot to a charity bazaar on condition that not a penny of the proceeds should go to the Juvenile Court work.) I was elected chairman of a building committee of the Y.M.C.A. (from which I afterward resigned when I found that my chairmanship hindered the work of raising money for the Association). I was made a member of the Board of Trustees of the Denver University. (And Miss Ida Tarbell could not have been removed from the Board of Rockefeller's Chicago college more shrewdly and softly than I was "transferred" from the Denver University Board when the days of my offence against the "interests" developed.) In short, I was receiving the same applause in Denver that Heney received in San Francisco before he turned from prosecuting grafters to prosecuting the big business men and "leading citizens" who *made* the grafters.

I had as yet done only one thing to offend business: that was the enforcement of the child-labour laws in 1902. Cotton mills had been established just outside of Denver, and poor families had been imported from Alabama and the Carolinas to work as operatives. I went through the factories, visited the homes and talked with the children; and I found that the awful labour conditions of the Southern cotton mills had been transplanted to Colorado. The workers were practically slaves, for they had been imported under contract and had assigned part of their wages, in advance, to pay for transportation; and boys and girls from ten to twelve years of age were at work in the mills, without education and subject to the temptations of bad moral conditions, trying to help free their parents from the bondage of debt.

We took proceedings against the company—in spite of an outcry that we were interfering with a prosperous industry that added to the wealth of the state—and we fined the owners and the superintendent the limit allowed by the law. One of the men of wealth interested in the mills came to my chambers and protested. He had lived in the community a good many years, he said, and he was no criminal. It was all right to fine the superintendent; the superintendent was responsible for the conditions at the mills. But it was all wrong to fine *him*, the owner; for he had a reputation and a good name and he did not propose to be branded a criminal. "We have never had any trouble," he said, "until this fight started. We're helping Denver, and we ought to be encouraged instead of being persecuted. I warn you, right now, that if this thing is kept up, we'll shut down the mills and you'll have to take the consequences."

The thing *was* kept up. The children were forced to go to school. The mill shut down. And I became "an enemy of prosperity"—prosperity founded upon the slavery of children and the stunting of young lives.

The child-labour problem is a problem of the Beast. If you, who read this, live in a city or a state where the mill and the factory are enslaving helpless little children, understand that these children are the victims of the Beast. It lives upon them. You must fight *it*, if you would save *them*.

We have had no child-labour problem in Denver since; but our work in ridding the city of it did not weigh heavily against the court, for the loss of the mills was not great enough to be offensive. The court continued to be popular; the politicians were aware of its popularity; they decided that its popularity would be a valuable political asset; and as I approached the end of my term of office, I was met by various advances on the part of those Democratic "leaders" who had so indignantly shunned and repudiated me at the time of the printing-steal exposures. I had, however, learned to be suspicious of politicians, especially "when they come bearing gifts." And I soon learned that the gift they offered me in this instance was a "gold brick." Let me explain how I learned it.

My experience on the bench and in politics has convinced me that the confessional fulfils a need of humanity that is almost as instinctive as the need of religion itself. I have found that among young criminals the desire to "snitch" on themselves is practically irresistible; on the slightest encouragement they blurt out the truth as if their tongues spoke in spite of them. Strangest of all, the "bad" politicians, like the "bad" boys, have come to my chambers in scores, even while they were publicly fighting me, and confessed their crimes (sometimes before they committed them!) with a pitiful eagerness that would soften the heart of the bitterest cynic who ever sneered at human frailty.

(The Beast could make them do its work, but it could not make them wholly bestial. There always remained in them some generous relentance that made them betray their faith with injustice. And in all the attacks that have been made upon me, in this curious struggle with the System, there has scarcely been a blow aimed at me of which I have not been forewarned. That, too, is one of the experiences of my life that has made me always hope.)

While I was in forced retirement politically—because of my exposure of the grafting County Commissioners—I was kept constantly informed of the secrets of the System by these confessions of the System's tools. I was informed, particularly, of the way elections were managed so as to keep the Beast in power.

Under the law, as we had it then, the County Clerk appointed the deputy clerks before whom the prospective voter appeared to have his name registered on the voters' lists; and the applicant had to bring with him two witnesses to swear that he had a legal right to vote. Well and good! His name was duly entered on a sheet of paper, and these sheets were returned from the various wards to the Clerk's office, there to be copied into the registration books. But then the original sheets were destroyed; there was no way of tracing a fraudulent registration back to the clerk who had made it; and these clerks, at the bidding of the men who appointed them, turned in sheets of "phony" names copied from the pages of directories from Omaha and Kansas City (for example) and kept a list of such names for use on election day.

On election day, the election "judges"—appointed, to guard the ballot-boxes, by the same men who lowered the assessments and rebated the taxes of the corporations—were given the lists of "phony"

THE BEAST AND THE BALLOT

names registered in their precincts; and the judges would check off the fraudulent names on their poll books, and for each name deposit a ballot in the ballot box in support of the System! Could anything be simpler? Certainly nothing of the sort was ever more barefaced. I have seen typewritten lists of these "phony" names that were made out at the Democratic Club and furnished to the Democratic workers, so that no election judge might make the mistake of depositing a ballot for any voter who might later appear at the polls to vote for himself.

One day one of the county clerks of this period came to my chambers and said: "Ben, I don't know what I'm going to do about the lists of names that are coming in from the lower wards. They are bringing in thousand of names that I know are false." I advised him to refuse the names and expose the fraud. He did not do it. He has told me, since, that he tried to stand out, but the organization forced him to give way. He got his reward!

Long afterward, Mr. "Jim" Williams, a political henchman of Wm. G. Evans, president of the tramway company, confessed to me: "Judge, it's really a shame when the thing gets as raw as it was that year. Why, one night, before that election, I carried $20,000 down to the Democratic Club and I sat there around a table with Bill Davoren and Tom Phillips, with a bottle of whiskey between them, and dickered about how much we ought to pay per majority per precinct!" And observe that the henchman of Evans, then "Republican" boss, supplies the Democratic ward healers with the money necessary to obtain fraudulent majorities for the "Democratic" ticket. (The Beast is bi-partisan!)

The result was that in one of the precincts of a ward of which "Billy" Green[*] was the "leader," the election returns showed 717 votes for the straight Democratic ticket and 9 votes for its opponents. The precinct, as everybody knew, did not have more than perhaps a hundred legal voters. And on one election night, when the returns were

---

[*] Green is now a city detective in Denver.

being announced, I stood outside a newspaper office and saw such returns, from "Billy" Green's ward, received by the crowd with shouts of laughter. A heart-tickling joke! And the people who applauded it were being plundered of the money that bought this laughable majority!

Did these people know it? Certainly not. They did not see the cat. I did not see it myself in *this* matter in those days. I thought the little "bosses," like Frank Adams of the Police Board, were alone responsible for the election frauds; and when the Honest Election League was formed and I was invited by the League to address mass meetings, I attacked the little "bosses" and the successors of the County Commissioners, and "bawled them out" amid the hisses and threats of their friends—threats that were made with the clenched fist brandished in my face. It was exciting work, but it was wasted. The Beast must have grinned like a Cheshire cat as it listened to me.

The other speakers of the League—with the one exception of Father Wm. O'Ryan—blamed the mere tools who stuffed the ballot boxes, an association of Democratic ward-heelers called "the Savages." They blamed the Savages as the good citizen of New York blames Tammany Hall. I knew a number of these Savages well; I had worked with them in the ranks of the Democratic party; and I knew that they had been corrupted by the political conditions, and that they had in them qualities of daring loyalty and unselfishness of which their employers had no trace. They would have followed honest leaders as unflinchingly as they followed these corrupt ones.

And the corrupt ones were not only corrupt; they were so greedily selfish that they had not even the human loyalty for the Savages that the poor Savages had for them. Note what they did:

In the spring and fall of 1903 were held the "charter elections" in Denver, by which the city and county of Denver were to be given a new instrument of consolidation; and under this charter the powers of the utility corporations were to be largely limited and the rights of the people protected. The corporations, through the agency of the Democratic machine, defeated the charter drawn up by the honest-charter convention, elected a convention that was more to their taste and obtained a charter that gave them more power than ever. In this campaign the election frauds were most open. "What chance have youse people got?" one of the Savages asked me. "Boss Evans and his crowd has fellows like me, good for 500 votes in a precinct, when fellows like you is only good for one vote. What show have *youse* got?" A watcher for the Honest Election League was thrown out of a polling booth by the Savages, and when an attorney for the League threatened the election judge with arrest and a sentence in jail, the ballot-box stuffer replied: "I don't care a damn for your district court. We'll take it to the Supreme Court, and then you'll see what happens." As a matter of fact, the League prosecuted in the district court but the case was appealed to the Supreme Court and the ballot-box stuffer won.

Similarly, in the elections of the spring of 1904, the utility corporations used the Democratic machine and the Savages to elect our old friend Robert W. Speer mayor of Denver, along with a Democratic ticket; and, according to the confessions of the agents of corruption themselves, there were 10,000 fraudulent votes counted at the polls. But six months later, in the fall of this same year 1904, the corporations for their own purposes wished to elect a Republican ticket in the city and the state; and the Democratic Savages were warned by their leaders—particularly by the mayor, Robert W. Speer—that they must not stuff the ballot boxes. They did not obey the voice of their master. They did, for themselves, what they had so often done for the corporations—although the frauds were not as great as usual—and they succeeded in electing the Democratic ticket in the city. Court proceedings were at once begun against them, and by an unprecedented use of the Supreme Court they were sent to jail. I went to them there and sat in their cells and talked with them.

Their indignation was almost tearful. They were like a family of "bad" boys who had been taught by their father to steal for him and had been handed over to the police by their unnatural parent when they stole for themselves! And the blind public rejoiced in their punishment and degradation! And the Supreme Court handed over to the corporations the "swag" which the young thieves had tried to keep for themselves!

This, however, is by the way and in advance of my story. The point I wish to make is merely that I knew the ballot boxes were being stuffed and knew how successfully it could be done. I knew too that in my previous campaign the Democratic machine had used frauds in an attempt to defeat me. One of the Savages had confessed to me that in his district, when the ballots were being counted, hundreds of straight Democratic votes had been "scratched" against me by the Democratic election judges who marked a cross against the name of my Republican opponent. If that had been done when I was a comparatively inoffensive opponent of the System, what would they not do now, after my four years of "grand-stand" plays and exposures? I knew what they would do. They would put me on the Democratic ticket—because they wished to use popularity of the Juvenile Court in support of the ticket—and then would "scratch" and "stuff" to defeat me. Their nomination was the gift they offered me; and it was the gift I feared.

I decided that I would not accept *their* nomination *alone*. The Juvenile Court had been helped by citizens of all political parties, and there was no reason why I should make a partisan campaign for re-election. Moreover, the Republican organization had been deserted by the public utility corporations, for the time, and a number of young reformers had seized it and hauled down the skull-and-cross-bones. Several were old and close friends whom I had known since my schooldays. All were favourable to my candidacy; and, though I did not believe I could be elected on the Republican ticket alone, I knew I could be nominated on it. I was even offered the Republican nomination for the mayoralty, privately, by Mr. John W. Springer, and Mr. Greeley W. Whitford, in the office of the Continental Trust Company, before Mr. Springer had accepted that nomination himself; and I refused it because my work was in the Juvenile Court and I did not wish to abandon that. But Mr. Springer was fighting Evans; and I agreed that if the Republicans endorsed my candidacy for the judgeship I should accept their support, so that the popularity of the Juvenile Court might not be wholly an asset of the Evans Democratic ticket.

I made my decision known to my friends, and immediately I received an anxious visit from Harry A. Lindsley, the District Attorney who served the Beast so faithfully while he was in office. He took me out to luncheon, and for two hours he laboured with me eloquently over the restaurant dishes. The registration, he assured me, had been fixed for the Democratic party to win, and if I did not agree to take the Democratic nomination, and refuse any other, I would go down to defeat inevitably. Worse than that: once out of the Juvenile Court, I would find that I could not make a living in Denver with the insulted Powers against me. "You'll not be able to make a hundred dollars a month," he said. He named lawyers who, as I knew, had failed in Denver because they had fought the System; they had been unable to get any big cases to handle, because the corporations would give them none; and they had been unable to win even their little cases, because the corporation judges were against them. He painted a vivid picture of me, shabby, soured, and a failure in life; and I knew, from my own observation, that the picture was not overdrawn. Some of the most honest and promising young men in Denver have been driven from us in just such a state of crestfallen destitution.

However, I knew all this before Lindsley told it to me, and the scarecrow had lost its terrors. I told him I would not refuse the support of any party. My court was non-partisan and I proposed to make its judge the same.

Next came a visit in my chambers from Earl Hewitt,* a "fixer" and "man-Friday" of Robert W. Speer: and after he had shut and locked my door, he drew from his pocket—so to speak—a gold brick of a peculiarly winning glitter. If I would promise to accept a Democratic nomination for the judgeship and refuse the Republican nomination, and support Speer for the mayoralty, the Democrats would elect me

---

* Hewitt is now a member of the Fire and Police Board in Denver.

Governor of Colorado in the fall! I must have looked dubious (though I tried not to) for he used all the eloquence of a horse trader in order to persuade me. He succeeded in convincing me that the trap was set and sure, since the bait was so large and alluring. And after he had gone I wrote a letter to the newspapers refusing to bind myself to the Democratic party and announcing myself as a non-partisan candidate for re-election to a non-partisan court.

"You have signed your political death warrant," a friend assured me; and I believed that he was right. A friendly ex-governor had written me a letter to the same effect. Milton Smith and "Bill" Davoren and all the other agents of the Beast saw my "finish." I saw it myself. But I was resolved to meet it on my feet and fighting.

The women rallied first. Mrs. J. B. Belford, Mrs. Sarah Platt Decker and Mrs. M.A.B. Conine of the Woman's Club, organized indignation meetings, protesting against the opposition of the Democratic machine to my renomination; and the newspapers spread reports of the protest, written effectively by such able newspaper women as "Polly Pry" and Winifred Black and Ellis Meredith. The pulpits took it up. The newsboys began to parade the streets shouting:

"Who, which, when?
Wish we were men,
So we could vote for our little Ben."

(And for the first time in my life I found it an advantage to be "five-foot-six" and weigh ninety-eight pounds!) The Democratic leaders began to fear that if the Republicans nominated me and the Democrats did not, the women would vote the straight Republican ticket, in their blind resentment, and turn the whole election. The children marched and countermarched with songs and banners, and even mobbed the doors of the Democratic Club with insults and cat-calls. "Little ——," a Democratic "leader," said, "They're stirring up the whole town!" A professional politician is as cowardly as a gambler is superstitious. When the Democratic convention met, I did not attend but I was nominated.

I was nominated—but not for love. A Democratic candidate, named Robert J. Byrne, went to one of the young Republican "leaders" and said: "We had to nominate Lindsey because we thought you people were going to. But if you'll put up a Republican, we'll support him and bury Lindsey so deep he'll never be heard of again." Other Democrats made the same proposal to other Republicans. And we felt it necessary to hold a mass meeting, to give the reform Republicans the moral support of some public enthusiasm. We met in the opera house, under the auspices of the leading women of Denver; and Father Wm. O'Ryan, Rabbi Wm. S. Friedman and Rev. John H. Houghton spoke in behalf of my candidacy. In the midst of the enthusiasm the news was brought that the Republicans had nominated me; and we adjourned with cheers.

My election was assured. There was no doubt of it. It was impossible to defeat me. But I knew another fact that was equally assured, namely, that my election would be declared void by the courts. I did not join in the cheering.

You see, those elections were held under the new charter consolidating the city and county of Denver. The charter provided for the election of two county judges; but the constitutional amendment that had provided for a convention to draw up the charter, had particularly prohibited the convention from providing for the election of such judges. These judges should have been elected under the state statutes, as they had been previously. The charter convention knew it. I knew it, and I had written to members of the convention about it. But the System had seen an opportunity to get rid of me. "Let's mix it up," I was told that one of the Democratic bosses had said. "We'll see if we can't drop the little devil in the shuffle." If I were elected and my election declared void, the County Commissioners, under the law, would have the right to name a judge to take my place; but there was nothing for me to do but go ahead with them and try to provide that after the "shuffle" they should find me on top!

CHAPTER X

THE BEAST AND
THE BALLOT (CONTINUED)

A NEW ENGLAND PHILOSOPHER HAS SAID that the great virtue of a college education is to teach a man how unavailing it is. I have never been taught that. I have always had an envy of those men who have been able to live four years of their youth among the ideals of a university, protected from the disillusionments of the world, novitiates of culture and the liberal mind, happy among the boyish comradeships of the lecture room and campus. It had always seemed to me that my life had been spiritually orphaned by this loss of an *alma mater*. And when—just after my re-election in the spring of 1904—the Denver University, through its chancellor, the Reverend Henry Augustus Buchtel, offered to confer an honorary degree upon me, I felt as humbly flattered as if I were a quondam street waif whom some almost noble family now wished to adopt. (Intellectual snobbery? No doubt of it!)

On the night that my degree was to be conferred upon me I went proudly to the Commencement exercises in the Trinity Methodist Church. Mr. W. G. Evans, president of the tramway company, had been showing a new interest in the Juvenile Court and had sent me word, through a friend, that he thought my work for the children ought to be publicly recognized by the university. I knew that the university had been founded by Mr. Evans's father, and that Mr. Evans himself had assisted it with large and frequent contributions. I knew that Dean Shattuck of the university had been a household friend of Mr. Evans and his family, that he had been elected a member of the charter convention that betrayed the city to the corporations, and that he had not opposed the betrayal. But all this meant nothing to me. The college had remained in my thought something as unworldly as a convent. The Honourable Henry M. Teller was to receive an honorary degree with me; and there was nothing but pride in my heart as I walked up the aisle of Trinity Church, with Senator Teller and Chancellor Buchtel, to the raised platform on which I was to receive my patent of intellectual nobility.

The church, of course, was crowded—crowded with the young men and women of the college and their fond parents. I looked at them from the platform and saw their happiness, and knew—better than they did—their good fortune, and thought of the little waifs of our Juvenile Court, and was glad that here, at least, youth was what it ought to be. They looked up at me, and I was proud to be there, honoured among them and raised in their innocent estimation by an academic distinction. The chancellor, in his address, was eloquent in his praise of our court; he made me blush till I could scarcely see. "If Christ came to Denver," he said, "He would go straight to your court; for there you are doing the Master's work." He put my precious diploma in my hand, and I sat down with tears in my eyes, amid the generous applause of all those enviable young people. I felt that I had never been happier, never been more fortunate, never been more honoured—and never *could* be.

While I was still blinking, in a flattered daze, a message was brought to me from Milton Smith written on a calling card; he wished to see me after the meeting, on a matter of great importance; and I came back to earth and politics with a chill shock. He was the chairman of the Democratic State Central Committee. It was he, you remember, who carried the case of Cronin, the dive keeper, to the Supreme Court in Washington. He was attorney for the telephone company and its associated corporations. I wished him at the ends of the earth.

I suspected what he wished to see me about. The Democrats, with the assistance of Wm. G. Evans, the Republican Boss, had elected Democratic Boss Speer and his ticket; but the election frauds had been so gross and palpable that the Republicans and their mayoralty candidate, Mr. John W. Springer, had filed suit in my court, contesting the election. The matter was to come up, on the morrow, on a motion to appoint watchers for the sealed ballot boxes. I guessed that Milton Smith wished to see me about this. I wondered, for a moment, what he could have to say to me; and then my eyes returned to the young graduates who were receiving their degrees at the threshold of their college, with their faces to the unknown world out of which I had been momentarily uplifted; and I forgot Cronin's attorney in the spectacle of hope and youthful innocence beginning its career, like a bride turning from the alter—on the arm of an old rake! Would she reform him? I wondered.

Milton Smith was waiting for me, with a young man whom I shall leave nameless (because he was, I believe, a guiltless participant in what followed). They were waiting for me with a closed cab; for a thunderstorm had broken over the city and the rain was coming down as if the skies had burst. They invited Senator Teller and his wife into the carriage, and we drove first to Teller's home—a few blocks away—and nothing passed between us but congratulations on our academic honours and condemnations of the weather that had made such a sodden ending for the young people's Commencement.

But when the Tellers had left us—and I sat back with my precious degree buttoned up in my breast pocket—Smith suddenly began: "Ben, we thought you wouldn't care to try those election cases." "Why?" I said, surprised. "Well now," he replied, "I'll tell you. You ran for election yourself, didn't you?" "I ran," I answered, "on both tickets." "Yes," he said, "but we don't want to embarrass you. There's no need for you to take the responsibility of deciding about elections in which you ran yourself. We feel that everybody would be better satisfied if you called in an outside judge." I asked: "Who, for instance?" He named a judge who has since become a notorious party crook.

The thunder was battering down the heavens overhead, with flashes of lightning and torrents of rain. The carriage splashed and jolted through the intermittent darkness. Milton Smith insinuated his way persuasively into his proposition that I should "job" the election cases for Boss Evans and his Democratic agents; and I wondered whether there was any mark of the Beast on the diploma that I had been so absurdly proud of a half-hour before.

They did not doubt my honesty, he said, but they were afraid that I was prejudiced, perhaps. I had been addressing mass meetings on the subject of ballot-box frauds; I had been a good deal wrought up, it seemed; I might not be as impartial as I ought to be. Besides, I ought to know what election cases were: both sides generally were equally guilty, and a judge was expected to stay with his party. They were afraid that I was squeamish. If I granted the Republicans this right to appoint "watchers" over the sealed boxes I would be giving the ballots into the hands of the enemy; at least, that was what they feared.

I confess I was curious to know how far he would go in this attempt to persuade a judge to decide a case before it came to court. He did not go very far. Under my assurances that I would not shirk my responsibility, that I was not prejudiced, that I would give him a square deal, he lost his temper; and pounding his fist into his hand he declared they would get a change of venue, and to get it, they would file affidavits that would make my "ears ring." This threat spoiled the whole situation, as far as I was concerned. I looked out the window to see how near home I was, and a flash of lightning showed me headed for the City Park—which was no neighbour of mine. "Here," I said, "where are we going? Take me home."

It seemed that they had mistaken my address. Smith calmed down. The cab lurched around in the darkness; and the rest of the conversation was in a descending scale of irritation. We drew up, at last, at my door, and there we stayed talking uselessly, until, finally, I said: "Well, it's for you to determine the propriety of this business. All I have to say is that I intend to hear the case. Produce your affidavits, and if they convince me I'll give you a change of venue. But I don't intend to shirk my responsibility. I was non-partisan in my election, and I'll be non-partisan on the bench."

I got out. The door was slammed angrily behind me; and the carriage drove off. The rain had ceased. I went slowly into the house with my honorary "Bill-Evans" degree.

I have often wondered whether any of the younger participants in those Commencement exercises found as little gilt on their gingerbread as I did when I got home with mine out of that storm. Or is it only I who so often find the honorary bouquets of the world a bunch of thistles when I close my flattered hands on them? I hope so. Well——

The case came before me next morning, but neither side was ready to argue. Both asked a continuance, and I granted it. I was leaving town, that night, on a long trip to Portland, Maine, where I was to speak to a charities convention about our Juvenile Court work; and I arranged that Judge Frost should hear the preliminary motions in the election case during my absence, but keep the case itself till I returned. I had begun to suspect that the System had trapped itself in those sealed ballot boxes, and I wished to be at hand with a judicial club when they were opened.

That evening, when I was packing my valise before I left my home to catch my train, I had a caller—a visitor from the past—my old partner in law, Senator Gardener. He was fatter; he looked more cynical and prosperous, but he was the man with whom I had first been under fire in politics, and I was glad to see him. We talked of old times, as old friends do. We talked of our present, and I did not resent his complacent boast of a financial success that must have contrasted

THE BEAST

in his mind with my own circumstances. (I knew him too well to resent it; I knew that to him I was still the same impractical simpleton I had always been.)

We finally came down to the last elections and the case that was before my court. He said that he had been talking to Mr. Evans and to "Bob" Speer; in fact, Mr. Speer had been to his office to see him. He had been told that Chas. J. Hughes, Jr., was to appear before me in my court and argue that I had no jurisdiction. "I'm to appear too," he said. "You see, I'm a Republican and Hughes is a Democrat, so the thing will be non-partisan. Hughes has an argument that'll convince any one. It'll let you out. You needn't hear the case at all. And you know your election as County Judge is no good; and if you had to decide this case against the Democrats, you could never get another nomination."

This sounded plausible—all but. There was one point I wished explained: why did Mr. Evans feel that Chas. J. Hughes, the corporation light of the Colorado bar, needed the support of such a lesser luminary as Gardener in the argument?

I said: "The statute of the state says that my court shall have jurisdiction in such cases, and the city charter expressly declares so. But if they have any law that will convince me to the contrary, you know well enough I'll do my duty." He did not seem satisfied. "To be frank with you," he explained, "they have never quite understood you, Ben. They're afraid you're not just right—that they'll not get a square deal. All they want is a square deal." (They have their own idea of "a square deal.")

"You can tell them," I assured him, "that they will receive absolute justice. I can't say more than that, can I?"

He fidgeted in his chair like a bad boy who is about to "snitch." I waited. "Well," he hinted, "they want to employ me in the case."

I saw it coming. "I'll be mighty glad, for your sake," I assured him, "to see you in it."

He looked up with a half-sickly smile. "Ben," he said, "you know I don't want to do anything wrong." (Surely not!) "But you and I have

80 122 08

always been friends, and you know what politics are. One side's just as bad as the other, and you know it." He hesitated. "Besides, if you do go ahead and try to hear the case, the Supreme Court will enjoin you."

"That's for the Supreme Court to decide," I said—and waited for him to come back to the secret that had stuck in his throat.

He talked around it for a long time. If I did open the ballot boxes, he said, I could put half the Democrats in town in jail, but it would not be enough to change the results of the election. It would do no good. He believed in taking a practical view of the case. I could resolve the reasonable doubts, in the matter, in favour of my own party. If I did not, I could never get another nomination.

"Well," I said, "you've been out on the Republican platform attacking the Democratic frauds. And now here you are defending them!"

He turned red. "It's all damn politics. They said they would pay me a big fee." He looked at me with a dubious expression of guilt and pleading shamefacedness. "It'll be the biggest fee I ever got in my life. And you know I'll be square with you." This last was given with an insinuating slowness.

I remained dense. "I have no objection to seeing you in the case. I don't see what *that* has to do with it."

"Well," he said, "unless I can guarantee that you'll dismiss the case, they'll not employ me."

I do not know whether they had expected me to ask how much of the fee I was to receive; or whether it was supposed that because of my old friendship with Gardener I would help him earn the money!

I looked into his face, as I try to look into the faces of the "bad" boys who come to my court. "Don't you see," I said, "that these fellows are either trying to trap me, or trying to make me disgrace my calling—and they're just *using* you? Why do you let them do it? You know they sent you here with this message." He rose from his chair, looking ugly and mean. "*I* know it," I said. "Why do you play cat's-paw in such a game?"

He looked about him for his hat, scowling. I saw that it was useless to talk to him. "Well," I said, "you can go back to them, then, and tell them this case will be tried fairly and justly. I have done nothing to make them think I'm 'not right.' Their own conduct is the cause of that suspicion."

He stopped at the door. He asked, guiltily: "Can't you get me out of here without any one seeing me?"

There was only one way out, and that was through the front door. He took it—and he left behind him the last faint sense of our old friendship. It was he who soon after introduced in the Senate a bill forbidding the Judge of the County Court to leave Denver, except in the month of July, under a penalty of forfeiting fifteen dollars a day during his absence; and it was he who introduced another bill, at the same time, forbidding the County Judge to call in an outside judge to assist him with the legitimate work of a crowded docket. At that time our court was doing 60 percent more work than the four judges of the district court, combined; and I was doing it practically alone. We had held 104 night sessions in one year. We were turning into the county nearly ten thousand dollars a year from litigants after all our salaries and expenses had been paid. (And this was one of the complaints the politicians had against us. We should have used the surplus to provide "jobs for the boys," as the other courts did.) Instead of taking the holidays allowed judges by custom, I had spent my spare time lecturing, in various states, in support of juvenile-court laws and the work of the Juvenile Improvement Association, which, as a children's protective and betterment league, was becoming a national organization. President Roosevelt had only just recommended our laws to the District of Columbia, and I had personally induced many governors in many states to do the same thing. However, this attempt of the "interests" to hamper me in a work that was being approved all over the country, is out of its order of consideration here. The fight against Senator Gardener's "spite bills" did not begin till some time later, and I shall save the story of it for its proper place.

Meanwhile, I went on my trip to Maine. The Supreme Court granted the predicted writ of prohibition temporarily enjoining the County Court from trying the cases, and before this writ was made permanent something else happened. Our old friend Boss Graham, of the Republican machine, went to Mr. John W. Springer, the Republican candidate for the mayoralty (who was protesting the election of Speer, the corporation Democrat), and told Springer that if his protest was not dropped and his case in my court withdrawn he would be ruined. He and his trust company would have "the four utility corporations of the city to whip financially." Graham claimed that the threat came from Evans.

Mr. Springer said publicly: "I conferred with the others interested in pushing the cases and said: 'Boys, we had better quit before we begin. We haven't enough money to beat four utility corporations.'" The tools of the Beast had first threatened him with the ruin of his reputation; they had showed him "fake" photographs of himself in company with various indecencies; and he had replied that he "would clean them out with a gun" if they attempted any such vilification. Some offensive articles about him were printed in a corporation paper of special circulation*; and an attempt was made to get copies of a scurrilous pamphlet delivered to Mrs. Springer who lay fatally ill at the time. (Oh, the Beast has no compunction!) Mr. Springer was not intimidated. "But," he said, "I could not fight them on the other issue. I could not jeopardize the savings of the widows and orphans that were invested in our trust company. They had me there. And they knew it."

---

* Perry Clay's *Review*. Perry A. Clay, its proprietor, is a man whom I saw among the armed gamblers on the steps of City Hall, defending the corrupt Fire and Police Board from Governor Waite's militia. He turned up again among the Negro deputies who precipitated the election riots in 1900, and he was undersheriff to the Democratic Sheriff who sold the use of his office for $20,000 to the Republicans during that campaign. Clay has since been politically rewarded with the clerkship of the District Court. His *Review*, long supported by the advertisements of saloons, dives and brothels, is now disguised as a temperance advocate; and in this disguise, delivered free, from door to door, whenever the Beast needs aid, it carries the arguments of the corporations to the homes of "the church element." B.B.L.

Of course they knew it. Widows and orphans were nothing to them. They live by making widows and defrauding orphans. It is part of the profits of the System. (It is cheaper to make a wife a widow than to pay her husband a living wage, or protect him at his dangerous work!) Mr. Springer had some human feeling of social responsibility. The others have nothing but the animal cruelty of the preying Beast in their hearts when they are on the hunt. (Mr. Walter S. Cheesman, president of the water company, afterward told a well-known banker: "It cost us more to defeat Springer than any other man who ever ran for office in Denver!")

Mr. Springer withdrew his protest on condition that the Evans candidates should pay the court costs thus far incurred. This was agreed to. Mr. Evans saw that the money was deposited to the credit of the Republican chairman; and $1,000 of the sum came from Chase—Ed. Chase! Do you understand? He was, and is, one of the "leaders" of the gambling syndicate in Denver. *There* you have the Beast scratching its right ear with its left hind leg—so to speak. Evans and Chase!

And do not for a moment imagine that this unholy alliance of Evans and Chase is peculiar to Denver. You will find it in every American city in which the heads of public utility corporations and the other "captains of industry" are trying to obtain special privileges to steal from the people. The Evans of your city—whichever one it is— is a partner with your Chase, your Cronin, your Tammany "Savages," your Frank Adams, your Billy Adams and all your enemies of law, promoters of graft and buzzards of public loot. Chancellor Buchtel is only the Chancellor Day of Denver. The Beast is everywhere the Beast, and its agents are always its agents.

CHAPTER XI

THE BEAST AT BAY

THE ELECTIONS THAT FOLLOWED, in the autumn of 1904, were marked by the most lawless and far-reaching contrivances of power on the part of the corporations in Colorado. In that huge turmoil of injustice, of subsidized treason and legal anarchy, my own small struggle was the merest flurry. But I am not trying to compose a history of the gigantic activities of the plutocracy, out of the conflicting testimony of various witnesses and the disputable interpretation of incidents of which there may be more than one sense. I am only seeking to make plain to you what I saw with my own eyes—to put before you the evidence of a personal experience of which there can be no doubt—to show you clearly, in the little, what was actually going on in the large.

My election had been declared invalid, as I had known it would be; and it became necessary for me to run again. The corporations, having put their Democratic tools in power in the city elections of the spring, now bought back the Republican machine so as to elect a corporation Legislature and governor in the state elections of the fall. I expected, therefore, to have the Republicans against me, and we began to organize the usual committees and arrange for the usual public meetings in advance. But several days before the Republican convention was to meet, a number of Republican "leaders," in newspaper interviews, announced that there would be no opposition to my nomination on the Republican ticket; and Mr. "Jim" Williams, one of the most intimate of Wm. G. Evans's personal agents, invited me to meet him in a room in the Brown Palace Hotel and assured me that it would *not* be necessary to "organize" my friends. "There seems to be no use trying to fight you," he said with a smile, "and we have decided to nominate you when the convention meets next week."

I felt relieved. The spring campaign had been a nervous trial that I did not wish to repeat. I thanked Williams for saving me the anxiety of several days' uncertainty, and went back to my court work.

Some days later I spoke to a Republican friend about the interview with Williams, and he said: "That's strange. Jim has been quietly sending the word 'down the line' that the party caucus is to put young Bert Shattuck (Hubert L. Shattuck)* on the slate, to-night, for County Judge." I thought my friend was misinformed. The Denver *Republican*, the official organ of the party, had been proclaiming in large headlines and leaded type that I was to be nominated unanimously on the party ticket. Bert Shattuck's father, the former Dean of the Denver University, had publicly declared that I ought to have the position of County and Juvenile Court judge for life; and he had come smilingly to my chambers and promised me his loyal support. His son had been Clerk of the County Court when I first took office, and we had never been anything but friendly. It seemed to me impossible that my Republican informant could be right.

The night on which the Republican caucus met, to make up a slate for the convention, I made no attempt to find out what was being done;

---

* Shattuck is now (Jan., 1910) a District Judge in Denver.

but at midnight I was roused from bed to answer an urgent call on the telephone, and a friend announced: "The Republicans have selected Shattuck for County Judge. Evans sent a telegram from New York saying it had to be done. The corporations are against you. They're going to prevent you from getting a nomination on either ticket."

I dressed in haste and hurried down to the office of the *News*—which paper, like the Denver *Post*, was then friendly to me—and a special edition was rushed to the presses with a flaming exposure of "Treachery" on the front page. In the early morning I went to the editor of the *Post* and a special edition was issued by that paper too. But the *Republican*—the paper that had been promising my unopposed nomination by the Republican party—inserted only an inconspicuous five-line paragraph announcing that Shattuck had been selected by the caucus!

We had been prettily betrayed. There was no time now to arouse the public sentiment that, at the previous election, had "scared the wits out of the Boss," as the *Post* had said. There was no time to organize the women and children.

We had just twelve hours in which to prepare, before the Republican convention should meet to ratify the choice of the caucus; and it might as well have been twelve minutes. The Democratic machine was against me. Mayor Speer, it was reported in the newspapers, "on the very best authority," had obtained the promise from Evans that I should not be nominated. "Chairman Davoren, for the Democrats, smiled pleasantly when these matters were being discussed." I had been "effectually blocked." Opposed by both parties, with both machines using election frauds and corporation contributions against me, I could have no more hope of winning my way back to the county court on an independent ticket than of getting an election to the White House itself.

Some of the young Republican reformers who had nominated me in the spring campaign came to my chambers, that morning, and talked the situation over with me. They suggested that I should appeal to Mr. David H. Moffat, who was president of the First National Bank of Denver and a large stockholder in the utility corporations. But I did not know Mr. Moffat. The only man of the sort whom I knew was Mr. Walter S. Cheesman, president of the Denver Union Water Company and head of our Society for the Prevention of Cruelty to Children. "Then see Cheesman," they advised.

I knew Mr. Cheesman well. I had first gone to him to get his aid in obtaining the public baths and playgrounds for the children, and he had been helping us in our work for the children ever since. I had more than once accompanied him, in his automobile, on little jaunts around Denver; and once, on our way to inspect the waterworks dam, which his company was building outside Denver, I saw him stop his car, pick up a stray cat mewing by the roadside, and take it to the dam where we caught fish to feed it. I thought him a gentle and compassionate man of wealth—and I hurried, now, to his office to appeal to his philanthropy, to his interest in our court work, and above all to his influence with Mr. Evans and his power on the corporation boards.

I went to the offices of the Denver Union Water Company, and was ushered down the inner passageways, past clerks and secretaries, to Mr. Cheesman's private room. He was seated at his mahogany writing desk, a typical business man in his business clothes—bald, elderly, with a round and kindly face but shrewd, cold eyes.

He received me genially enough. "Mr. Cheesman," I said, at once, "I've come to see you about the convention."

"Yes, yes, Judge," he said; "sit down." I sat down. He always spoke in a sort of half voice, that at times became a whisper, leaning forward, as if confidentially, because his hearing was defective. "Yes, I've just been talking to Mr. Field about it over the telephone." Mr. Field, of course, was Mr. E. B. Field, president of the telephone company.

Thus encouraged, I went on to explain my situation. I told him that I had made a lot of enemies among the Democrats because I had exposed the grafting County Commissioners and attacked the Police Board for protecting the wine rooms and denounced the ballot-box stuffing that had been done by the Democratic machine. I could not hope for the Democratic nomination, but I had been led to expect a place on the Republican ticket. Now I had been betrayed by the Republican caucus. "It's not square," I said. "It's not honest. It's not fair."

He listened, but I saw that he listened unmoved.

Then I appealed to his interest in the work we had done for the children. He heard me politely, but with a blank eye. "You know," I pleaded, "that I'm entitled to a renomination on every count. The court has been honest; it's been efficient; it has served the public interest every time. The people will elect me; you know that. Nobody's against me but Mr. Evans, and it's Mr. Evans that's standing in my way. He sent a telegram from New York saying I wasn't to be nominated. That's the whole trouble. If we can get Mr. Evans to keep his hands off, I'll have no difficulty. Won't you help us? We can do it if you'll help pull off Mr. Evans."

"Yes," he said, "I understand that Mr. Evans is against you. And I've been thinking the matter over. I'd like to see you returned to the court. You've been doing good work there . . . Yes . . . Personally Mr. Field and I admit all you say. You are entitled to be renominated. But Mr. Evans represents our interests in politics, and, of course, you understand, politics with us is a matter of business. Mr. Evans represents our interests and we cannot very well question his judgment. If Mr. Evans were here, I'd make an exception in your favour and see him about it. But he's in New York——"

"Send him a telegram," I put in eagerly, "I can get it rushed through. I know them—down at the telegraph offices. We can get an answer back before the convention meets."

He shook his head over it, judicially. "I'm afraid it's too late. Mr. Evans insists that Mr. Shattuck must be nominated by the Republicans. He has arranged with Mr. Speer that Judge Johnson (Henry V. Johnson) is to be nominated on the Democratic ticket. I'm afraid I can't go behind him."

"Well! What about *the people?*" I cried.

He replied, benignly: "You have been long enough in politics to know the people have nothing to do with these things." He spoke as if I were a personal friend come to borrow money from his company, without security, and he regretted that he could not lend it—as a matter of business—though personally he would have liked to. I felt the ground slipping from under my feet. I made a frantic appeal to him—for the sake of the work for the children which would be discredited all over the country if I were refused a nomination by both parties. Every one would think the Juvenile Court had been a failure. In other cities, where I had been lecturing, they would think so. They would not understand why I had been defeated. The movement was growing. A check to it might be fatal now. The other cities were looking to Denver. It would hurt the work for the children all over the states.

"Tut, tut," he said. He thought I was "over-exercised"—"unduly" alarmed. Mr. Shattuck was an intelligent young man. He could continue the work. Or Judge Johnson.

By this time I had lost my self-control. I knew that neither Shattuck nor Johnson could do the work of our court; they had no training for it, no knowledge of its methods, no understanding of its aims. Besides, it was the work of my life; it was the one thing left to me; I had fought and suffered for it, struggled and succeeded with it, when no one believed in it. And now—

I jumped up from my chair and began pacing about the room, arguing, pleading with him, almost beseeching him not to join Mr. Evans in crushing our court because we had done what was honest, what was right. "It's an outrage!" I cried, backing up against the wall before him. "It's an outrage that Mr. Evans should be the man to say whether I'm to work for the children in this community—or not!"

He seemed embarrassed, as if he were a public executioner who pitied his victim but could not help him. "Sit down a minute," he would say; and I would sit down, only to spring up again when his unyielding "business" considerations forced me to face again the hopelessness of my situation. "I'll run any way," I said in desperation.

"No," he warned me, "don't do that. As a friend, I wouldn't advise you to do that. If I thought you had a chance, I'd like to see you run. But you know it's impossible under our ballot laws. The people don't know how to 'scratch.' It's impossible." He was afraid that I was such a "headstrong young man" I might make an expensive independent campaign, and mortgage my house (he even thought of that!) and lose all I had. And while he spoke, calmly, the anger rose in my throat. I could guess why Mr. Evans was to give the Democratic nomination to Judge Johnson; wasn't it because Judge Johnson, while mayor of Denver, had signed a franchise for the tramway company against the protests of the whole community and in violation of the platform on which he had been elected? I could guess why Mr. Evans had insisted that I should not be nominated by either party; wasn't it because I had refused to job the election contests? Weren't these the "business considerations" that put Mr. Evans against me and joined Mr. Cheesman with him? Mr. Cheesman might pretend to be as friendly and as fatherly as he chose, in his advice; my anger dried the blur in my eyes and I saw through him. I saw through him and I despised him. Business demanded that I should be crushed. The Beast required it. The tools of the Beast—like the grafting Commissioners who had rebated taxes for Mr. Cheesman's corporations—insisted on it. The ballot laws made it possible—the very laws which Cheesman deplored and his corporations took advantage of!

I struck my clenched hand on his table, furious with indignation. "I'm going to make a fight," I challenged him. "Will you stand by me?"

"I can't," he hedged, "if you run independent. You have no chance."

That was the end. That was the "showdown." I caught up my hat. "I'm going to fight," I said, "and fight like hell." And without waiting to hear his fluttered remonstrances I flung out of his office, trembling with an agitation I could not conceal from the clerks who stared at me as I hurried by.

It was the Beast again, the whole Beast at last, self-acknowledged and unashamed. The people had "nothing to do with these things." The united corporations ruled the town. I had offended *them* when I fought graft, ballot-box stuffing, the wine rooms, the Police Board, and all the other effects, means and agents of their rule. And here I had wasted a valuable hour appealing to one of the patrons of this corruption to help me fight it! I do not know whether I despised Cheesman more than I despised myself for my trusting simplicity as I hurried back to my chambers that morning from my appeal to the head of the Children's Aid Society to save the Children's Court!

I had only a few hours left. The Republican convention was to meet that afternoon. I telephoned to all my friends among the young Republicans, telling them that Cheesman would not help, that we must fight alone and at least go down fighting. They must hold the floor in the convention until we could get in the women—the children—anybody who would shout for us and intimidate the machine. I got all the men who had fought for me in the Republican convention in the spring—E. P. Costigan, James C. Starkweather, Wm. W. Garwood, Willis V. Elliott, Horace Phelps, James H. Causey, Rodney Bardwell (who had not yet gone over to the corporations)—and they got the aid of their friends. When the convention met, there was not a quorum present, but within half an hour the old Coliseum Hall began to fill and the fight commenced—on a resolution offered by ex-Judge George W. Allen* delegating the work of the convention to a committee so that the machine might "knife" me privately behind closed doors.

Costigan, Causey, Starkweather, Garwood, and the other young reformers held the floor against Allen, fighting for time. Delegates were pouring in from all parts of the city; the galleries were filling up with cheering men, women and children. In an hour the place was jammed, and it was jammed with opponents of the machine. The "Treachery" extras of the morning newspapers had done their work, and the public enthusiasm that had "scared the wits out of the Boss" in the spring now scared the wits out of his henchmen. They lost control of the convention. It was less like a convention, as the newspapers said, than it was like the gathering of a mob. The machine speakers were howled down, hissed and jeered. The young reformers were

---

*Allen is now (Jan., 1910) a District Judge in Denver.

applauded and cheered on. The galleries hooted and clapped. In a confusion of cat-calls and insults, Ex-judge Allen withdrew his motion;
and my friends spoke for my nomination in the midst of an enthusiasm that carried all before it—in one of those waves of emotion that
sometimes sweep conventions and wreck the best-contrived plans of
the most astute politicians. In vain did tramway agents like C. W.
Varnum try to stand against it. In vain did Mr. Fred J. Chamberlain,*
a pillar of his (and Mr. Evans's) church, cry: "You fellows *mustn't* nominate Lindsey. You *can't.*" They did. To the waving of handkerchiefs in
the galleries, with "staid lawyers tossing their hats in the air" (as the
papers said)—with Bert Shattuck withdrawing his nomination, and
pandemonium let loose upon the angry and helpless machine men
who could not make themselves heard—my nomination was moved—
was carried—was made unanimous—and the wild cheering of the
convention drowned the ragtime of the brass band!

We had won again. At least we had carried the first line of the System's defence. The second fell when the Democratic Executive Committee, alarmed by my apparent popularity, also nominated me. But
the System still had the courts to appeal to. It had particularly Judge
Peter L. Palmer, who had protected Cronin and the dive keepers; and
on the application of Milton Smith he granted a temporary injunction
enjoining me from running—on the ground that my previous election
was valid. (It seems impossible—doesn't it?—but it is all on record in
the courts of the county.) One of the attorneys in the case confessed to
me: "The whole thing's fixed up. They're afraid more election protests
will come into your court, and something has to be done." When we
went before Palmer to argue against making the injunction permanent, we found him closeted with the machine politicians; and when
he mounted the bench he rendered his decision against us without
even allowing my lawyers to open their mouths. (This was not in
Russia under a Czar. It was in Colorado under the System.)

---

* Mr. Chamberlain is now a member of the Colorado Railroad Commission, and
Varnum of the City Civil Service Board.

The public outcry was effective. The Supreme Court reversed Judge Palmer. Another suit was promptly trumped up and Palmer granted another injunction this time, in effect, forbidding the election commissioners to print my name on the official ballot as a candidate of the conventions that had nominated me. But he was reversed again on a ruling of the Supreme Court that such suits must be brought after the elections, not before them; and I was allowed to make my campaign, the System meanwhile having discovered a less public way of getting rid of me.

I was allowed to make my own campaign, and I took the opportunity of making another, directed against Harry A. Lindsley, who had been renominated as District Attorney, and against "Len" Rogers, a notorious election crook, whom the Democrats had put on the ticket as State Senator. I fought Rogers on general principles; his candidacy was an outrage to decency. I fought Lindsley because I hoped to hamstring the Beast by putting in an honest District Attorney. We succeeded in defeating both Lindsley and Rogers, but the man, George Stidger, who took Lindsley's office, proved little better than the corruptionist whom we displaced. (He confessed to me afterward that he, too, had been nominated by Evans, and that Evans, personally, had given him money for his campaign.)

In the fight against Lindsley and Rogers all the old tricks of the Beast were used against us. False affidavits were obtained, from two unfortunate women of the streets, accusing me of unmentionable vices; but I was warned of it in advance, by a friendly physician who heard of it, and when Rogers came to my chambers to threaten the publication of this perjured slander, I was able to defy him. I had found out who the women were, and one of them had admitted her guilt. Fortunately for Rogers he went no further with the affair. I continued to make public my knowledge of his record, and of Lindsley's. One day Rogers, crazed with whiskey, came to the Court House and lay in wait for me with a loaded revolver in the corridor outside my chambers, but a friendly deputy sheriff (Edward G. Shaffer) came upon him there and got the revolver from him and coaxed him away.

"Judge," Rogers confessed to me afterward, "Those fellows down at the Democratic Club put me up to it. They kept saying 'Len, if the little —— said things like that about me, I'd shoot him!'" (Exactly the same tactics that ended in the shooting of Heney in San Francisco!) "I got drunk, and they egged me on to it." And that poor tool, in tears, almost went down on his knees, in my chambers, to ask forgiveness for the slanders he had circulated about me, the attempts he made to ruin me!

Forgiveness? I could forgive him a thousand times over. I had never had anything but pity for him in my heart. But I could not forgive the men who had brought him to that posture before me—who had debased him in his own tears—a man like myself, crawling in spirit through the degradation of remorse for the crimes with which *they* had polluted him. O you rulers of Denver—to whom "politics is a matter of business"—this was *your* work! The bleeding Clerk in the Capitol, the poor Negro shot in the gutter, the would-be murderer weeping over his shame—these are among the spoils of your triumph. Let your clerks and bookkeepers write them down in your ledgers beside the columns of millions which their dishonoured lives helped you to gain. Cheesman——

Cheesman is dead. I wish to say nothing but good of the dead; but "the evil a man does lives after him"; and of that evil I propose to say nothing but ill. What else can I say of the part that his corporation took in the system of evil which I have described? What else can I say of the history of the Denver Union Water Company, with its record of taxes rebated, assessments reduced? What else can I say of the preparations that are now being made—this day, as I write— to force the people of Denver either to pay $14,400,000 for the water works or to grant the company a new franchise? What else can I say of the fact that after Mr. Cheesman's death, it was proposed to a complaisant City Council that our Congress Park—donated to the city by the Federal Government and valued at a million dollars—should be named in his honour "Cheesman Park," on condition that his heirs spend $100,000 erecting a public monument to his memory there;

and the City Council dedicated that public park to the private glory of this——

No. Let us say nothing but good of the dead. Let us say that on the highest point of "Corporation Park," where the view of the Rockies is most beautiful, the rulers of Denver are building a marble pavilion, with fountains and electric lights, to perpetuate the dishonour of the Beast and immortalize the success of its knaveries! Let us not join the name of the dead to this edifice of public shame. Let us see in it only a memorial to the Beast, erected by the Beast, as a mark of its power over a free community betrayed and corrupted; and seeing in it only such a memorial, let us realize that a monument in Washington to Benedict Arnold or to Wilkes Booth would not be a sorer insult to the sun that shines on it, the rain that wets it. Let us citizens of Denver look up at that pavilion, when we pass, as the disfranchised patriot of a subject race looked at a Roman Arch of Triumph in his capital, with the blood of indignation swelling against the iron collar on his neck. Let us leave the dead to their rest—forgiven. Our war is with the living.

CHAPTER XII

THE BEAST AND
THE SUPREME COURT

I N A REPUBLIC, SUCH AS OURS, where the law is the only
king, "there is a divinity doth hedge" the courts; and it is right that
it should be so. If our democracy is to endure, we must obey the
law and respect its agents. The man who wilfully tries to impair the
public credit of our courts, when those courts are just, is the greatest
traitor that our country has. But what if a court is not just? What if it
does not impartially administer the law, but does the bidding of a ruling faction of the community, and oppresses the helpless many in the
interests of the powerful few? Must we respect the corrupt priest and
minister of justice who degrades his almost holy office and defiles the
very temple of justice with his iniquities? Must we obey the court that
crushes us? Or is it true with courts as it is with monarchs that "resistance to tyrants is obedience to God"?

Throughout this story I have been careful to accuse no judge of corruption, by inference—to relate nothing of him but what I personally

knew to be true. I have refrained from arguing any conclusions; I have left the facts to plead for themselves. I have particularly respected the Supreme Court of Colorado, the high altar of justice in our state; and even when the evidences of corruption there were more than arguable, I have drawn no inferences of guilt. I have waited until I had followed the trail of the Beast, step by step, from the dives to the Police Board, from the Police Board to the lower courts, from the courts to the political leaders who nominated the judges of the courts, and from the political leaders to the corporation magnates who ruled all. But now the trail goes one step farther. It leads from the offices of the corporations to the doors of the Capitol; it ascends the steps of the State House; it enters the sacred precincts of the Supreme Court itself. And I propose to follow it.

I thought I had seen the footprint of the Beast in the Supreme Court's decisions on our three-fourths-jury law. I thought I had seen it in the decision that protected the ballot-box stuffer who was prosecuted by the Honest Election League. I thought I had seen it in the injunction that prevented me from opening the ballot boxes in the spring of 1904. I thought I had seen it in 1893 when the tramway company claimed a perpetual franchise in Denver, contrary to the provision of the constitution that declared: "No law making an irrevocable grant of privileges, franchises or immunities, shall be passed by the General Assembly"—and Justice Luther M. Goddard first held that the franchise was void, and then, allowed a rehearing and reversed himself! (So that the tramway company was able to sell its stocks and bonds in Wall Street on the representation that it had "a franchise without limit as to time, and therefore, perpetual," in spite of the constitution, the law and the courts.) But these were merely strongly suspicious circumstances; I needed proofs that were above suspicion. I got them in the memorable elections of the fall of 1904.

Six months before, in the spring, the corporations had elected Mayor Speer and his Democratic machine men by ballot-box frauds that were open and admitted. But the state was normally Republican; and the corporations now turned Republican in order to elect their candidates to the Legislature and the governorship. The Democrats were warned that they must not "stuff" the ballot boxes; and Speer in person carried the warning to the Democratic "Savages," ward heelers and election crooks—as they themselves afterward confessed to me. The Savages, having candidates on the Democratic ticket, from their own ranks, took the warning with a countenance that did not promise well; and before the balloting began—on the application of a corporation attorney acting ostensibly for the Republican party—the Supreme Court issued a blanket injunction enjoining the election officials from committing ballot-box frauds, and appointed "watchers" who were responsible to the court alone.

The injunction was printed in the form of a poster and pasted up all over the city. I saw it, and read it, with amazement. Not only was it without precedent in the whole history of American jurisprudence, but it was without legislative or constitutional authority, and it was in contravention of all the specific provisions made by law for the conduct of elections. It was an exercise of "kingly prerogative" that was declared by lawyers and law journals to be the most amazing act of lawlessness ever committed by an American court.

It was done avowedly to prevent the Savages from stuffing the ballot boxes; but the Savages—as I have related in a previous chapter— were not wholly intimidated. Some of the usual frauds were perpetrated (though in a much milder form than usual) and the Democrats carried the elections. All the candidates on the Democratic county ticket were returned, excepting Lindsley and Rogers, against whom I had made a campaign. The Republican Governor, Peabody, was defeated for re-election. And the Senate was given a Democratic majority.

Here was a dangerous slip in the plans of the corporations. A constitutional amendment had been carried, by which the number of Supreme Court justices was to be increased from three to seven. Two were to be promoted from the Court of Appeals, but two were to be appointed. A Democratic Governor would have the appointment of these, and a Democratic Senate would confirm the appointments. There was no time now to buy up the Democratic state machine, even if it could be bought in its hour of triumph. Something had to be done. It *was* done—and done promptly.

The Supreme Court prosecuted the Savages for "contempt" and imprisoned them. Then Gabbert and Campbell—with Justice R. W. Steele dissenting—ordered that certain election precincts, in which frauds were alleged, be not canvassed; the hundreds of honest Democratic votes in these precincts were thrown out with the few dishonest ones;* and, by eliminating these votes, the Supreme Court succeeded in declaring elected three Republican State Senators, eleven Republican representatives, and the entire Republican county ticket—although the returns showed that the Democrats had carried the county by majorities ranging from two to five thousand; and even with all the "fraudulent" votes eliminated, the Democrats would have won.

But this was not the end. The Democrats still had a majority of two in the Senate. So the State Canvassing Board, upheld by the Supreme Court—although the Board had properly only clerical powers to canvass and make its report—illegally threw out the returns from certain precincts in the counties of Boulder and Las Animas, and issued certificates of election to a number of Republican Senatorial candidates, and so manufactured a Republican majority in the Senate.

Pardon these tiresome details. They are necessary to make plain how the cards were "stacked." Without them, the deal that followed would be as bewildering as sleight-of-hand.

The constitutional amendment that provided for the appointment of the new Supreme Court justices expressly stated that the court so constituted should not come into existence until the first Wednesday in April, 1905, when Governor Peabody would have been out of office and his Democratic successor sworn in. Governor Peabody did not wait for the passing of April's Fool day. He submitted the names of the new justices to the manufactured Senate and got them confirmed.

---

* In a subsequent investigation thousands of votes that had been held fraudulent by the Supreme Court on the testimony of handwriting experts were proved honest and valid by the sworn evidence of the voters who had cast them.

Finally—as the climax and triumphant crown of the whole conspiracy—the Supreme Court assisted the manufactured Legislature in preventing Alva Adams, the Democratic governor-elect, from holding his office—although he had been elected by a plurality of more than 10,000 votes. And, after an interval of legislative uproar, with troops ready in the Capitol and the machinery of government at a standstill—while the corporations quarrelled among themselves—a sort of compromise was effected by which Adams was unseated, Peabody was declared elected, his appointments to the Supreme Court were accepted, but he himself resigned in favor of his lieutenant, Jesse McDonald.

All this, no doubt, was nothing to the public but more political chicanery. I knew that it was corporation treason; and this is how I knew:

At the time that Governor Peabody was considering the appointment of the new judges, I happened to mention to Mr. W. G. Brown—then president of one of the Denver banks—that I intended to speak to the Governor on behalf of a friend who was seeking a place on the Supreme Court bench. "The Governor?" Mr. Brown said. "Why, he hasn't anything to do with it. Don't you know the deal is to let the committee name the judges?"

I asked "What committee?"

"A committee," he explained, "agreed upon by the various 'interests.'" He named the men. They had been chosen, he said, by the public utility corporations of Denver, the railroads, and the Colorado Fuel and Iron Co. "If your friend is to have any show," he told me, "he will have to see this committee. They are 'the big ones' who will pass on his qualifications. He'll be especially strong if he can get Mr. Evans's endorsement. He'll have to satisfy these gentlemen that he's 'right' on certain questions in which they're interested. And if he can be depended on to decide such matters 'right,' he'll be considered. Otherwise, he needn't apply. They're going to have a court they can depend on."

What were these important questions in which the corporations were "interested"? The most important, Mr. Brown said, was the right of the Governor to declare martial law in case of labour disturbances so that the right of habeas corpus might be suspended and the labourers prevented from applying to the courts in defence of their liberties.

And it was not Mr. Brown alone who admitted the deal with Governor Peabody. Peabody's nephew, Mr. Geo. P. Steele, was a candidate for one of these appointments, and his friends had given it out that the Governor had promised him the place. One day I met Steele on the corner of 17th and Welton streets and asked him why he had not been appointed. "Why, Ben," he said, "it was the darndest farce you ever heard of. The corporations had him absolutely. He had to appoint Bailey and Goddard. He had to appoint whoever the corporations wanted. I wouldn't go up there unless I could go 'straight.'"

Does this seem incredible? Read then the Colorado Supreme Court Reports, Volume 35, page 325 and thereabouts. You will find it charged that the Colorado and Southern Railway Company, the Denver and Rio Grande Railway Company, and the public service corporations of Denver had an agreement with Governor Peabody whereby these corporations were to be allowed to select the judges to be appointed to the Supreme Bench. You will find it charged that Luther M. Goddard had been selected as a proper judge by the public utility corporations, but that the two railroad companies objected to him as "too closely allied with the interests of the Denver City Tramway Company and the Denver Union Water Company." "As a last resort," the statement continues, "the agent and representative of the said Colorado and Southern Railway Company was induced to, and did, after midnight on Sunday, the eighth day of January, and at about one o'clock in the morning on Monday the ninth day of January, repair to the home of the said Luther M. Goddard, in a carriage, calling him out of bed, having then and there such conversation with the said Goddard that the said railway corporations, through their agents, withdrew their opposition to his confirmation, and they did on said morning at about three o'clock thereof announce to the remainder of the said corporations through their said agents and representatives, that their opposition had been withdrawn, and the withdrawal of the said opposition, having been announced, the said Senate of the

Fifteenth General Assembly did, almost immediately upon its convening on the morning of Monday, the ninth day of January, confirm the said nomination of the said Goddard."

The brief containing these charges is signed by Senator Henry M. Teller, Ex–Cabinet Minister and United States Senator, and by Ex-Governor Thomas acting as counsel for Senator T. M. Patterson, who had made the charges in his paper, *The Rocky Mountain News*. These gentlemen offered to prove the charges before the court, but the court, in a most amazing decision, refused the offer, held that no matter how true such charges might be, it was "contempt of court" to make them, and fined Senator Patterson $1,000! Senator Patterson, rising to receive his sentence, protested against it, to the court, in one of the most scathing arraignments ever addressed to an American bench of justice. "If constructive contempt," he ended, "is to be maintained as it has been maintained by this court, it can simply mean . . . that we have in each of the states of the union a chosen body of men who may commit any crime, who may falsify justice, who may defy the constitution and spit upon the laws, and yet no man dare make known the facts. . . . From this time forward I will devote myself . . . to deprive every man and every body of men of such tyrannical power, of such unjust and dangerous prerogative."

His protest was no more vigorous than Justice Steele's dissent from the decision—Justice Robert W. Steele, the judge whom I had succeeded in the County Court—an honest man who was in the minority in so many of the corporation cases that came before the court. He has fought the people's fight for years, often single-handed, in that court; and he is still fighting. But his term of office expires in the fall of 1910, and he will have as much chance of being reelected as any other honest man who is not "right" on those "important questions" in which the corporations are "interested."*

---

* No charge of corruption against Judge Campbell is here made or implied. Even the labouring men during these troubles recognized that Judge Campbell's decisions were those of an honest prejudice, due to his training and his temperament.

I understood why the corporations wished the Governor to have
the right to declare martial law and suspend the habeas corpus in case
of labour disturbances. The Cripple Creek "labour war" was being
waged. I do not hold a brief for either the miners or the mine owners in that struggle. I do not defend the lawlessness of either. But I
went to Cripple Creek at the time and talked to the labouring men
and learned that they knew, as well as I did, who controlled the
Supreme Court and Governor Peabody and the corrupt Legislature
that betrayed the people. An intelligent labourer, who had opposed
the calling of the strike, said to me: "No one thing ever caused so
much ill-feeling among the labouring men of this state as what we
considered the treachery of Judges Gabbert and Goddard in deciding against us on the eight-hour law!" (Both these judges had been
"Populists" at the beginnings of their careers and had been first
elected by the votes of the labouring men.) The strike claimed to be
a strike for an eight-hour day in certain mills. The Legislature had
passed an eight-hour law, but the Supreme Court, composed at that
time of Campbell, Gabbert and Goddard, had declared it unconstitutional—although the Supreme Court of the United States, in a similar
case, had held the contrary!

When the question of the validity of my election of the fall of
1904 came before the Supreme Court, my counsel argued that I had
not been legally elected in the spring of 1904—because the charter
convention had no right to provide for the elections of county judge,
district attorney, or district judge, since these offices had been specifically excepted from the jurisdiction of the charter convention by
the constitutional amendment that provided for the convention. But
the Supreme Court calmly held that the charter convention had no
right to consolidate *any* county office with a municipal office—a question that had not been brought before the court at all in this case,
except by distant implication. And the effect of this decision was to
throw out of office *all* the Democratic county office holders who had
been elected with me in the spring of 1904. They had been renominated and reelected in the fall, but the action of the Supreme Court,

in throwing out the precincts in which the Democrats had obtained their majorities, had given the Republicans the offices. And now these Democrats found themselves on the streets—the very Democrats who had "mixed it up" in the hope of losing me "in the shuffle." I was far from lost. I had been elected twice, by both parties. If one election was not valid the other was. If one party's plurality was declared fraudulent, I had still all the votes of the other party to elect me. I could laugh at the Beast, its frauds and its courts.

But I did not feel like laughter. Some of the decisions of the Supreme Court had already had an awful result. They had had a result that not only convulsed Colorado but horrified the whole civilized world.

In the spring of 1904, Chas. H. Moyer, president of the Western Federation of Miners, was arrested by the military authorities at Ouray on a charge of desecrating the American flag by using a printed representation of it in a campaign handbill. He had obtained a writ of habeas corpus from the local judge, but the military authorities in power in the strike district refused to surrender him—on the ground that his "reasonable further detention" was required by "the ends of public justice and the restoration of public tranquillity." His attorneys appealed to the Supreme Court in Denver, and the judges decided against him—all but Judge Steele again.

Judge Steele held, in his dissenting opinion: "If one may be restrained of his liberty without charges being preferred against him, every other guarantee of the constitution may be denied him. When we deny to one, however wicked, a right plainly guaranteed by the constitution, we take that same right from every one. When we say to Moyer: 'You must stay in prison, because if we discharge you, you may commit a crime,' we say that to every other citizen. When we say to one governor: 'You have unlimited and arbitrary power,' we clothe future governors with that same power. We cannot change the constitution to meet conditions. We cannot deny liberty to-day and grant it tomorrow. We cannot grant it to those theretofore above suspicion and deny to those suspected of crime, for the constitution is for all men—'for the favourite at court, for the countryman at plow'—at all times and under all circumstances."

The corporations and their court did not think so. Having denied the labouring man his representation in the Legislature and his appeal in law, they now denied him his most elementary constitutional right to liberty itself. What happened? The inevitable happened. Harry Orchard writes in his terrible autobiography: "They wanted us to work on Judge Gabbert and see if we could not bump him off, as they were very bitter against him—especially Moyer. Judge Gabbert was Chief Justice of the Supreme Court, and had decided against Moyer when they brought him to Denver from Telluride on a writ of habeas corpus, when he was in the hands of the militia." And again: "They were very bitter against Judge Goddard, as they said he had written up most of the opinion in the Moyer habeas-corpus case, and had been instrumental in declaring unconstitutional the eight-hour law that had been passed by the Legislature a few years previous, when he was on the Supreme Bench before." Lawlessness had its inevitable result in lawlessness.

As I walked home, one midnight, with my friend Dr. C. B. James, the city and county physician—from a performance of "Dr. Jekyll and Mr. Hyde"—we passed Judge Gabbert's house, and saw on the porch a man crouching, like the horrible Hyde himself, at the sill of Gabbert's front window, while a confederate watched from the shadow of a veranda pillar. These two men—as we have since come to believe— were Harry Orchard and Steve Adams. They made off rapidly across the lawn and down the street as we approached; and after trying in vain to find a policeman we met Judge Gabbert's stepson returning home and we warned him of the burglars, as we thought they were. Some time before this, Dr. James had received a telephone message from an unknown friend in the middle of the night telling him not to walk down to the Capitol in the morning with Judge Gabbert, as had been his custom; and Orchard's confession shows that he and Adams were then planning to kill Gabbert, with a bomb, on his way to court. They killed, by accident, a man named Walley, in a vacant lot a few blocks from my house. I heard the explosion of the bomb. They planted another bomb at Judge Goddard's gate, but it did not explode. They tried to waylay and shoot Governor Peabody, but they failed.

And why did they do these things? Why were murderous outrages committed in Colorado that are only paralleled by the outrages of the revolutionists in despotic Russia? Because like conditions breed like events. The government of Russia has been described as "a despotism tempered by assassination"; and the government of Colorado, in the spring of 1905, was just that! The crimes of Orchard—that horrified the whole country and blackened the name of Colorado in the estimation of the world—were the inevitable result of the crimes of the corporations that made the government of Colorado an insufferable despotism of lawless men. The crime of the oppressed is a demand for justice!

From my chambers, in which I am writing now, I can look out my window and see the little shop in which Orchard says the casings of his bombs were prepared; and from another window I can see the Majestic Building from which the corporations govern the state. What a government! And what an opposition! The millionaire uses his power of wealth to rob and starve and pollute a whole community with protected vice and thwarted justice and laws defied—and the exasperated labourer, finding himself denied the common rights of man, declares war against his oppressors with the bomb and the bullet! Who is the more to blame—the criminal who makes the conditions or the criminal who is made *by* the conditions? The one goes in broadcloth to his church, sleek, smug, respected, feared for his power and honoured for his successes. The other, branded with his guilt, a moral leper by his own confession, imprisoned for life, a shuddering horror to the whole world, appeals to the same God for forgiveness Whose church the man of wealth so proudly enters—one of its "pillars," its powerful benefactor, its generous patron, its bland communicant. I do not presume to voice the judgment of Providence upon these two men. I do not even predict the decrees of human justice. But if I had to make my choice of their fates and elect between the burdens of their iniquities, I should prefer to crouch before the altar of Orchard's prison chapel, trembling, with all his clotted murders on my hands.

CHAPTER XIII

THE BEAST AND REFORM

S O ENDED THE GREAT CONSPIRACY of the corporations
of Colorado in the elections of 1904. And with the triumph of
that conspiracy, the government of Colorado changed from a
democracy to a plutocratic oligarchy. I saw it then; I have seen it
more clearly since. I saw that the people of Colorado were not free
citizens, but enfranchised serfs. They could be killed by their masters with impunity, and the jury would "hang." As a rule, they could
elect no man to a political office unless he served their masters—and
my own election was merely "the exception that proved the rule." If
they rose, in mass, to vote for an eight-hour law, and the Legislature
passed such a law, their masters, through the mouth of the Supreme
Court, declared it unconstitutional. If they rose again to pass a constitutional amendment permitting such a law, their masters, through
the Legislature, refused to pass it. If they rebelled against this tyranny, and went on strike for their constitutional rights, and were

lawless in their opposition to lawlessness, their masters, through the Governor, called out the militia, suspended the last pretence of justice, and drove them from the state. The citizen of Colorado had no more right to "life, liberty and the pursuit of happiness" than a yellow dog on the streets of Denver, unless he wore the corporation collar and tag, came to the whistle of his master and ate scraps from his hand.

And it was not only that the American citizen in Colorado had no rights as against his masters; he had none as against the favoured slaves of his masters. I had seen it in numerous cases that had come to my court. For example: a junk dealer had been employing boys to steal bars of lead from box cars, and after trying the boys I advised the prosecution of their employer. He retained a corporation lawyer to defend him before a justice of the peace who aspired to a judgeship; and the case against him was dropped. Or again: a man was once accused in my court of seducing a little girl; the District Attorney declared he was a "regular degenerate"; and his lawyer offered to plead guilty if I would put him on probation. I refused to. A new lawyer was brought into the case—a corporation tool who was then County Attorney—and there was an immediate change in the fervour of the prosecution. The District Attorney reported that he had investigated the charge and found no evidence against the man; and I was compelled, under the law, to accept a "nolle," which amounted to a dismissal of the case. This sort of thing prevailed even in divorce suits. It prevailed in every sort of suit that a corporation lawyer could be retained to defend before a corporation judge. Just as the king's favourites in France, before the Revolution, were free to commit any outrage upon the citizens who had no court influence, so, in Colorado, the favourite who wore the livery of the corporations—or was able to retain a favourite who *did*—could spit upon the freeman, could debauch the son of the freeman, could violate the daughter of the freeman, and then appeal confidently to the corporation ministers of justice to protect him. Our boasted "government of the people, for the people and by the people" had passed away.

Does this seem an intemperate statement of the facts? I hope not. It would distress me to have any one suspect me of impatience. I am trying to relate my experiences, in the Jungle, with the Beast, as dispassionately as possible, without any colour of prejudice, coolly, for the benefit of those of you who live sheltered private lives, purred to in prosperity. I do not raise my voice. If I say that you are not a citizen of a democracy but a sort of enfranchised house slave of an oligarchy of corporate wealth, I say it, believe me, in the politest tone conceivable. It is merely a condition which I wish you to recognize. If, after you have recognized it, you are still content to sit by your fireside and leave politics to your masters, at least you can do so without having been unnecessarily annoyed. If the democracy is to die, by all means let it die decently, with resignation, on a feather bed. Let it not make a noisy finish, like a stuck pig, dragged from its comfortable pen and prosperity's full hog trough, to have its throat cut, squealing shrilly, while the rest of the world jeers.

In the spring of 1905, I admit, I was not so philosophical. I had just come through a hot campaign and my blood was still intemperate. I was prepared to stir up an insurrection among my fellow-serfs, and I believed that such an insurrection could be made successful. I had not been, for so long, an opponent of the Beast without having learned the sources of its power. I had seen that whenever it was attacked in its jungle, it took refuge up a tree. I believed that we could fell that tree, with the animal in its top—bring the brute down, stunned by its fall—and dispatch it where it lay, before it could recover. In other words, I had seen that the corporations derived their power from their control of politics, and that they controlled politics largely through the election laws. If we could reform the election laws so as to make the will of the people effective, we could overturn the throne of the plutocracy and have the king sprawling at the feet of his subjects. After that, we could make what terms with him we pleased.

We needed, first of all, a registration law to prevent ballot-box stuffing, so that Boss Evans might not have voters "good for 500 votes" each, while the people had only voters of a vote apiece. Then, if we could get a real Australian ballot law, with a headless ballot—so that the people might be able to vote for candidates instead of parties—we would make it possible for an independent man to succeed in an independent campaign, and prevent Boss Evans from using the name of Roosevelt or Bryan to elect a ticket of corruptionists. Next, with an effective direct primary law, we could abolish the machine caucus and convention—in which the corporations choose the candidates for whom the people are to be allowed to vote—make it possible for the voters to choose their own representatives and free the honest politician from the necessity of going to Big Steve, or Boss Speer, or any other corporation favourite, for permission to aspire to a political office. And finally, with a "corrupt practices act," we could limit campaign expenses, make it unnecessary to appeal to the wealthy corporations for contributions, and make it possible for an independent candidate to compete against a party man without mortgaging his house or selling his independence.

In short, what we most needed—and do still need—was not laws *against* trusts and corporations, limiting their powers and restraining their activities, but laws *for* the people, permitting them to use *their* power and restoring to them the tools of democracy, which the corporations have taken from them. It is useless to agitate for "government control of trusts" as long as the trusts are able, through our machinery of elections, to control the government that is to control *them*. Once let us regain control of our legislatures, our courts and our public officials—by regaining control of the process of electing them—and we shall have the corporations where the sans-culottes had King Louis and his favourites before the Reign of Terror. Then 'ware the figurative guillotine!

With this pleasing prospect in my hope, I began to work on a series of bills to reform the election laws, and I began to stir up a popular demand for such laws by means of public speeches, newspaper articles and the like. And because this same campaign will have to be fought in every state in the union in which it has not yet been fought, I wish to chronicle it here in sufficient detail to explain the tactics that were used against us, the methods by which we succeeded and the reasons for which we failed.

We opened fire in the newspapers—and especially in the Denver *Post*, through a clever editorial writer named Paul Thieman who had given me a vital aid in my two previous election contests. The *Post* was then as independent as a highwayman. One of its proprietors, H. H. Tammen, had begun life as a barkeeper, and he would himself relate how he had made money by robbing his employer. "When I took in a dollar," Tammen said, "I tossed it up—and if it stuck to the ceiling, it went to the boss." He had a frank way of making his vices engaging by the honesty with which he confessed them; and he had boasted to me of the amount of money the newspaper made by charging its victims for suppressing news-stories of a scandalous nature in which they were involved. He admitted that he supported me merely because it was "the popular thing to do"—it "helped circulation." I knew it was a very precarious support, although the editorial writer, Paul Thieman, seemed to me an honest and public-spirited young man.

The *Rocky Mountain News,* the official organ of the Democratic party, also aided us. (It was owned by Senator Patterson.) But there was a wing of the Democratic party for which it could not speak—the corporation machine faction led by Boss Speer—and I had yet to learn how strong that faction was. The Denver *Republican*, of course, was not in our camp; it is a corporation organ simply. But the Republicans were not unwilling to have the popularity of the children's court as an asset of their ticket, and their paper did not openly oppose our reform of the election laws.

There, then, were the three typical newspapers of a typical American city; and we had two of them with us and one preserving a sort of armed neutrality. After a preliminary cannonade of articles and editorials, our reform bills were given to Senator W. W. Booth, whom we had elected by defeating "Len" Rogers; and Senator Booth introduced them in the Senate.

This immediately "developed" the position of the corporation tools in the Legislature. The Republican sub-boss, George Graham, held a parley with Senator Booth, and Booth reported to us: "They say there's absolutely no hope for the direct primary law or the Massachusetts ballot. Neither party organization will stand for it. But there's been a big fuss about padded registration in Denver and in Pueblo, and something may have to be done in that matter for fear the party will be injured. I think we can get them to give us a show to put through the registration reform, but they say that if I try to pass the other two bills, they'll not even let us have the registration law."

I understood, of course, that the "they" who spoke were the corporation representatives. The Democratic chairman, Milton Smith, and other Democrats, like Senator Billy Adams, always faithful to the public-service corporations, opposed the bills as stubbornly as the Republicans did. The corporation lobbyists worked with a will against them. William R. Freeman, a corporation lobbyist whom I met one day on the street, said frankly, in reply to my arguments for a reform of the election laws: "Yes, they do give us the power to rule the people, but why shouldn't we have it? You know the corporations give this state good government. Look what Speer has done for Denver. Suppose the corporations have got millions of dollars' worth of franchises; they know how to use them and the people don't. Now be honest! You know the people aren't fit to govern themselves. If the corporations of this state didn't do it for them, what kind of a state would we have?" He pointed to some workingmen digging in the street. "Do you think we are going to be ruled by a lot of cattle like that? What do *they* know about government? No, sir. We rule, and we're going to continue to!"

Freeman was frank. The men in the Legislature were not. They had been elected by the votes of "the people not fit to govern themselves" and it was necessary to add hypocrisy to treason. The bills were referred to committees and the doors of silence were locked on them. We battered at the doors.

Thus far the corporations had been apparently on the defensive, entrenched and silent; and we were preparing to push the assault, when suddenly we discovered a flank movement that had been weeks afoot and was now sweeping in triumphantly upon us. In the very first days of the session my old law partner, whom I have called Senator "Gardener," had introduced two bills that would have made my position as County Judge untenable, and one of these bills had almost passed the Senate before I knew that it had been even introduced. They provided that County Judges in counties of the first class (which referred only to Denver) should not be permitted to leave the city except in July, and should not be allowed to call in a judge to assist in the work of the County Court. It was humanly impossible for one man to do the work of my court, and Gardener and his corporation masters knew it. We were forced temporarily to use all our efforts in the Legislature to defeat these "spite bills," and we were put on the defensive thereby. It is an old trick of the Beast, but an effective one.

The newspapers came to our rescue; the women held meetings in their clubs; the boys marched through the streets with banners; and Senator Gardener found himself beaten upon by a storm of public abuse that has marked him for life. The people, though they did not yet see the Beast, saw that the Juvenile Court was in danger, and rallied at once to the support of a "moral issue." (Woman's suffrage in Colorado has done *that*, at least, for our politics.) The women packed the legislative committee rooms at the Capitol when I spoke against the bills; and the House did not dare to pass them.

A few days before this, while I was at luncheon in a restaurant, Mr. R. D. Thompson—the lawyer under whom Gardener and I had served our apprenticeship—came to the table at which I sat and gave me a warning from Gardener. If (Gardener had said) I dared to say anything publicly that would reflect on him or any of his friends they would "spend a thousand dollars in circulating a story" that would ruin me in the estimation of the women, and end my career.

"Well," I said, "what the deuce does he mean?"

Mr. Thompson replied: "I don't know. He didn't tell me any more than that—and he said I'd better tell you, because they believe you're going to go before the House at the hearing on these bills and make some statements reflecting on him—something that *he* did, which you claim is the animus behind these bills."

I knew, then, that Gardener referred to the visit he had made to me in my home and his request that I should "job" the Springer election contest for him. I went straight to Gardener's office to demand what he meant by his threat. He was not in. I wrote him a letter and told him that if he knew anything reflecting on my character it was his duty to make it public, and I released him from every confidential or friendly obligation to conceal it. He wrote in reply that he knew nothing against me, and he denied having made the threat.

This was all very well. But he continued to circulate his slanders. He poured them into the ear of Senator William L. Clayton, for example, and Senator Clayton repeated them to me. They came to the knowledge of my brother and my friends. It was evident that the Beast had turned "polecat" again. I went to the newspapers and gave them the whole story of Gardener's attempt to influence me into jobbing the election cases and I challenged him to substantiate any of his slanderous charges against me. In other words, I set the dogs of publicity upon the Beast and drove it to its burrow.

Do you think I was done with it, then? Gentle reader, you do not know the "animal." Slander is one of its choicest and most effective weapons. Come to Denver to-day and hear some sweet and motherly little woman, at her dinner table, among her children, tell you, "Yes, I voted for Judge Lindsey—*in spite* of his private life." Abominable stories about me, circulated privately, are privately believed, despite the fact that there is not a corporation crook in Denver who would not dance with joy if he could find the slightest evidence on which to base a charge of immorality against me. My private life has been gone over with a microscope. I have been followed by detectives. Faces have peered in my library window at night when I have been sitting there, talking with friends. My chambers in the Court House have been broken into, my desk drawers forced open, and my letter files searched. Bribes have been offered the officers of my court to find or manufacture evidence of my moral turpitude. Nothing has been found on which the harpies could build even a presumption of guilt that would endure the light. And yet the slanders circulate!

I have proof, too, that they are deliberately circulated. In 1904, when I was opposing the election of "Len" Rogers and District Attorney Lindsley, Paul Thieman, of the *Post*, came upon a young brood of slanderous lies that had been hatched out at the Democratic Club. He spoke to a politician about them. "*You* know Judge Lindsey," he said. "You don't really believe those stories, do you?"

"No," the politician replied, "but we've got to get the little —— some way. There'll be a lot of people believe them." And he described how some sensitive reformer in San Francisco—whose name I have forgotten—had been overwhelmed by just such calumnies.

If this method of attack were peculiar to the Beast in Denver, I should not refer to it here. But do you know what stories were told of District Attorney Jerome in New York, of Senator La Follette in Wisconsin, of Governor Folk in Missouri, of Heney in San Francisco and even of President Roosevelt? O you citizens of the United States who are "not fit to govern" yourselves—the manufacture and circulation of these stories is one of the operations of the powers that govern you. It is this defilement that has helped to make our politics so dirty. It is your credence of these lies that has made the honour of public office so often a garment of torture to the man who wears it. Beware your Beast when it turns "polecat"! Remember always that if there was a word of honest evidence on which to defend these stories, they would be printed in every corporation newspaper in the country!

Well, we defeated Senator Gardener's spite bills and turned again to our campaign of reform; and by this time it was evident that we could hope for no more than the passage of our registration law. The other bills were pigeonholed in committees, guarded by corporation representatives like the Democratic Senator "Billy" Adams, who has sat for more than twenty years in our Senate, sunken-lipped, glint-eyed, with the beak of a buzzard, waiting silently like an old scald-head hawk to pounce upon any reform measure that threatens the "plum tree" of the corporations.

But our registration bill apparently had a chance of becoming law. It passed along quietly through the Senate—to my amazement—a little mutilated now and then by an amendment, but still effective. I watched its course with interest, puzzled by its success. I began to hope that the public outcry against the ballot frauds had put the fear of the popular wrath into the hearts of the machine politicians. And certainly the outcry had been loud. We had defeated the Democratic candidate for District Attorney in Denver, and elected a Republican, who had instituted a vigorous prosecution of the Democratic "stuffers." In Pueblo, the Republican District Attorney had been defeated, and a Democratic District Attorney was prosecuting the Republican "stuffers." The public was applauding both. The henchmen and ward heelers and even some sub-bosses of both parties were in danger of the penitentiary; and on the wave of this "reform movement" our new law seemed to be borne gaily along.

And then the mystery was explained to me by Senator W. W. Booth. He had discovered that the two corporation bosses had come together and agreed "to swap prisoners." Our registration bill had a clause that repealed the old registration law "save and except as to all violations thereof and prosecutions pending thereunder"; and when the bill came up for the final vote, this "saving clause" was struck out.

I hastened at once to see Governor McDonald, explained the plot to him, and besought him, upon receiving the mutilated bill, to return it to the Legislature with a message exposing this premeditated jail delivery and demanding the reinstatement of the "saving clause." He replied calmly that the facts were probably as I had related—that he had been so advised from other sources. (The District Attorney in Pueblo had telegraphed him that the passage of the amended bill would free some 200 ballot-box stuffers against whom there were indictments.) But he said: "You can't get the law, in my judgment, unless you get it in this way." And we had to take what we could get.

The ballot-box stuffers immediately appealed to the Supreme Court, under the new law, for a stay in the proceedings against them.

The judges decided that the passage of the new law repealed the old one, and they held that since the clause "save and except as to all violations thereof" had been stricken out—and a repeal of all penalties for crimes thereunder deliberately inserted—it was no doubt the intention of the Legislature to grant a pardon to the criminals. We lost the thieves, hut we got the instrument against them; and it has been effective. Billy Green, the notorious election crook, has since borne unwilling testimony to that effect. In districts where there had been 5,000 voters registered in the old days, less than 1,000 were now on the books. The corporations had lost their voters "good for 500 votes apiece," and the people of Colorado were one step nearer freedom.

I was elated. We had not only forced a reform, but it proved practical; and of all our bills the registration measure was the only one of whose effect there had been any question. Our direct primary law was after Senator La Follette's ideas, some of which had been adopted in Wisconsin.

The headless ballot law had shown its strength in Massachusetts. If we could get those two laws, now, we should be able to hear Lincoln's Gettysburg address read in Colorado without turning pale.

CHAPTER XIV

A CITY PILLAGED

HAVE I CONVINCED YOU YET? Do you still think I am crying "Wolf! Wolf!" when there is no wolf, or do you believe that we indeed *do* have our fabled dragon, to which some of us are daily sacrificed—that lives upon us—that the daughters of the poor are fed to, no less than the sons of the rich? Or do you think that it is, after all, a rather harmless brute whom some of us in Colorado have goaded to a natural rage—a domestic animal properly—a milch cow, perhaps, that has to have its fodder but repays us in the rich cream of prosperity? Do you agree with the candid Freeman that government by corporations is not so bad a thing? Then let me—before I proceed with the story of our struggle for a reform of our election laws—let me add one more instance of what that kind of government entails. Let me show it as I saw it in my court room in the spring of 1906. Let me put you on the bench there to judge it, and decide.

Under the constitutional amendment that had granted the city of Denver in 1902 the right to make its own charter, it had been provided that the citizens should dispose of franchises to public service corporations by the direct vote of the taxpaying electors, and not, as in the past, through the City Council. In 1906 the Denver Gas and Electric Company applied for a franchise for twenty years, and the tramway company applied for an extension of some of its franchises, without, however, waiving its claims to a perpetual franchise. The gas company wished also the power to take over the electric plant of a local company that by its charter could not sell except to the city; and the Denver and Northwestern Railroad wished an entrance to the city and a right of way. For these monopoly rights in the streets of Denver nothing was offered to the citizens of Denver except by the gas company, which agreed to pay $50,000 per annum, and by the street railway company, which engaged itself to pay the city $60,000 a year on condition that a certain part of the money be spent on the public parks and for park amusements (to which, of course, the tramway company would carry the crowds!).

These franchises were voted upon in the spring elections. Before election day it began to be freely charged that in the offices of the County Assessor and the County Treasurer, where the lists of taxpaying electors were being made up, great numbers of citizens were being assessed upon trivial articles of personal property, so that they might be qualified to vote. It was charged, too, that "fake" tax receipts were being issued to employees of the utility corporations. And a league of citizens, through their lawyers, at once applied to the District Court (Judge Frank T. Johnson*) for a writ similar to that issued by the Supreme Court in 1904 against the "Savages," to prevent election frauds. Judge Johnson held that if the Supreme Court could grant such a writ the District Court could do the same.

---

* Judge Johnson did his duty to the community bravely in these cases. The System crushed him at the next election.

He issued it. The elections were held, and on the face of the returns the franchises were granted.

But the majority in favour of the grant was very small—ninety-nine for the tramway franchise and about five hundred for the gas franchise on the official recount. The tax-receipt frauds were evident. Hundreds of votes had been cast upon taxes of a few cents levied on almost worthless land that lay out on the prairies. And the league of citizens, under Judge Johnson's writ, applied for an investigation in his court. He decided to hold it.

Subpoenas were issued to the boys who had voted on the "ten-cent" tax receipts and to the woman in the Treasurer's office who had made out these receipts. The woman promptly fled from town. The County Treasurer rose from his sick bed to deny responsibility for having issued the receipts, discharged the chief clerk under whose instructions the work had been done, collapsed in his office and died that same afternoon at his home. It was charged that more than 2,000 fraudulent receipts had been issued. It was proved that the receipts had been issued wholesale and distributed among the clerks of the gas company office. The clerks, called to the witness stand, either per-jured themselves by swearing that they had bought the land through Mr. Frank W. Freuauff of the gas company, or practically confessed their guilt by refusing to testify lest they might incriminate them-selves—a privilege that every criminal has under the law.

Does this sound merely technical? Ah, you should have been in that court and watched those poor boys—honest sons of good fami-lies, who had been driven at the bidding of their employers to com-mit a crime—standing there before the bar of justice, admitting their shame while their wives and mothers watched with tears in their eyes. You should have heard them floundering through their per-juries, red-faced and guilty, while the officers of the gas company watched them with a cynical smile. And you should have seen Henry L. Doherty, president of the gas company, when *he* was called to the stand and refused to testify—refused to do for himself what he had let these boys do for him—and with a contemptuous sneer on his face denied the jurisdiction of the court and would give no evidence before it.

That court represented the sovereign power of the people. But Henry L. Doherty was protected by the sovereign power of the Beast. That court had the right under the law to hear the case and give judgment upon it; and the question of its jurisdiction should then have been decided, upon appeal. But Henry L. Doherty had the lawless power of the Beast to smile at court procedure, to despise law, and to teach anarchy by example. Judge Johnson sentenced him for contempt. He went out smiling in the custody of a deputy sheriff. One of his attorneys rushed to the telephone and called up the Clerk of the Supreme Court and said in the voice of a man talking to his office boy, "Hurry up with that writ." Doherty made a triumphal descent of the Court House staircase, smiled at by the crowds in the halls, as if he were the hero of some huge practical joke that was admirable in its insolence; and he was taken by the Sheriff to a neighbouring hotel where he waited until Judge Gabbert directed his release under a writ of habeas corpus—a proceeding which the Supreme Court itself afterward repudiated as illegal.

However, the Supreme Court granted a temporary writ restraining Judge Johnson from proceeding with his investigation; and later, a majority of the judges of the Court made that writ permanent and so held that Judge Johnson had no right to do for the people in 1906 what the Supreme Court had done—for whom?—in 1904. Judges Steele and Gunter dissented. They held that though the action of the Supreme Court in 1904 was "without precedent" and "not based upon any recognized rule of equity jurisprudence," it was "nevertheless, until reversed, the law of this state." They held that the decision of the Supreme Court in 1904 declared that it was "in the power of a court of equity to supervise elections by injunction." They held that the Supreme Court could not claim such a right for itself and deny the same right to the District Court, for by doing so the Supreme Court "arrogates to itself an exclusiveness expressly disavowed in many other opinions and assumes a superiority denied it by the constitution." The other judges overrode this dissent. They did not propose to strain at a gnat after having swallowed a camel. They denied Judge Johnson's jurisdiction, and his investigation collapsed.

Balked there, the league of citizens applied for a grand jury investigation; but since their complaint alleged a conspiracy of the corporations to buy up and control both parties in the elections, the League asked the appointment of a special Sheriff and a special District Attorney on the case. Judge Mullins granted the investigation, and appointed officers in place of the suspected Sheriff and District Attorney Stidger. Another appeal was taken to the Supreme Court, and the Court again intervened and stopped the proceedings, on the ground that the Sheriff and the District Attorney could not be displaced—in the face of Justice Steele's dissenting opinion, that the case came "within the doctrine announced in the People *vs.* District Court, 29 Colorado, 5, where the right of the District Judge to appoint a special officer to advise the Grand Jury whenever he has reason to believe, from information which he considers reliable, that crimes have been committed and that the officers' conduct in connection therewith is such that it should be investigated, is expressly confirmed."

The franchise investigation was finally brought before me. As judge of the County Court, I had the right, under the charter, "to hear all election contests." The lawyers for the corporations filed affidavits charging me with prejudice and demanding a change of venue. I refused to grant it. An appeal was taken to Judge Malone of the District Court, and the corporation lawyers argued there that I had no jurisdiction. "Some of the counsel for the petitioners," Judge Malone said in his decision, "were frank enough to tell the Court that they did not think there was any court that had jurisdiction to consider, investigate or pass upon the validity of the franchises in question, or as to whether they were lawfully carried. They say that there having been no court or tribunal established or named for the purpose, there is a radical defect in the legislation upon the subject, which can only be corrected by further legislation. . . . I cannot believe this to be true."

He resolved the doubt in the case in favour of the people, and held that the County Court had the right to hear the contest. He has since admitted that he had been warned that if his decision went against the corporations he could not be renominated to the bench; and he has not been renominated!

The case before me continued. There continued also a general exodus from Denver that became one of the jokes of the newspapers. "Bill" Evans, president of the tramway company, had gone East. Freuauff, the manager of the gas company, had taken an early train. "Bill" Davoren, chairman of the Democratic City and County Central Committee had flown, and a friend of his came to my chambers to ask that I grant him immunity on the promise that the organization would back me as a candidate for the Governorship. Scores of young clerks made off, their travelling expenses paid (as some of them have since confessed to me) by the gas company. The mothers of others—or their wives—came to my chambers with pitiful tales of poverty and lack of employment, and told me that their sons or their husbands had been compelled to cast fraudulent votes or lose the work on which they depended for their daily bread. (The victims of the Beast!) One of the guilty clerks was the son of the Bishop of one of Denver's churches, and I was besought for the sake of his father, for the sake of the congregation, for the sake of religion and public decency, not to put him on the witness stand. (He finally escaped the process server and got out of town.) A young man came to confess to me that he had committed perjury in Judge Johnson's court, believing that the corporations would "square it"; "for," he said, "it's been common talk that the corporations control the Supreme Court and wouldn't let us get into trouble." All day in my chambers, every evening in my home, these trembling slaves of corporation government besieged me with their petitions for clemency; and the pitiful guilt and moral degradation of it all made life a nightmare. These people were not the "lower classes" of the slums whom you are accustomed to think of as born to shame and suffering. They were not the working men who are "cattle" to such as Freeman, and in his opinion "not fit to govern themselves." They were those whom you, "gentle reader," are accustomed to consider as good as yourself. And yet they were dragged through the mire of fraud and perjury just as *you* and *your* children and *your* wives and *your* mothers will be dragged, if the Beast in your community ever finds the need to drag you. Never doubt it!

The case continued. Party workers were put on the stand and admitted that they had received money from the party organizations and had voted for the franchises. The clerks and their wives who had voted on the fraudulent tax-receipts either refused to testify lest they should incriminate themselves, or perjured themselves so flagrantly that the court was compelled to warn them. Scenes similar to those that I had watched in Judge Johnson's court were repeated in mine; and Henry L. Doherty, and those of his fellow officials who had not succeeded in getting out of town, smiled as they listened.

Then, in order to prove that the money paid by the political organizations to their workers had come from the corporations, Doherty was ordered to the witness stand. He refused to testify. With his arms crossed, backed by his lawyers, he denied the jurisdiction of the court and silently dared us to punish him.

I pointed out to him, mildly, that the question of the jurisdiction of the court was one to be settled by appeal from the judgment of the court in the case; that no citizen had the right to interrupt court proceedings by such an arbitrary defiance as his. And I fined him $500 and sentenced him to imprisonment in the County Jail until he should decide to testify.

I passed the same sentence on Mr. Fred. Williams, chairman of the Republican City and County Committee, on the president of the Election Commission, and on Mr. J. Cooke, Jr., who followed Doherty's example. They reflected his amused smile. He was not only president of the gas company in Denver, but he was (or had been) president of gas or electric companies in Madison, Wis., Lincoln, Neb., Quebec, Canada, Milwaukee, Wis., Grand Rapids, Mich., St. Paul,

Minn., Binghamton, N. Y., San Antonio, Tex., and St. Joseph, Mo. He crossed his arms on his importance and defied the law.

I summoned the Deputy Sheriff ("Ed" G. Shaffer) and warned him that the court's order must be obeyed, that Doherty must go to jail and that if any special privileges were granted to him or the other prisoners I would punish for contempt of court any officer that granted such privileges. The corporation lawyers interposed with a request that I merely leave Doherty in the custody of the sheriff till writs could be obtained to free him, pending an appeal. I refused the request. They asked, then, that I suspend sentence until they could get up the record of the case on which the writs had to be obtained. I refused that request also. "If any poor man came to this court," I said, "and refused to be sworn, no such privileges as you ask for would be granted him. I have never known any one to show such contempt for a court as this man has. I refuse to stop the court proceedings so that the Clerk of the Court may write up the record. The defendant will get strict justice from this court and no more."

By this time Doherty's smile was more defiant but less contemptuous. He went out, in charge of the deputy, with the expression of face that I have seen a hundred times upon the incorrigible bad boys who had been sentenced in the Juvenile Court. He went to jail; and he and his fellows were entered on the warden's books with a prisoner who was held on a charge of murder.

There—judging from the newspaper pictures of him behind the bars—his smile rather faded. The county jail was not built to furnish millionaires with luxury. The cells are clean but bare; the bars are tastefully painted with aluminum paint; the floors are made of iron plate filled with rivets; the beds are hammocks that are not slung until nightfall; when the prisoner wishes to sit down, he sits on the floor.

Doherty remained there while the court record was being prepared. The Clerk took no more time than usual with that record— but no less. And if the reports that came to me are to be believed, Mr. Doherty became rather angry, as night followed day, and day night, and no writ arrived to free him. He expressed a very low opinion of his lawyers. He was, I believe, the first and only trust magnate in this country who ever found himself in such a pitiable situation; and his indignation was natural. He remained there during three days and two nights, before a new act of court lawlessness freed him.

The Supreme Court was on its vacation, and a single judge was unable to stay the proceedings of a lower court. The only action a single Supreme Court judge could take was the granting of a writ of habeas corpus; and, under the ruling of the court in the previous case in Judge Johnson's court, a writ of habeas corpus was not the proper remedy in contempt cases. But there was still sitting in the District Court the notorious Judge Peter L. Palmer; and Judge Palmer issued a writ of habeas corpus freeing Doherty and his associates on the ground that the Supreme Court was not in session.

Judge Palmer had no more right to issue such a writ than one of the gas company's office boys. He was as lawless, in doing so, as Doherty had been in refusing to testify. I immediately ordered the Sheriff to recapture his prisoners and return them to my court. But they had fled. "I have searched the entire city," the Sheriff reported, "but I can find none of them." The newspapers found Doherty in Lincoln, Nebraska, safely beyond the jurisdiction of the court. The others remained in hiding until the Supreme Court met and decided substantially that though my court, under the charter, had been granted jurisdiction in all cases of contested elections, the franchise investigation was not such a case and the legislature had not specifically empowered the court to hear franchise cases.[*]

I have written all this as baldly as possible, so as to have the facts before you uncoloured by prejudice. But do you realize what these facts mean? Do you realize that the citizens of Denver, robbed of millions of dollars by a franchise steal, found themselves in 1906 with

---

[*] A ridiculous quo warranto suit was subsequently prosecuted by District Attorney Stidger (!) before Judge Peter L. Palmer (!). Do I need to say that the result of that suit was favorable to the corporations?

no court under heaven to which they could appeal for redress?* Do you realize that the robbers, caught in the act, were able to laugh at their victims and defy the law? Can you consider what an example of citizenship was set for those young men and women who were compelled to betray their city, to perjure themselves on an oath before their God, and to see Doherty and his associates smile upon this treason and this perjury? Doherty—the millionaire president of a score of power companies, rich, honoured, admired! Freuauff, the manager of the Denver Gas Company, ex-treasurer of the Board of Deacons of the Central Presbyterian Church, an active religious worker, a most "respectable" man! Williams, chairman of a great party committee, ex-superintendent of a Sunday School in the Central Presbyterian Church! Who may not be the victims of the Beast in *your* city when such men as these are its active agents in *ours*?

Nor was this all. Months after the court investigations ended, Mr. Freuauff lost—or had stolen from him—some pages of the memorandum book in which he had kept an account of his briberies. Those pages were published in facsimile in Senator Patterson's paper, the Denver *Times*. They were in Freuauff's handwriting and he never repudiated them. They showed that he had corrupted the political workers of both parties in the franchise elections, that he had bribed candidates of both parties, that he had paid Mayor Speer $4,500, had spent $3,551 on newspapers, had given $550 in church contributions, had paid Judge Gavin $400, the president of the Board of Supervisors $1,600, the State Oil Inspector $4,490, the Commissioner of Supplies $300, the City Clerk $200, "Len" Rogers $256, Soetje, an election commissioner, $200, Julius Aichele, former county clerk, $670—and,

---

* We had a bill introduced in the Legislature of 1909 providing that the county court could adjudicate upon franchise election contests. The bill was defeated by the corporation representatives. Now, under their contentions—already sustained in part by the decision of the Supreme Court of 1906, in the case before Judge Malone—a corporation that has obtained a franchise by whatever bribery, corruption, or ballot frauds, cannot have its right to that franchise legally contested in Colorado!

in short, on the evidence of those five pages of memoranda, had used $67,690 to corrupt the guardians and sentries and officers of the public, so that the corporation banditti might find open gates and defenceless citizens when they came to pillage.

Pillage? Rich and plenty! No free town of the Middle Ages, sacked by the robber barons and their retainers, ever paid such a ransom or yielded such a haul of loot. The income of the Denver City Tramway Company for the year 1908 was more than three million dollars. If the company paid for its franchises as the street railway does in Toronto, Canada (a city not much larger than Denver), the people of Denver would be receiving, in concessions on fares and in actual cash paid for the use of their streets, more than a million dollars a year instead of a beggarly $60,000. (And it must be recalled that for this beggarly $60,000 the company has had its car taxes of $10,000 remitted!) If the citizens of Toronto paid the fares that the citizens of Denver do, their street car travel would have cost them $889,721 more in 1908 than it did.

In a recent case in the Federal Court in Denver City Attorney Harry A. Lindsley—always the friend of the Beast—stipulated away to Mr. Charles J. Hughes, attorney for the tramway company, valuable rights in a case involving the tramway franchise, so that the Federal Judge on the bench was compelled to concede the right of the tramway to a fifty-year franchise,* leaving still undetermined its further persistent claim to a perpetual franchise. If the Denver Tramway Company can continue to defend that illegal claim, its "rights" in the streets of Denver are worth $500,000,000, to put it modestly. The physical value of the tramway plant does not exceed $7,500,000. Its stocks and bonds aggregate about $21,000,000; an additional issue

---

* Our new Supreme Court, in December 1909, held flatly against this claim in "the Leadville sewer case."

In the appeal of this case now pending in the Federal Court of Appeals (Jan., 1910) the special attorney for the city is Mr. N. Walter Dixon, who is also attorney for Mr. Evans, president of the tramway company, in private litigation!

of $25,000,000 of bonds has recently been authorized—of which $13,000,000 is to retire prior liens, etc.—and it is predicted in the brokers' offices that an old issue of $6,000,000 of stock will be increased to $20,000,000 as soon as these liens have been retired. Loot! Beyond the dreams of all the thieves, highwaymen, pirates and gentlemen of fortune in the history of crime.

The Denver Gas and Electric Company is earning sufficient to pay dividends of 20 percent It charges $1.00 a hundred for gas. And now Doherty and Freuauff have announced a plan to reorganize with a bond issue of $25,000,000 and "a stock reorganization at a later date." The amount of the stock issue depends, in the language of the railroad, upon how much the traffic will bear.

The Denver Union Water Company, piping water into the city from the mountains, from great watersheds and water rights belonging to the people—and conceded to the company without any reservations to the people of their rights—charges three times as much for its service as the citizens of Boulder, for example, pay for theirs. Surely, as the frank Mr. Freeman said, "the corporations give this state good government." They give us a government that is an outrage, and charge for it a price that is a robbery.

It is a *robbery*, and duly declared so by the Supreme Court of the United States. That court, in the case of Wilcox *vs.* Consolidated Gas Company (of New York City), decided that the rates charged by a public utility corporation must be sufficient to pay a reasonable return on the "property devoted to the public use"—not on the watered stock, not on the probable value of the franchise and the "good will" of the business, but on the valuation of the physical plant. It decided that a reasonable return in New York City for a gas plant is 6 percent. Under this ruling—which is the law of the land—the Denver Gas and Electric Company should be charging the citizens of Denver not more than 6 percent on the actual value of its plant instead of a sum that has yielded over 20 percent on stocks. The Tramway Company should be charging not more than 6 percent on $7,500,000, instead of seeking to extort from the people a sufficient sum to yield interest on

$40,000,000. But of what avail is the law when the robbers so often control the officers and the courts that should enforce the law, and control them for the express purpose of preventing its enforcement? Here is the secret of the Beast, its first cause and its final reason for being. It rules to rob. It must rule in order to rob. And as long as it rules, it will continue to rob.

Mayor Speer, on the night before his last election, officially opened an electric fountain in City Park. A crowd of fifteen thousand people (of whom the tramway company had taken its usual toll) applauded the sky-high spurt of water glittering like fireworks in the glow of coloured lights; and on all sides, when the first shouts of delight had subsided, there sounded the heartiest praises of Mayor Speer for what he was doing for Denver. He was reelected. Some day, let us hope, an electric fountain will be dedicated in City Park to the memory of that well-meaning and unfortunate County Treasurer who, when he found how his office had been corrupted at the time of the franchise steal, died of the disgrace. It should bear the inscription: "To the civic official of Denver who died of shame. Erected by the others who have only blushed themselves into insensibility."

As the philosopher said: "There are times when one laughs that he may not weep!"

CHAPTER XV

THE BEAST, THE CHURCH
AND THE GOVERNORSHIP

THE INVESTIGATION OF THE FRANCHISE VOTE had had one hopeful issue: it proved that the corporation ballot-box stuffers were afraid of the teeth of our new registration law. Behind every vote that we counted there was a voter—although it was evident that at least a thousand of these had been "qualified" by fraud. The Supreme Court writ arrived in time to prevent us from investigating the fraud; and, by one of those suspicious strokes of luck that seem to happen only to the corporations, our very proof that the votes were not "phony" by wholesale, only redounded in the public mind to the greater profit of the Beast! The Denver *Republican* celebrated the fact that the election had been probably "the cleanest held in Denver since it became a city." And it claimed the credit for itself and the Republican party.

Said this official voice of the Beast, sweetly disguised: "It required an enormous amount of work to bring about this condition. It is a thing with which parties and courts grappled for years; it became necessary even to invoke the Legislature and the Supreme Court to wrest from corrupters of the ballot the fruits of illegal victory." Do not let your smile be cynical. "Hypocrisy is the tribute that vice pays to virtue." There is still hope so long as the animal must wear its sheep's skin—so long as it recognizes that if the people knew it in its true stripes they would promptly cut its throat. I have that hope yet; and I had it very strongly in the campaign of exposure in which we were engaged throughout these years. It seemed to me only necessary for the people to "see the cat" in order to set them on it; and I continued, with all the power of my lungs, to "bawl out" the corporations and recite the list of their crimes.

The corporations replied through the Board of County Commissioners by refusing to pay an outside judge for helping me in my court and by disallowing bills incurred in the work of the court by probation officers. During the five years that I had been in charge of the court, we had done more than twice as much work as any two courts in the history of the state, and we had done it for less than half the usual expense. In Indianapolis, there were three judges and three courts doing the work of our one court in Denver. The judge and the clerks in our court had more than returned their salaries to the county in fees paid by litigants. Although the four district judges together had less work to do than I had, they were continually calling in outside assistance and the County Board was paying for it.

I appeared several times before the Board to ask for help, and I usually found in attendance, as the Board's confidential adviser, Mr. "Jim" Williams, the right-hand man in politics of "Bill" Evans and the tramway company. I was even, on one occasion, referred to Mr. Williams, by the County Attorney, for the answer to my plea that I should have help with my court work. I did not get the help—avowedly because I refused to allow the Board to appoint extra officers, whom I did not need, at a cost of about six thousand dollars a year to the county.

One of the officers of the Democratic party of the City Hall came to me and said: "You ought to go and see Mr. Field, president of the telephone company. He's willing to help you out." I did not go, but, subsequently I accepted an invitation from a friendly county official to meet Mr. Field at luncheon, and I found him very suave and conciliatory, despite the fact that I had been publicly naming him, with Evans and Cheesman, as one of the corporation rulers of Denver.

Mr. Field is a desiccated, small man who came to Colorado as a "lunger" and here regained his health. He was known in Denver, then (as he is now) to the politicians as "the brains of the System." Before I was talking to him very long I guessed that he had been deputed to "take me in hand," to try friendship and gentleness where force and enmity had failed.

He blamed "Will," as he called Evans, for having opposed me in 1904; and he said he remembered well the conferences between Evans, Cheesman and himself about my candidacy for a return to the County Court, and he confessed that they had played "poor politics" in opposing me. He did not think, however, that I quite understood the gentle Will—who was "really a good man" and wanted to help me. They all wanted to help me. They all admired the work I was doing in the Juvenile Court. But they all felt I was mistaken in my charges against the corporations.

However, he concluded by agreeing that I ought to have help in my court work and he promised that he would take the matter up "with Will" on the following Sunday, when he and Evans were to meet. He subsequently sent me a check for $250 toward the expenses of the Juvenile Improvement Association. Did I accept it? I certainly did. Why? For the same reason that I once accepted the aid of a woman in Denver who conducted a disorderly house.

I sent for that poor creature, and an officer of my court brought her to my chambers. I took her by the hand, looked her in the face, and said: "Madam, I want to thank you for your good deeds and I want to tell you how I despise your evil ones. I accept the good you did, but I shall not shut my mouth about the evils of your business." She was a procuress, but her business was no worse than that of the corporations. She corrupted young girls; they corrupt whole communities.

(A secretary of Mr. John D. Rockefeller once wrote me from New York to ask my views upon "tainted money." I replied with this story about the procuress. He did not send me a contribution, but if he *had* done so, I should have accepted it.)

I did not receive any help from Mr. Field, but I had a visit from Mr. "Jim" Williams and found him very friendly. Mr. Gerald Hughes also came to tell me how mistaken I was in my enmity to Mr. Evans and how Evans had had nothing whatever to do with my "turndown" by the machine in 1904. (Gerald Hughes is the son of Chas. J. Hughes, Jr. He was counsel for Evans and the tramway company in the franchise investigation; and when his father became United States Senator from Colorado, the son nominally succeeded him as attorney of the tramway company and its allies.) They were all very pleasant, and I enjoyed their tacit admission that they and their master, the gentle "Will," controlled the appointments in my court as absolutely as if I were a chief clerk in one of the tramway offices. But I made no promises; I accepted their advances without being deceived by them; and finally I was informed by one of their agents: "There's nothing doing. They're still scared of you and Will isn't going to tell the Board to give you help yet."

The fact that they were crippling the administration of justice in the community had no more weight with them than it would have had with any band of criminals. And they were not moved by the consideration that they were hampering us in the work for the children which they professed so much to admire!

I tried to force the County Board's hand by "grand-standing" in an appeal to the public through my annual report, published in the Denver *Post*. But nothing came of it. I accused two of the County Commissioners, including the chairman, Mr. William Lawson, of committing the "crime of cheap graft and repeated perjury," but even *that* did not move them. I had to arrange to become personally liable for the salary of the judges whom I called in to help me, and it cost me hundreds of dollars.

I relate all this merely to show "the cat"—and as a warning to any one who is ambitious to carry the banner of reform in his own state, that there are "other ways of killing a dog besides choking it with melted butter." I was almost dead from overwork. I realized that I could not go on as I had been; my health would not permit it. And then I was galvanized into new activity by a confidential report that the Powers, at the next legislature, were going to divide the County Court from the Juvenile Court and "lose" me in the shuffle. *That* meant that I must watch the coming elections and use my influence for candidates who should help me in the "deal."

They were state elections. Governor McDonald's term was to expire; so was Judge Gabbert's; and a United States Senator was to be elected as well as a new legislature. It was certain that Alva Adams, who had been defrauded of his election as Governor in 1904, would again be the Democratic candidate on a "vindication" platform; and it was common talk that Simon Guggenheim, the head of the smelter trust, was to have the support of the corporations for the United States senatorship.

As far back as 1902, my name had been used in preelection gossip as that of a "dark-horse" candidate for the governorship; and I have already related how the corporation Democrats had tried to bribe me, on more than one occasion, with the promise of their machine's support in obtaining the office. For several years I had been receiving, from people all over the state, enthusiastic encouragement to run as a reform Governor; and the newspapers had been continually prophesying my candidacy and predicting my success. All this was very flattering, but I knew—probably better than any one else—that whatever the people might wish, the corporations were united against me; and the corporations ruled. I knew, too, that my work in the Juvenile Court was as important as anything I could do as Governor, and I was not willing to give up my court until I had evolved an efficient legal procedure to promote its purposes and had firmly established it by law.

In the early summer of 1906 there began to come to my desk hundreds of clippings from country newspapers and letters from friends, acquaintances and strangers, urging me to be a candidate for the governorship and promising to support me. The men with whom I had been working for the reform of the election laws saw an opportunity to carry our laws by electing me on a platform embodying them. Mr. Paul Thieman, of the *Post*, was particularly confident. And finally, in order to put a stop to plans that I considered hopeless, I wrote to Mr. Alva Adams, privately, and urged him to come out as the Democratic candidate, so that I might be relieved of the expectations of my well-wishers.

I have made many mistakes in my life, but that was the most foolish. I had been fighting the Adams family for years, and I should have understood that there is no enduring virtue, as Mark Twain says, "in the good end of a bad banana." Frank Adams, as chairman of the Denver Police Board, had been the acknowledged agent of the Beast in controlling the saloons, dives and disorderly houses for political purposes; and Senator "Billy" Adams had always been the crafty leader of the corporation agents in the Legislature. Alva Adams, however, had seemed to me a man of another stripe; he was the logical candidate, I thought, of the Democratic party; and, in any case, if he would announce his intention of making the campaign, it would leave my friends without the support of any party for my name.

Alva Adams replied that he would "rather take to the woods" than run again. I wrote a second letter, but it received no reply—except a newspaper interview with Adams saying that he would not be a candidate. His son, Alva Adams, Jr., came to my court and told Mr. Gerald Hughes and a number of politicians that his father did not intend to run and was favourable to my candidacy. I received similar assurances from other sources.

This left me in greater uncertainty than ever. A labour leader of national reputation, passing through Denver, came to my house and advised my candidacy. He assured me that the labouring men would never support Adams; he was equally sure that they would support me. The whole state was up in protest against the rule of the corporations and their use of the Supreme Court, and the hour had come to lead a reform movement to success. He asked me what newspaper support I could count on.

I told him that Senator Patterson's papers were calling on Adams to accept the Democratic nomination on a "vindication" issue, but that the Denver *Post* seemed favourable to me. We went to see Mr. Paul Thieman together, and Thieman was as enthusiastic as ever. I began to see visions and dream dreams of being able at last to attack the Beast with a united public opinion behind me—but I still hesitated.

A few days later the *Post* endorsed me editorially as a candidate for Governor, and there was a flurry in the corporation camp. The paper was no more than on the streets before Mr. Field, as Thieman afterward told me, made a frantic effort to have the edition stopped and the paper's support reconsidered. But the *Post* had just lost in a fight with Evans about a public franchise deal, and the proprietors were eager for revenge. Their newspaper rivalry with Senator Patterson made them ambitious to defeat him as leader of the reform Democrats, by forcing my nomination in spite of him. I found myself in the stormcentre of a small political cyclone. An independent body of Republicans in El Paso, Conejos and other counties offered me their support; the independents among the Democrats seemed all favourable; it began to be evident that if I could get the Democratic nomination, the success of our whole reform movement would be sure.

And then, at the solicitation of Senator Patterson, Alva Adams came to Denver and signed a written pledge—published in the Patterson newspapers—in which Adams declared he would accept the Democratic nomination, and salved his conscience by adding: "Judge Lindsey has a right to run for Governor if he wishes."

Have you ever played politics with the Beast? It is as puzzling as the "con" man's shell game—as bewildering as a masked ball—as dizzying as a kaleidoscopic ballet danced in a transformation scene. I got my first clue to what was going on when one of Simon Guggenheim's personal friends explained to me: "I was out at a little party last night with Simon and he told me I could say to you that if you will only keep out of this race for Governor and let things progress so that Adams can be nominated, he will promise you anything you want in the next Legislature. He says he can guarantee it. He told me the deal is all shaped up with Evans, and Simon is to name enough candidates for the Legislature to give him absolute control. And by the way, he's going to nominate good men—men of good standing and not the ordinary cheap skates that usually go into the Colorado Legislature. Of course they're going to make him United States Senator. He told me frankly that he thought you could be elected Governor if you were nominated, and he's satisfied that Adams can't be. This vindication issue is all rot. They are prepared to show how the Democrats have taken the money and accepted the help of the corporations when it was offered them and how they have stolen elections the same as the Republicans." And so forth.

It was not news to me that Guggenheim was to have the senatorship. He made no secret of it himself. He had told Mr. John W. Springer that he intended to get it, even if it cost him a million; and in an interview with Frederick Lawrence, published in *Ridgway's Weekly*, after the elections, he admitted that he had bought his place.

But the part that Alva Adams was to play was matter for thought. I looked up his record as Governor and found that during his régime the corporations had fared better than they had under governors who were acknowledged corporation favourites. I recalled a conversation I had had with Field in which he said he had been one of Alva Adams's best friends and had obtained money for Adams's campaign fund, from the corporations, at Adams's request. It was, therefore, no surprise to me when Adams, in the Democratic convention, accepted, as the chairman of his campaign, Milton Smith, the corporation agent and attorney—and this on a platform that denounced the corruption of the Supreme Court, demanded the initiative and referendum, advocated the direct primary law and the election of United States senators by the vote of the people and denounced the rule of the corporations with all the eloquence of a new declaration of independence!

I believed that Senator Patterson was honestly deceived; that he accepted Milton Smith in good faith. His paper, *The Rocky Mountain News*, has since said editorially: "If anything is clear in the political field of Colorado, it is that the Democracy cannot afford to have Smith

in charge of its affairs. . . . So long as he is at the head of the state organization, the reform promises of the Democratic party will be greeted
with derisive jeers, and its denunciation of political corporations will
be a subject of mirth." This fact was as evident to me then as it is
now. It was as evident to the independent Democrats. They advised
me to stay in the fight and they circulated the petition to nominate
me. They argued that Adams, carrying Milton Smith, was hopelessly
out of the running and that thousands of both parties would vote for
me and a legislative ticket to defeat Guggenheim. I went to El Paso
County to help the independent Republicans fuse with the independent Democrats against the Guggenheim outrage; and a committee
was appointed in Denver to name an independent county and legislative ticket that was to be subject to my approval.

But when this latter ticket was named I found it largely composed
of Speer corporation Democrats. Mr. Fred. G. Bonfils, one of the proprietors of the Denver *Post*, (which was still supporting me) assured
me that Speer and his city organization would aid me if I would agree
to lend my name to this ticket. I received assurances of the same character from Mr. Speer himself. Mr. Solomon Schwayder, who had been
in the law office of Chas. J. Hughes, came to my house twice and
urged me to head this corporation ticket, promising me Hughes's support, on the ground that Hughes would be the choice of my proposed
legislators for the office of United States Senator! In short, the corporations being sure of Adams, now wished to make sure of me by tying
me to the candidacy of a lot of corporation tools who would never
allow us to obtain a reform law.

I refused to lend my name to any such business, and I lost thereby
the support of the *Post* and the Speer Democrats. I had already lost
the Patterson papers and the Patterson Democrats by refusing to support Adams unless he repudiated his corporation chairman. There
was now no longer the faintest hope that I could be elected Governor,
and I felt rather relieved, but I still had the backing of some independent Republican organizations, and I endorsed the Democratic legislative candidates in the El Paso and Denver Districts in the hope that

we might defeat Guggenheim, at least, by putting in a Democratic legislature.

Evans, meanwhile, had been casting about for a gubernatorial candidate to carry the corporation flag in the Republican party. Mr. Philip Stewart, of Colorado Springs, had accepted the rôle and then revolted, after his nomination, when he found that he was to carry Judge Gabbert on his ticket. According to the newspapers of the day several other prominent men also declined the nomination. The situation was grave. Open public gambling in Denver and the progress of the Anti-saloon League had made a "moral issue" that threatened the hindquarters of the Beast. Churches and religious organizations all over the state were entering the campaign. It was necessary to have a candidate who should give respectability to corruption.

Mr. Evans found his man in the Reverend Henry Augustus Buchtel, D.D., L.L.D., a minister of the Methodist Church, who was Chancellor of the Denver University! And after a harmony meeting at which Mr. Buchtel accepted the nomination, he invited Mr. Evans's emissaries to rise with him, join hands and sing "Blest Be the Tie That Binds"!

The tie that binds the Beast and the Church? Yes, and the Beast and the College! During the Peabody campaign (according to the *Rocky Mountain News*) a young student named Reed had been practically driven from the Denver University because he criticised the corporation Governor. Later a university professor was sent to Europe to gather data which was used in the campaign against municipal ownership in Denver; and the professor was "exposed but not forced into retirement." Later still, Buchtel reprimanded a student named Stanley Bell for volunteering as a worker in one of our Juvenile Court campaigns. Mr. Evans was president of the Board of Trustees of the University, and the Reverend Henry Augustus Buchtel was his Chancellor.

The use of Buchtel in the campaign that followed was a huge success. Everywhere people said to me: "Why, the Chancellor will never stand for the sale of the senatorship to Guggenheim!" Or the "dear chancellor" will never permit this or that undesirable thing in politics.* But Buchtel had already admitted to a ministerial friend that he believed Guggenheim ought to be elected—though he said nothing of it from the platform, you may be sure. After he was Governor, he not only endorsed Guggeheim but vigorously defended the Legislature for electing Guggenheim, honoured Evans with a place on the gubernatorial staff, and gave a public dinner to the corporation heads who had most profited by the rule of the System in the state. They reciprocated by sending the Denver University handsome donations; Evans led with $10,000, and Guggenheim, Hughes, and others followed with fat checks.

The keeper of a gambling hell, whom I summoned to my court and forced to make restitution to one of his victims, said to me: "I have some respect for Mayor Speer. He tells these preachers that he believes in our policy of open gambling. But I have nothing but contempt for that old stiff up in the State House who talks about 'the word of God,' and gets his nomination from a boss who protects *us*, and gets elected on money that *we* contributed to the organization!" It is one of the saddest aspects of this use of the Church that the Beast gains respectability thereby, and the Church contempt.

I yield to no man in my admiration for what "the church element" has done to fight the saloon and the gambling house and the brothel, in Denver. It was these good Christian people who conquered for us in all our earlier encounters with the "wine-room gang" and the political supporters of protected vice. It was they who helped the women and children to save the Juvenile Court when the attempt was made to destroy it. They are the hope of society in every fight for public decency and moral reform. But in a community where the "cohesive power of public plunder" has united criminal corporations with criminal politicians and the criminal poor, has put the dive into alliance

---

* At that time I did not believe he would, wittingly. We were, and had been, the best of personal friends. It was not until later that I learned all the facts given here. B.B.L.

with the dishonest public official, the unjust court and the predatory millionaire—in such a community do you suppose that the churches by some miracle have escaped clean? I know that they have not. I know that the agents of the Beast have even dared to enter the house of God itself—to intimidate the minister—to cajole and deceive the congregation—and to use the religious organizations of a Christian community to increase the vicious power of the System and to punish its opponents. And I shall tell how I know.

I am well aware that what I am going to write will be quoted out of its context by the agents of the System and used by its newspapers to prove that I am an enemy of the religion in which I have been raised, and a traitor to the churches that have again and again saved me from political destruction. I can foresee, from my experience in the past, that when I attack the Beast where it hides behind the Church I shall be accused of attacking the Church—and so accused by the very agents of the Beast that I am attacking. But I hold that I should be a greater enemy of religion, a more cowardly traitor to the Church, if I were to keep my peace about these enemies within the camp of righteousness, these traitors who are trying to betray the very pulpit to corruption, to pollute the altar of God as they have polluted the court of justice, and to use the churches for the same purpose that they have used the dives.

When a petition was recently being circulated to renominate me as Judge of the Juvenile Court, a pastor of one of the most influential churches in Denver refused to sign the petition because I had "offended so many business men." "I can't come out publicly," he said. "I like Judge Lindsey. I think he is right. But *we have to build.*" For the same reason a Denver prelate who was raising money to build a new church wrote to one of his clergy, who was making platform speeches on behalf of the Anti-saloon League, and ordered him to be silent. The Christian Citizenship Union—during my last nonpartisan and non-political campaign for the judgeship—endeavoured to obtain the use of a downtown church in which to hold an afternoon meeting in support of my candidacy, at which Father O'Ryan, Rabbi Kauvar and a number of other clergymen were to speak; no such church would allow them to hold the meeting under its roof. During this campaign, a meeting was to be held in a downtown Baptist Church, and permission to hold the meeting was revoked when it was learned that I was to speak; and the reason given for the refusal was the fact I *was* going to speak. At a time when practically every labour union in Denver had adopted resolutions endorsing our work, a member of the Christian Citizenship Union went before an association of ministers and proposed that they, too, should endorse me; they silently declined to do so. The Citizenship Union had printed at its own expense a number of non-political circulars advocating my reelection on nonpartisan grounds; the pastor of the Trinity Methodist Church refused to allow these circulars to be distributed to the congregation; and at the Central Presbyterian Church they had to be distributed on the sidewalk before the doors.

The young men of the Christian Citizenship Union were members of the Y.M.C.A. But an assistant secretary of the Y.M.C.A., during this same non-political campaign, told me frankly that I could not be allowed to speak from the platform of the Y.M.C.A. hall, because, he said, "We have to get our subscriptions from the business men to run the Association." And to descend to an incident so petty that it can scarcely be believed—the officers of the Union had been asked by the members of the boys' department of the Y.M.C.A. to give them a portrait of me to hang in their meeting room, and they were informed that the Association refused to allow the picture to be hung. Now, I had been at one time chairman of a building committee of the Association, and had voluntarily resigned when I found that my chairmanship was an offence to the "interests" and hindered the work of raising money for the association. I had maintained my friendly relations with the young men of the Association; and I do so still. The picture was in no way offensive. The photographer had done his best to make me handsome in it. If it was not a beautiful work of art, this perhaps was because, as Whistler said, the sitter was not a bewilderingly beautiful work of Nature. But it was not so hideously ugly that the objectors could not endure it. I shall never believe that! Never! The Beast is not so aesthetic!

These young men of the Y.M.C.A. who are banded together as the Christian Citizenship Union, have done more for the enforcement of the laws and the maintenance of public decency in Denver than any other similar body of young men that I know of, in any city in the United States. I could say nothing too much in the way of grateful praise of them or of the Association that gave them their ideals. But what I wish to say is that even *they* found the influence of the Beast above them, met it in the management of the churches of which they were members, and were punished by it in the houses of business in which they worked—for two of them received their "notices" from their employers because they had been conspicuous in the work for reform.

At a session of the Colorado Legislature in the spring of 1909, we were attempting to force the passage of a bill limiting the hours of work for women in laundries to eight hours a day. Revival meetings were then being held by "Gipsy" Smith in the Auditorium, and a resolution had been carried at one of his meetings endorsing the work of the Anti-saloon League. It was proposed, at a conference of the men and women interested in the laundry bill, that we should attempt to get a similar endorsement of our work to protect the unfortunate slaves of the laundry. And I was astonished to find that every one at the conference recognized the uselessness of such an attempt. Why? Well, it may be enlightening to notice—for example—that the Denver Gas and Electric Company had mounted upon the roof of its office building a huge electric sign advertising the revival meetings, and did not charge any rental for that aid to evangelism!

Mr. Ray Stannard Baker, writing of "The Godlessness of New York," in the *American Magazine*, has pointed out: "The churches . . . are still dallying with symptoms: offering classes and gymnasiums to people who are underfed and underpaid, who live in miserable and unsanitary homes. . . . They devote tremendous energy in attempting to suppress vaudeville shows while hundreds of thousands of women and children in New York are being degraded, body and soul, by senseless exploitation—too much work, too small wages, poor homes, no amusement. They help the poor child and give no thought to the causes which have made him poor. They have no vision of social justice; they have no message for the common people."

Is this the fault of the churches or of the powers that are trying to dominate the churches? There are ministers in Denver—like Father Wm. O'Ryan, the Rev. A. H. Fish, D. H. Fouse, Frank T. Bayley, Frost Craft, Bayard Craig and Rabbi Kauvar—who have not only recognized that I was right in my charge that the corporations were corrupting our politics and exploiting our defenceless poor, but have dared to support me publicly in those charges. And I know, from more than one of these men, what influences were brought to bear to silence him and what authority he had to defy that he might continue to speak. The ministers are in the same position as the rest of us. They are allowed to do what they can—and they do much—to palliate the hardships of poverty and rescue the victims of economic wrong; but as soon as they propose to attack the causes of some of the greatest hardships of poverty and attempt to alleviate the injustices of corporate greed, our masters speak. As long as the ministers are content to dip the water out of a tub into which the faucet is still running, they are encouraged. But as soon as they attempt to turn off the faucet—to cure the cause instead of relieving the result—the strong hand of the System is laid upon them. How can the churches have any "vision of social justice" and any "message for the common people" when the rulers of their congregations exist upon active social injustice to the common people? We must be free of the Beast in our congregations before our ministers can be free. When the slave holder sat in the pew, there was no Abolitionist in the pulpit. Where the Beast is deacon, the minister is dumb!

CHAPTER XVI

HUNTING THE BEAST

D ID YOU EVER HUNT THE SACRED MONKEY among the Hindoos? Have you been a revolutionist in Russia? Or were you an Abolitionist near the Mason and Dixon line before the war? Well, did you ever make an anti-corporation campaign in a corporation-ridden community? It is an experience without which no man's public life can be said to be complete. No politician, till he has tried it, can truly boast, "I have lived!" My memories of my tour of Colorado in the autumn of 1906 I would not exchange for a copy of the best novel ever written, a seat for the most moving drama ever staged.

In the first place, having repudiated the corporation candidates of both parties, I was free to speak the truth of them all. Having no expectations of being made Governor myself, I did not need to consider how my words would affect my own candidacy. Being a candidate I was sure of a hearing, no matter what I said—thanks to our

American courtesy in such cases. And having no party claque to serenade and applaud me, I could speak of things as I knew them to people who were eager to see things as they are.

When either of the other candidates arrived in a town, on his special train with his staff of politicians, he was received at the station by a committee, escorted to his meeting by a brass band, and introduced—with all the praises of a hired eloquence, from a platform crowded with "prominent citizens"—to a hall half filled with apathetic listeners who knew the whole proceeding was a lie. When I arrived in the town, I found at that same railroad station a few curious idlers who stared silently; I made my way to the hall as best I could. I found my platform empty even of a chairman, and in most cases introduced myself to a silent audience that packed the hall to the doors. But when, having paid my respects to both parties, I proceeded to explain how both were the tools and agents of the Beast, we did not miss the absence of the brass band. My fellow-slaves recognized the small voice of rebellion and greeted it with a shout.

The "prominent" citizen would whisper to me afterward: "It's a shame you had to introduce yourself. I'm with you, but, you know, I can't come out openly. They'd simply salivate me." Personal friends, speaking under the voice, would congratulate me and add: "We wanted to have you down to dinner, but we didn't dare. You know how things are." In the towns where there was an independent ticket that I could be on, there was no lack of reception and platform backing. And down at Montrose, in the fruit country, where the independent farmers did not depend upon the corporations for their bread and butter, the platform was as well filled as the body of the hall. But for the most part I was preaching a proscribed doctrine in a country where no one— under pain of a corporation interdict and excommunication—dared to give me any conspicuous support.

I do not write this pessimistically; for I knew, then, that the people were with me, and I know, now, that not a word of what I said was lost. Many thousands voted for me, even though they knew their votes would be thrown away. And our exposure of the political conditions and our explanation of their cure through a reform of the election laws—however clumsy, however feeble—started a demand for reform in Colorado that has not been stilled yet and cannot be stilled ever, until it has been granted. Therein lies the virtue of such apparent Quixotism. That is the eternal weakness of the Beast. It can only rule through fear. Let but one man in your community defy it, and the revolt of thousands has begun. The days of the Beast in Colorado are numbered. It is masking itself now in one disguise, now in another—this year as one party, next year as another—but the people have seen it; they are beginning to track it down, through every devious winding, in all sorts of unsuspected lairs. It cannot "fool all the people all the time." We shall get it yet.

During the governorship campaign it even stole a "Lindsey" ticket to hide its stripes in El Paso County, and put up for election, under my name, a gang of corporation candidates who would oppose to the last breath the passage of any of the reform laws that I was advocating. I appealed to the court in Colorado Springs, and an outside judge, named Armour, was called in to hear the case.

(It is an old trick of the Beast to bring a judge from one county to decide its suits in another. By this means an outraged public cannot bring its anger to bear upon the traitor to its interests!)

Judge Armour at first expressed some sympathy with our indignation at the theft of my name, but he had a change of heart over night, and in an outrageous decision he finally ruled against us. We took the case to Denver, to the Supreme Court—which, under the statute of the state, has the right to hear such election cases, at its discretion. The Supreme Court decided not to hear it, on the ground that there was not time to do so before the elections. Consequently, we had to change the designation of our ticket in El Paso County, but we had no time to explain the fraud to the electorate, and we lost several thousand votes through the confusion of the ballot and the despair of our supporters.

Then in Denver, where we threatened the Guggenheim "deal" by endorsing a reform ticket of Democratic candidates for the Legislature—after they had pledged themselves in writing to support our election laws—another trick was played on us. On a Saturday, ten days before election day, our nominations were taken to the office of the Secretary of State to be filed, before five o'clock in the afternoon. The office, always open at such times until midnight, was found locked. The Secretary of State was not at his home. We heard that he was leaving the city, and a messenger intercepted him with the papers at the railroad station and forced him to accept them. That was ten days before the elections, and the law required that the papers should be filed eight days before election day.

The Secretary of State wrote us on Monday that since his office had not been reopened until Monday, the eighth day, the nominations could not be accepted. We obtained a mandamus from Judge Mullins ordering him to accept them. Guggenheim's campaign manager obtained an order from Judge Peter L. Palmer to the contrary effect. The dispute was carried to the Supreme Court—the same court that had decided, a week previous, that it was too late to hear election cases. And the Supreme Court justices not only heard it, but—with Justice Steele and Gunter dissenting—they reversed Judge Mullins's decision, and ruled that our nominations had not been filed in time and could not be printed on the ballots.

I shall never forget that hearing. It was held in chambers, informally. The seven judges sat around a table at their ease, in a private room carpeted and quiet. I appealed to them for justice—my own counsel—hoarse with the fatigue of a campaign that had worn me out. I was so weak that for the first and only time in my life, I wept before a court. Five of the seven listened as if they had been the Grand Inquisition and I a heretic who must be exterminated. I saw their decision in their faces, and the blood went to my head. I turned and hurried out of the room lest I should reach across the table and seize one of those men by the throat. Fortunately such emotions do not endure. (If they did, life for some of us in Colorado would be a poisoned rage.) Crippled in my campaign by having my name stolen from me in El Paso County and our ticket refused in Denver—continually recalled from the platform in one town to defend myself before the courts in another—without a campaign fund to defray even legitimate expenses, and with no organization except in the few places where there was an independent movement to aid us—we came to election day with the certainty that our independent fight would prove itself the greatest failure in the history of the state. We had no watchers at the polls in Denver. One of the Democratic watchers in a polling place near the Court House, after the elections, offered to take his oath for me that, of 83 votes cast for me in his district, 40 were counted for Buchtel, 40 for Adams, and 3 for myself! But even so, on the face of the returns, we polled the largest vote ever counted in the state for an independent candidate. Had we been able to elect the representatives from the El Paso and Denver districts—whom the courts had prevented us from endorsing—the defeat of Guggenheim would have been certain, and the object of our campaign attained. Buchtel ran nearly ten thousand votes behind his ticket, and Adams only two thousand behind *his*; we cut into Buchtel's vote almost five times as much as into Adams's.

Buchtel was elected. His candidacy proved a successful disguise for the Guggenheim "deal," and the "church element" was used as well as "the dive element." A corporation legislature was put in power. It only remained for the corporations to deliver the United States senatorship to Simon Guggenheim "for value received," and to betray the nation as they had betrayed the state. Simon Guggenheim had no more claim to represent Colorado in the Senate at Washington than John D. Rockefeller has—or Baron Rothschild. He was the head of the Smelter Trust, and he had been financially interested, of course, in the election of Peabody in 1904, and the defeat of the eight-hour law and the suppression of the eight-hour strike. These things entitled him to the gratitude of the corporations only. He was unknown to the people of Colorado. He had never been seen by them except in a picture. He had never been heard by them except in a newspaper interview. He had not, as far as I know, ever spoken or written a word publicly on politics. "I don't know much about the political game," he told one of his campaign managers, "but I have the money. I know *that* game." He does.

During this contest, a young man whom I knew—ambitious to be a state senator—was summoned to the tramway company's Majestic Building and was promised a nomination on condition that he pledge his vote for Guggenheim. He refused, and he was not nominated. Another, of similar aspirations but less strength, after denouncing the proposed sale of the senatorship to Guggenheim (at a public meeting of young reformers) accepted a nomination from the Republicans, and explained to his reform friends, after his election, that he had to sell himself in order to "get anywhere." He voted for Guggenheim, and he became one of the most efficient tools of the corporations in the House. Boss Evans had controlled the Republican conventions, and resolutions had been passed providing that all members of the Legislature in voting for candidates for the United States senatorship should be bound by the caucus—that is to say, should be bound by the corporations to vote for Guggenheim. Many of the legislators, thus sold and delivered, did not get money for the prostitution of their manhood. One of them, whom I knew, was an insurance agent, and he received a big insurance policy from which his fees were large. Another, a young lawyer, had been paid in corporation cases to prosecute or defend; he had received, in the course of a few months, thousands of dollars in fees; and he had received them through the boss who had helped to buy Gardener. This same young lawyer had come to me, after his election, like a man who had made a bargain with the devil, full of abhorrence for the betrayal of public trust that was now demanded of him. I counselled him rather to resign than to sell himself. He had not the strength. He voted for Guggenheim, and he is now one of the most notorious corporation advocates in the Legislature. Others received fees, corporation business, or political favours and rewards of various sorts. The corporation Democrats joined the corporation Republicans in supporting Guggenheim. (At the Democratic Club during the election campaign, Mr. Gerald Hughes, son of Chas. J. Hughes, attorney for the tramway company, had made a speech in support of the Evans-Guggenheim Republican candidates; and the corporation Democratic machine had openly supported that ticket.) Guggenheim received his senatorship.*

Do you suppose that he is the only member of the Senate in Washington who has been so elected? Do you suppose that senators, so elected, represent any one in the councils of the nation except the powers that put them there? Whether these men be called Republicans or Democrats, do you think their votes are cast for any law, any tariff, any reform that will hurt "the interests" whom they represent? If you *do*, you do not know the Beast. It is not only Denver that lies beneath its paw. It is not only Colorado. It is this whole nation. The System controls the machinery by which we elect our national representatives as well as our state and city representatives. It picks the same sort of legislators to rule in the Capitol at Washington that it picks to rule in the Capitol at Denver. The men so elected give to the nation the same sort of government that they give to our state. And our fight in Denver is not a fight to free Denver alone—nor to free Colorado alone—but to help free the whole nation, and to reestablish a free government of a free people in a country that shall be free. It was for this we fought in 1906. It is for this that we are fighting still.

Our fight in 1906 had some disastrous results for me. We offended the blindly loyal party men among the Democrats as among the Republicans, and I lost the support of all the party newspapers. Senator Patterson's organs did not at once forgive my campaign against Adams. The Denver *Republican* treated me as an irreconcilable enemy of the corporations. And the Denver *Post*, having failed to tie me to a corporation Democratic ticket, turned to Buchtel and Evans, and enlisted under that black flag which it has served and fought for, ever since—with occasional independent forays after loot of its own!

This is not as small a matter as it may seem. It has been my experience that there are no agents of reform as powerful in our American

---

* Only two Republican members of the Legislature voted against Guggenheim: Hon. Merle Vincent in the House and Hon. Morton Alexander in the Senate. Both were defeated for renomination at the next election.

communities as the newspapers. They are the very eyes of the people. What they refuse to see, it is almost impossible to discover to the public. What they desire to see wrongly, it is almost impossible to show in its true face. And this is well known to the Beast. It not only uses the editorial pages: it applies its influence to the reports of the news columns; it supplements editorial arguments and abuse, with misrepresentations, with falsifications, and with downright inventions in the reporters' room.

For example: A complaint was made in my court, by the Humane Society, against a woman who was drunk and ill-treating her children. A Deputy Sheriff arrested her and put her in the county jail, at the request of the neighbours, "to sleep off her drunk"; and they agreed to take care of the children. One of the "interests" newspapers, on its front page, headed the story something like this: "Juvenile Judge sends poor washerwoman to jail, while six children starve. Kind-hearted neighbours take care of children separated from mother who languishes in jail." The reporter who wrote the story came to my chambers and explained: "Judge, I'm sorry about that article, but it wasn't my fault. The city editor told me I had to find something to roast you about, and I sent in that story—but it wasn't so bad when I finished with it. A lot of things were added, after I turned it in."

Or again: An Italian labourer, charged with neglecting his wife and encouraging his children to steal from the railroad tracks, came to my court drunk and used such vile language that I sentenced him to jail for thirty days for contempt of court. I suspended twenty-nine days of the sentence without telling him so, and next day—which was Sunday—I sent an order for his release, had him brought to my home and gave him a friendly lecture. He apologized, and—after the fashion of his people—he kissed my hand before he went away, promising to attend to his work and look after his family. (And the court officers afterward reported that he kept his promise.) Some days later, a newspaper printed a sensational account of how I had taken a poor Italian from his home where his family was starving, and sentenced him to thirty days solitary confinement in the county jail because his children had picked up a few cents' worth of coal from the railroad tracks. The article was headed: "A Jeffreys on the Bench."

Whenever a boy who had been put on probation in my court was arrested for a second offence, the "kept" newspapers joined in an attack on the probation system, accused us of encouraging young criminals, and advocated the abolition of the Juvenile Court. Such an attack was made on us, once, because two of our boys had been rearrested; and a railroad police officer (Mr. E. D. Hegg) in no way connected with our court, wrote to me that these boys were two out of 103 boys who had been before us from the district, and the 101 others had never backslided. Such misrepresentations, repeated and repeated for years, seriously hurt our work for the children. They seriously impaired the public credit of our court—and that is what they were designed to do. The Beast was preparing to "get" me at last; having driven me back upon the County Court with no political support and no newspaper to defend me, it was trying to alienate the sympathies of the independent voters so that when my next election should come I might not have even the "sentiment" of the non-partisan citizens to rely on.

My term would expire in the autumn of 1908. But in the spring of 1908 the city elections would have to be held. As judge of the County Court I would have power to hear all contests arising from those elections; and in order to get me off the county bench the Legislature in the spring of 1907 took up the "deal"—of which I had already been warned—to divide the Juvenile from the County Court by legislative enactment, and "lose" me in the division. Having failed in our attempt to elect any reformers to the House, I was left to face this "deal" without a friend among the legislators to defend me.

Mr. Geo. S. Redd was the man deputed to take the matter in hand. He was a cousin of George Stidger, who was then District Attorney, and he had been Stidger's law partner. He was a member of the Methodist Church, had been put on the legislative ticket by Evans, and had voted for Guggenheim. But he was not the sort of man that you might suppose from these antecedents. "Judge," he said, when he came to talk with me about the bill to divide the court, "I'm friendly to you. I believe in your work and I will tell you, now, that while I'm to introduce the bill, I'll do all I can to make it satisfactory to you." And he did.

I proceeded to draft a bill that would be satisfactory to me. District Attorney Stidger drafted one that was satisfactory to the System. I gave the Juvenile Court jurisdiction in all cases against minors and in all cases in which the protection of minors was involved, gave the probation officers complete police powers and gave the court the right to arrest and punish adults guilty of contributing to the delinquency of minors. Mr. Stidger took away from the Juvenile Court officers the power to file petitions in children's cases, denied the probation officers any police powers, and made the Juvenile Court an impotent little police court for children. In the House, Mr. Wilbur F. Cannon (the same Cannon who murdered our insurance bill so many years before) amended Stidger's bill so as to give the County Commissioners the power to appoint all the probation officers, the superintendent of the Detention School and so forth, so that, even though I remained judge, the court officers would belong to the System. I simply served notice on Mr. Redd that I would not accept the judgeship of any such court, that I would remain in charge of the County Court—knowing that this was exactly what they were dividing the court to prevent.

After some irritated conferences, they agreed that I should have the right to appoint my own court officers, but they still refused to allow the probation officers police powers and refused the court the right to try the gamblers and dive keepers who debauched girls and boys. District Attorney Stidger was very frank in his explanation of why I could not have this power. It would hurt the System. Pacing up and down his office, with the door shut, he spoke for the Beast and announced the ultimatum of the Beast. I was to be given a court in which I might try the cases presented to me by the System, but I was not to have a court that should give me any power to interfere with the System, by prosecuting those agents of vice who were protected by the System.

We kept up these quarrels and conferences until within a few days of the close of the legislative session, and then I served notice again that unless I were given a Juvenile Court with teeth, I should remain on the county bench. Stidger and my old law partner, Senator Gardener, finally compromised by accepting an amendment to their bill—an amendment providing that the Juvenile Court should have coordinate jurisdiction with the District Court in all criminal cases in which minors were involved and against all persons who violated laws for the protection of minors. Senator Gardener introduced this amendment in the Senate and had it passed.

This was all very well, but I had no proof that the amendment had passed the Lower House. In fact the Clerk's record showed that it had not passed the Lower House. I do not wish, here, to charge that there was a conspiracy to betray me—although one of the newspapers at the time freely made that charge. But I had been warned that there was a plot to get me into the Juvenile Court and then "pull out the slats" from under me; and I refused to accept the Court unless I had proof that Gardener's amendment had passed the House also— for, without that proof, the "slats" would be loose. I got the proof. I was given a transcript of the records, signed by the Secretary of State, the Clerk and other officials showing that the Juvenile Court Bill and the amendment thereto had passed both the House and the Senate! That transcript nailed down "the slats"—for the Supreme Court of Colorado has held that you cannot go behind the legislative records even if you have extrinsic evidence to show that they are wrong.

I accepted the judgeship of the new special Juvenile Court in July, 1907, with all the powers to protect children that I had had in the County Court for seven years, but of course with no power any longer to interfere with the System in election cases or to try adults for any offences in which the rights of minors were not involved. We have succeeded in getting from the Legislature laws that give the Juvenile Court not only power to go over the heads of the police in children's cases—so as to arrest offenders whom the System may wish to protect—but power also to act independently of the District Attorney in children's cases and to file complaints against offenders whom the District Attorney might wish to protect. It is true the Legislature did not seem to know it was passing such a law, but there it is! There are ways of getting the best of the Beast legitimately and honourably without beating the tom-toms of public clamour. When the newspapers refused to help us with our "grand-standing," we found a way to do some still-hunting after night, horribly disguised.

CHAPTER XVII

A VICTORY AT LAST

ICOME, NOW, TO THE LAST CHAPTER of this story of the Beast; but I come to it, in the reminiscence—thank heaven!—with a lighter heart than any of us had when we faced it in the fact. As the result of seven years of almost frantic agitation for legislative reform, we had gained—an effective registration law! Nothing more! In all our fights to obtain an honest charter for Denver, to prevent dishonest elections, to protect the city from the theft of its franchises, to defend the poor from exploitation and to check the corporations in their abuse of the courts, we had failed. We had founded, it is true, a Juvenile Court with laws that protected the children from the agents of the System; but we had gained no election law that would protect the court itself; and we were continually assured by the agents of the Beast that they would "get" *that* court yet. Governor Buchtel had gone about the country, in the summer of 1907, on a Chautauqua lecture tour, heralding himself as the man who had been called upon to "guide Colorado from the verge of political anarchy," and incidentally defending Guggenheim and the corporations that had elected him. The Denver Chamber of Commerce had passed a resolution declaring me an enemy of the state, because a false news despatch reported me as saying, in a public lecture in the East, that Guggenheim ought to be hanged if we hanged Orchard; and the members of the Chamber passed their resolution, although many of them afterward admitted to me that they thought I was "right" in my attacks on the corporations and their Senator. ("You told the truth," they would assure me, privately, "but, you know, it hurts business to tell it—it hurts the prosperity of the state.") The Denver *Post* followed the resolution with a demand that I be driven from town, and stirred up all possible enmity against me as a "defamer" of my state. In the city elections of the spring of 1908, the Anti-saloon League and the "church element" tried to elect a mayoralty candidate in opposition to Mayor Speer and the "dive element"; but the corporations, represented by Boss Evans, betrayed the League while pretending to support it, and Speer was triumphantly reelected by the Beast. We were all discouraged. I knew that I was regarded as hopelessly "discredited." I knew that the men whom I had fought believed that the public was tired of our crusading—for there is nothing more wearisome to a Western community than a "professional kicker." Men would come to my chambers and say: "Ben, what's the use? You're only butting your head into a stone wall. Why don't you settle down to some sort of peace and comfort? If the people want their state run this way, let them have it."

The trouble was that I did not believe the people *knew* how their state was run. I was determined that they *should* know, if I could tell them. And I went into the campaign for the judgeship, in the autumn of 1908—as I had gone into that for the governorship in 1906—with the single and forlorn purpose of making it a "campaign of education."

It was probable that I should be unable to get a nomination from either party, and we had first to consider the possibility of making an independent campaign; and we came to the immediate conclusion that there was no possibility of me succeeding as an independent.

During the county elections of 1906, a strong organization of prominent citizens had nominated a number of independent candidates for the judiciary, in an attempt to free the courts from the influence of the corporation machine; the independent ticket had been supported by a large campaign fund and an efficient organization; the candidates were men well known to the community for their honesty and public spirit; yet those candidates who did not also get a nomination on a party ticket received less than 3,000 votes out of about 60,000 cast. This result was pointed out to me, by the men who had conducted the campaign, when I consulted with them upon my own candidacy. They conceded that 90 percent of the people of Denver wished me to continue in charge of the Juvenile Court, but they believed—as I did—that with the straight-ticket ballot to vote on, not 5 percent would vote for me.

You see, the ballot used in Colorado is particularly designed to discourage "scratching" for independent candidates. If, for instance, I were running as an independent for a district judgeship, and a Democrat wished to vote for me, he would have to write "Democratic" in the blank space at the top of his ballot, put an X after my name, and run a line through the name of the opposing candidate on the Democratic ticket. If he did not run a line through the name of my Democratic opponent—although he put the X after *my* name—his vote would be counted for the Democrat. But if I were running independent for a place as County Judge or Juvenile Judge, the procedure was different. In that case, after writing "Democratic" at the top of his ballot, he would have to put his X after my name and carefully refrain from running a line through the name of my Democratic opponent. If he *did* run that line through the name of the Democrat, it was a mutilation of the ballot. These technicalities are always made more confusing by the party workers, who purposely give conflicting advice to the voter in order to mislead and intimidate him. The party newspapers play upon his fears by warning him that if he tries to "scratch" he will surely mutilate his ballot and lose his vote. And the party men, who act as election judges, in counting the votes take advantage of their opportunity to count scratched ballots very much as they please.

"Judge," a ward politician named Billy Arnett said to me, "unless you can get on one of the straight tickets, it doesn't matter if all the people in Denver are for you; you'll have no more chance than a snowball in hell. The people don't know how to scratch. They're scared to try it. And they *won't* try it; they know independents have no chance and they don't want to throw away their votes." My friends warned me that if I ran independent, I would be giving the corporation machine the very opportunity it was eager for. I would get only two or three thousand votes, and the word would go out from Denver that I was so discredited that the people of Denver had refused to reelect me.

Well then, could I get a party nomination? That was the next question. And it was at once evident that I could not get one through favour. My independent campaign for the governorship had piqued the leaders of both parties. Friends who had helped me in the Republican convention of four years before—men like E. P. Costigan, J. H. Causey, and J. C. Starkweather—were now marked men, "spotted" by the Beast; they could not even get credentials to a convention, much less raise a revolt in one. Many well-meaning men and women who had fought for me in 1904—because of a sentiment of admiration for the Juvenile Court—had since been intimidated by the opposition of "business" and the Beast. I was no longer fighting the petty grafters; I had raised more powerful enemies; and a sentimental following of kindly disposed people would not be daring enough, I knew, to force me upon an unwilling political machine.

There was one hope left. One of these two parties, at the last minute, might feel the need of having my name as an asset to a corporation ticket. I was not willing that my name should be so used, unless I could make it plain to the voters that I was not a sympathetic member of the company in which I was to be put. For this reason I published, in August, 1908, a pamphlet called "The Rule of the Plutocracy," in which I tried to set forth, in a brief form—with the aid of Ellis Meredith, an experienced writer—the facts which I have detailed here in these present articles. I issued 30,000 copies, at my own expense, with the money I had earned on a lecture tour; and I had thousands of copies delivered to the homes of voters in Denver.

A month later the conventions met. There was a factional fight in the Democratic organization; and at the preliminary caucus my name was included on the "slate." But before the convention met, Mr. Gerald Hughes, son of Charles J. Hughes, the attorney for the tramway company, interfered with the arrangement; the slate was altered; and Earl Hewitt, Boss Speer's "man Friday," nominated as Juvenile Judge a police magistrate who was one of the ward politicians. In order to put the machine on record, I proposed to one or two young Democrats, whom I had befriended, that they should try to nominate me in the convention, but they replied that such an act would mean their political ruin, and I did not press them further. My name was not mentioned in the convention. To several delegates who made bold to ask Gerald Hughes why I was not on the ticket, Mr. Hughes replied, "Because he has attacked our best friends—men like Mr. Evans."

I had a friend in the Republican caucus, and he said it would be good policy for the party to nominate me; but the caucus did not, and he admitted that it was because the politicians were afraid of the corporations. They nominated a man named Howze, who, after the elections, tried to collect a fund to fight some of our laws for the protection of children, on the ground that they were unconstitutional!

There was nothing for us now but an independent campaign. We tried to raise a campaign fund. My friends went first among the business men—and found their pockets buttoned. All our efforts ended in raising only $450. The business men said that I was "the man for the place," but that I was foolish to attack the corporations, and that it was dangerous for a man of business to support me. For the same reason, many of them refused even to sign a petition to nominate me.

I then tried the ministers. I sent a letter to every preacher in Denver—about one hundred and fifty in all—explaining my difficulties and asking them to meet me in the Juvenile Court on an appointed evening. Four or five sent letters of regret. Two or three came to the meeting. The others were silent. Later the young men of the Christian Citizenship Union sent a similar letter to the ministers, through their president, Mr. Harry G. Fisher. The same ministers came!

I talked to a number of school teachers who came to my chambers privately to promise me their support. They told me that many teachers were eager to help, but dared not make themselves conspicuous because it was known that the First National Bank and the Moffat-Evans-Cheesman interests controlled the School Board; and the teachers were afraid of losing their positions.

I tried the leaders of the Woman's Club. One able and wealthy woman, of whose support I was certain, confessed that she could not even sign my nominating petition. She said that if any woman of wealth wished to take part in such a fight, she would have to invest her money in another state. Her own investments were in Denver, and if she were to champion our cause publicly, the corporations would make her suffer for it ruinously. Another leader told me: "You know, Judge Lindsey, I would like to help you, but my husband is in business, and his business depends largely upon the good will of Mr. Evans. He has large contracts with the county. He has told me that I must not under any conditions attend your meetings or do anything like that. It would be very offensive to Mr. Evans and the business men." Another said: "I know you're right, Judge, but my husband is in the City Hall. Some day I hope he will be free—so that *I* may be free—but he isn't now." I went at the beginning of the campaign to practically all the women's suffrage leaders who, at national meetings, had been telling how much the women had done for the Juvenile Court in Denver; and none of them dared help me. Women like Mrs. Mary C. Bradford and Mrs. Lafferty (who was a member of the last Legislature) took the platform against me and supported the System in its attempt to "get" the Juvenile Court. Mrs. Scott Saxton of the Woman's Club stood practically alone in her open public support of our anti-corporation campaign.

Beauty and the Beast! I am, and have always been, an enthusiastic advocate of woman's suffrage. In our Juvenile Court campaigns, the women, like the "church element," have given us a loyal and victorious support. But if any one believes that woman suffrage is a panacea for all the evils of political life, he does not know what those evils are. The women are as free of the power of the Beast as the men are—and no freer. Their clubs in Denver have not dared offend it any more than the churches have. In a typical American community such as ours, where the Beast rules, the women are as helpless as the rest of us. They are bound by the same bread-and-butter considerations as the rest of us. Their leaders in politics are politicians; when they get their nominations from the corporation machines, they do the work of the corporations, and there is almost no way, under the Beast, to get a party nomination except from a corporation machine. Women in politics are human beings; they are not "ministering angels" of an ethereal ideality; and they are unable to free us, because they are not free themselves.

Do not misunderstand me. Woman suffrage is right. It is just. It is expedient. In all moral issues the woman voters make a loyal legion that cannot be betrayed to the forces of evil; and however they are betrayed—as we all are—in campaigns against the Beast, the good that they do in an election is a great gain to a community and a powerful aid to reform. I believe that when the women see the Beast, they will be the first to attack it. I believe that in this our first successful campaign against it, the women saved us. I have only tried, in the preceding paragraphs, to answer a question that is in the mouths of many Eastern opponents of woman suffrage: "Why don't the women cure the political corruption in Colorado?"

Well, we had gone to the business men, to the ministers, to the teachers, and to the women's suffrage leaders, in search of money or an organization with which to begin our fight; and we had gotten practically nothing but confidential good wishes. The corporation newspapers—the Denver *Republican* and the Denver *Post*—were, of course, against us. I went to Senator Patterson and asked him for the support of his papers, the *Rocky Mountain News* and the Denver *Times*; he replied that he would support me if I could get on a party ticket; but his managers seemed to object to wasting the influence of the papers in a hopeless, independent struggle. There was one other daily, the "little" *Express*, a Scripps paper that had been established in Denver by Mr. Scripps, at the solicitation of members of the Honest Election League, to aid in the fight for the people. It was sold for a cent a copy—the other papers sold for five cents—and it had gradually gained a circulation among the working people of the city. It had refused the free telephone service offered it by Mr. Field of the telephone company, and had kept itself clean of all corporation bribes and favours. Its editor was an incorruptibly fearless young man, Mr. B. F. Gurley, who had had experience in Cleveland and Los Angeles. He knew the Beast and understood how to fight it. When I sent out my first appeal to the ministers, asking them to come to a meeting in the Juvenile Court, Mr. Gurley gave notice of the meeting in the *Express*; and several labour leaders, whom I had never so much as met before, came to the Court and volunteered their aid.

That—though I did not know it then—was the first stir of the popular uprising that was to come. I had never made any particular appeal to the labouring people, but they are, in every community, the most bruised and beaten slaves of the conditions that I was fighting; and they knew it!

The next aid that came seems still to me an accident that was little short of miraculous. I was talking one day to some school teachers, in my chambers, about the impossibility of making a successful campaign without money to pay watchers at the polls, to employ workers to canvass the wards, to print election "literature" instructing the voters how to scratch, and to support an organization that should arrange meetings and direct the whole campaign. I said I believed that if we had $5,000 for these purposes, we could win. I believed that the people were with me, but my experience in the governorship contest had shown me that where we had a little money and an efficient organization we could carry a county, and where we had not, we failed. And I said that I was going into the election without money, without an organization, merely to make a "campaign of education" again.

There happened to be listening to me a lady whom I had met only a short time before. She had first heard of the Juvenile Court through Mr. Lincoln Steffens's articles in *McClure's Magazine* and she had later heard me lecture in the East. She had become interested in the work of the court; and now, after learning of our need of money to defend the court in an election, she went to one of the court officers and asked whether she might be allowed to contribute $5,000 to a campaign fund. She was not a wealthy woman, but she and her husband—she said—had set aside $5,000 to be devoted to philanthropic work and she felt that to use the money in defence of our court would be philanthropic. I took care first that she should learn how little hope there was that I could be reelected; I gave her as much discouraging political information as I could; and then, finding her still eager to help us, I gladly accepted her help. She has never allowed her name to be made known. She has never accepted any credit for her act. But there is not a shadow of doubt in my mind that she saved the Juvenile Court.

We began to organize at once. Mr. E. V. Brake, a labour leader, took charge. He got volunteers among his followers to act as ward workers and even coaxed many away from the other parties to join with us. About two hundred women, many of them volunteers, came to our headquarters, took instructions on how to teach the voters to "scratch," and began to go from house to house repeating the lesson. They reported a strong sentiment in our favour. The politicians of both parties recognized it too, and I began to receive the usual overtures from "leaders" who were willing to drop a dummy candidate in order to get my name on the party ticket. It was a presidential campaign, and the Republicans needed all the support they could get against Bryan. Mr. Vivian, the Republican State Chairman, held conferences with his committeemen and ward leaders, and advocated my nomination. He was opposed by the corporation attorneys and particularly by Mr. Field, president of the telephone company, who appeared in person to threaten that if I were put on the Republican ticket he would not give the committee the $8,000 promised by the company to the Republican campaign fund. H. L. Doherty, president of the gas company, had sent word that if I were nominated on either party ticket, every responsible official head in the gas company's office should fall! Mr. Vivian and other Republicans told me that many members of the Central Committee were eager, now, to have me on the ticket, but the corporation magnates, with their hands in their pockets, blocked the way.

The same sort of thing went on among the Democrats, and reports of it kept coming to me day by day. Mr. Field was the active head of the corporation opposition and he did not disguise it. When Mr. Gilson Gardener, the Washington correspondent of the Scripps papers, came to Denver, Field said to him—in one of the most important pronouncements ever made by the Beast: "Our company is in politics? Yes. Why? By virtue of necessity. Our company contributes to political parties and for political purposes? Yes. Why? Because this is the modern system. It began years ago. It exists for the same reason that we contribute to a state fair or a Y.M.C.A. It became the custom, long since, to expect corporations to contribute to all kinds of things. And finally, it was politics. Then it became necessary. There came the unfair acts, and we needed men in office who would be our friends.

"Our company is in politics in order to have friends. We never have asked for anything improper. I speak for no other corporation or person; but our company has always been above reproach. But we do have friends. We have them in both parties. They come to me and ask advice. They come and ask me to help them lay their plans. They come regardless of their parties and they hold meetings in my office. I am not a boss. I have carefully avoided being anything like that. But I can't help it if they come to me and ask advice."

He admitted that he had opposed my nomination in both parties. "My opposition," he boasted, "was effective. Yes, it was effective with both parties. Judge Lindsey's name was left off both tickets." He said he had opposed me because I had made attacks on his "personal character," but that statement deceived no one. I had never attacked him except as one of the corporation presidents who were debauching politics and maintaining the political system that united the law-breaking "dives," gambling hells and brothels with the law-breaking public-utility companies and their corrupted courts. He deceived no one—least of all his interviewer, Gilson Gardener, who wrote, in the *Express*: "Judge Lindsey has been left off two strong party tickets in defiance of the voters' will and in pure revenge, for the truth which he has told. It is the work of the corporation powers—the tramway-telephone-water-gas combination, manipulated by such men as Field and Evans."

He certainly did not deceive the labour men. I was admitted to the meetings of their unions and addressed them night after night. In company with Rev. A. H. Fish, of the Central Presbyterian Church, and Mr. L. M. French, a labour leader, I went to the factories and shops at luncheon hour, talking to the men and women workers. We made it plain that our fight was against the tyranny of the corporations. The unions passed resolutions endorsing our work, and the members of the barbers' union made every barber shop in Denver a centre of propaganda which their lathered customers could not escape. We sent out, from our headquarters, cards to the voters for them to sign, pledging their votes; and we received 23,000 of these pledges signed.

The women—not so much their suffrage leaders or their politicians, as the mothers in the homes and the working women in the factories and the shops—came out for us by the thousands. Our headquarters swarmed with newsboys and schoolchildren anxious to help; and some of those boys made the most effective campaign orators we had. It was tickling to the verge of tears to hear them, on a public platform, addressing a crowded hall with their pathetic earnestness and their childish arguments. If the "kids" were going to "stay wit'" me, they pleaded, why shouldn't "the folks"? One of these boys spoke to an audience of several thousand at a W.C.T.U. convention in the Auditorium, and raised a heart-shaking enthusiasm; and the aid and inspiration given us by these noble women was a power in the campaign. The corporation newspapers cut all mention of it from their reports of the meetings—maintaining a policy of concerted silence about my candidacy in an attempt to "bottle" us. But the Denver *Express* kept on hammering; the signed pledges kept coming in; and at last Senator Patterson's two papers swung into line and things began to move with a whoop. The Christian Citizenship Union had succeeded in reaching the "church element" in spite of the opposition of those wealthy churches whose boards were controlled by the Beast. The labouring men and their wives packed our meetings. In the foreign quarters, and particularly on the West Side among the Russian Jews, the poor mothers whose children I had befriended received us with tears running down their cheeks, so that I could hardly speak to them for the choke in my throat. The people were up—with a shout— with a shout that was at once angry and tearful with anger, for we did not yet believe we could win—and the politicians shut their ears to it, and orated about their presidential candidates, and placarded the town with "Rebuke Guggenheim—write Bryan on your ballot," so as to insure the election of Chas. J. Hughes, Jr., attorney for the tramway company, as another corporation senator to join Guggenheim in Washington! And the machine that called for a "rebuke" of Guggenheim was the machine that had elected Guggenheim! And the Hughes who was now to be elected, on that "rebuke," was the Hughes who, for years, in the courts, had fought for the corporations against the people who were to administer the "rebuke"! These are the tricks of the Beast!

As upon former occasions, when the Beast in Denver was in trouble, Mr. Bryan was summoned to act as the eloquent—but, I am sure, unconcious—"tout" and "capper" of the System's confidence game. In 1902, with the grafting County Commissioners on his platform, he appealed to the people to vote the Democratic ticket, and the grafters applauded him with all the enthusiasm of guilt. Now, in 1908, with Chas. J. Hughes, Jr., as the candidate of the local utility corporations, on a reform platform that has since proved to be the usual corporation "fake," Mr. Bryan called to the people to support Mr. Hughes, and used every eloquence of his oratory, unwittingly, to "stall" the voters into the corporation "deal." Great is the Beast; and Bryan—even Bryan sometimes—is its prophet!

Our campaign went on gaily, nevertheless. It was a straight campaign against corporation rule. I made no appeals to sentiment; I often left the question of our court work out of my speeches. I was determined that if I was to be beaten, I must be beaten as the opponent of the Beast; and that if I was to be saved, it must be by voters who saw who were their masters and revolted against them. All the usual tricks of the Beast were used against us. Many Democratic and Republican "workers," in going their rounds, whenever they were asked by a voter how to vote for me, replied: "Oh, that's all right. He's on our ticket. Just vote it straight." And our workers were kept busy explaining that I was on neither party ticket. In order to issue instructions to voters, we asked the clerks in the office of the County Clerk and Recorder where my name would appear on the official ballot; they replied: "In the fourth column about half way down." Accordingly, in our printed directions, we told the voters to look for my name "in the fourth column, half way down." But when the official ballot was issued, there appeared, half way down the fourth column: "For County Judge for short term, to succeed Ben. B. Lindsey," with the "Ben. B. Lindsey" in very large letters where it should not have appeared at all. Some distance below, in smaller type, my name appeared as an independent candidate for Juvenile Judge; and as a result of this trick, it was estimated, some eight thousand votes intended for me were lost. In an ordinary election, it would have been sufficient to defeat me.

But this was not an ordinary election, as the vote showed. When the polls opened, the betting was four to one that I would not get ten thousand votes. Early in the forenoon, it was known that at every polling place in Denver the people were "scratching" as they had never "scratched" before. Women wearing long white badges—"Vote for Judge Lindsey"—watched the approaches to the polling places all day long, without relief, and accosted every voter. A newsboy, on the previous night, had obtained a dollar from our committee for "campaign expenses," had bought a dollar's worth of coloured chalk and sent out a horde of boys to mark the sidewalks, the walls and the fences with "Vote for Judge Lindsey"—and the party henchmen with brushes and mops had not succeeded in entirely obliterating that "handwriting on the wall." By midday the betting gave odds in my favour, and the excitement among the politicians was breathless. The foreigners who could not speak English came to the polls with cards on which friends had written for them, "I want to vote for Judge Lindsey." The women, everywhere, made no secret of the fact that they intended to vote for me. We began to believe that the impossible was about to happen at last.

I was, myself, the last to believe. I had faith in the ultimate triumph of the cause for which we were fighting, but I did not believe that we could win in this campaign. I was resigned to the loss of the Juvenile Court to the agents of the Beast, and I had made arrangements to carry the fight on in a lecturing tour. I did not credit the first favourable reports from my friends when the polls closed. It was a presidential campaign; I was an almost wholly unsupported candidate for a small county office*; and never, of recent years at least, in a city like Denver, had any independent candidate in America carried a vote under such circumstances. When one of our committee telephoned me, at my house, that I had been elected by 10,000 majority, I refused to accept the report as even plausible. But the details kept coming in, from the well-to-do precincts on Capitol Hill, from the foreign quarters, from the home districts of the working men and women, and even from the wards where the "dives" were thickest; and all but three gave me pluralities. At last, late in the evening, I was summoned to the telephone by a call from my old opponent "Big Steve"—A. M. Stevenson—at Republican Headquarters; and he said "Ben, it's a d—— miracle. You're elected, and that's about all that's certain. There's been so much 'scratching' we don't know where the h—— we're at!"

---

* I had, however, been nominated on the Prohibition ticket.

Elected? Out of 65,000 votes cast, we had polled, on the official count, 32,000, which was almost as many as my two opponents had together. Even without the 8,000 votes of which we had been cheated by the trick in the ballot—and although these votes had been counted for my opponents—I had a plurality of almost 15,000. The people had at last "seen the cat" and they had "scratched" it to the bone! I went to bed that night, no longer a slave among slaves, but a freedman in a community that had at last risen against its masters and given them a warning of the wrath to come!

What matter that the legislative candidates elected on that day on a reform platform, refused, in the session that followed, to pass any of the election laws which they were solemnly pledged to give us? What matter that the corporations obtained the election of Chas. J. Hughes as United States Senator? The people see "the cat"! They know what influence prevented the passage of the election laws. They know who elected Hughes and they know whom he represents. They are on the trail of the Beast, and some day—soon—in Colorado, they will be cutting its hide into cat-o'-nine-tail strips for the backs of the legislative traitors and hired betrayers of public trust who have sold the community into slavery and been rewarded with an eminence of shame. This state, founded in liberty, cannot be governed by the criminal intelligence of corrupt men. Our people, born to freedom, will not see injustice bought and sold in their courts, laws purchased in their legislatures, cities robbed of their streets, vice protected in its dens, homes despoiled, girls debauched, children ruined, the poor starved at their work, and the hired procurers of political prostitution enriched with the profits of all this tyranny, this misery, this disgrace. The day is coming. The reckoning is due.

CHAPTER XVIII

CONCLUSION

I HAVE BEEN ASKED A HUNDRED TIMES: "Has the fight been worth while? Wouldn't it have been better to let the corporations alone and just devote yourself to the children? You have made enemies who have hampered you in your work. You can't get the contributions you used to get. The court has suffered because of the attacks upon it. And the corporations are just as powerful as they ever were." Let me answer that. Let me give a little summary of what we have gained, for the people, in this struggle. And let me first try to express a part of it in terms of dollars and cents.

According to Julius Aichele, a corporation politician who was at the time County Clerk in Denver, our fight against the grafting County Commissioners resulted in a saving to the county, in four years, of $300,000. After our exposure of these printing steals, a committee of the Legislature investigated the state printing and reported that $90,000 a year could be saved; an inspector of state printing was appointed, and he has since claimed, I understand, that he saved the state $50,000 a year—or $200,000 in the four years. The Clerk of the Supreme Court made a similar investigation of the court's printing, and effected a considerable saving; I do not know how much. But, you see, this one small fight against graft saved the people at least a half a million dollars.

As a result of my anti-machine decision in the licence-inspector case, $70,000 a year was collected from dive keepers and saloon men, which had been left uncollected before because the Police Board inspectors were "protecting" these men. This is on the testimony of Mr. Wm. Burghart, the inspector who succeeded the System's tools.

By obtaining a law forbidding the collection of fees for prosecuting children, we have saved the state $10,000 a year since 1903—about $50,000 to date. Before this law was passed two little girls who had stolen a few pennies' worth of bright beads from a shop were charged with burglary, and the fees for convicting them—paid to the constable, justice, sheriff, jurors, district attorney and court—amounted to at least $150.

By sending boys unaccompanied to state institutions we have saved in sheriff's fees at least $5,000. Our books show that the sheriff's fees for taking two boys to the State Reformatory at Buena Vista were $140. The County Commissioners held that I might not send prisoners to Buena Vista without a sheriff—that they were criminals and had to be treated as such—but our right to send them unaccompanied, on trust and honour, to other institutions, could not be denied.

By our reform of the probate laws we have saved estates in probate at least $50,000 a year—$300,000 to date.

By taking all children's cases into the County Court in 1901 and abolishing most of the fees for trying them, we saved the county about $10,000. By doing the work of the Juvenile Court—when it was first instituted—without salary, we saved the county the cost of an extra court, about $12,000 for a year. By calling in an outside judge and handling the Juvenile Court work in the County Court, we saved the public $10,000 a year for six years—$60,000.

In 1903 Governor Peabody sent an inspector to our court to compare the cost of our method of handling children's cases with the cost under the old system; and in his message to the Legislature he stated that in eighteen months our methods had "resulted in a saving to the county and the state of $88,827.68." This, in nine years, would amount to $500,000.

In 1901 there was a movement in Denver to establish a Parental School for chronic truants. The Legislature even passed a law providing for its establishment. It would have cost $50,000 to build and $25,000 a year to maintain it. Our probation and report system obviated the necessity of such a Parental School, at a saving, to date, of $250,000. Our Detention School, which takes the place of the jail for children, costs less than $10,000 a year for equipment and maintenance.

By refusing to allow the County Commissioners to appoint political "workers" to sinecures in the County Court, we saved in three years about $18,000.

During the seven years that I was judge of the County Court we not only paid all the salaries of the judge and the clerks of the court out of the fees paid by litigants, but we turned over to the county more than $50,000 earned by the court. So that while I was judge of the County Court, the county not only did not pay us a penny for our work, but we paid the county $50,000 for letting us do the work. And if you will add up the preceding items of saving, you will find that we paid the county $50,000 for letting us save it more than two millions!

But the real glory of our struggle has not been its saving of dollars and cents, but of flesh and blood. When I first visited the Industrial School at Golden, I found armed guards in the reformatory buildings and some of the boys shackled with ball and chain on the grounds; I found the iron boot in use, the boys being flogged in the presence of their fellows, and many of the usual prison brutalities practised on the miserable and rebellious children. To-day there are no armed guards, no chains, no prison restraints. The superintendent in charge—instead of being a ward politician—is an educated, trained and capable man, Mr. F. L. Paddleford, whose work is an honour to him and a blessing to the community. Most of the boys come alone to the school, stay there of their own will, receive visits from their parents, accompany them to the railroad station unwatched, and return themselves to their duties; they learn useful trades and receive the semi-military training of a good boarding school, with drill and a military band of their own and officers promoted for good behaviour. The whole school, on a recent gala day in Denver, marched in parade and enjoyed the freedom of the city; and every last boy of the four hundred, at the day's end, was back in his dormitory. They are happy; they are learning to be honest, healthy, useful citizens, instead of brutalized and rebellious criminals. Of a Sunday, in their chapel, it would lift up your heart with exultation to hear them sing. If we had done nothing else in our long struggle—if we had nothing to show for it but this reformed "prison"—that Sunday chorus of childish happiness and good will would be of itself a song of adequate reward, a chant of sufficient victory.

When I went on the County Bench the dive keepers, gamblers and saloon men who debauched boys and girls were not only protected by the police and other officials, but by the technicalities of the law. It was impossible to convict the saloon man or the gambler unless we could prove the serving of "liquor" to young people or their participation in the gambling game; and this was always difficult. Now we have "contributory delinquency" laws that require the keeper of a saloon or any disreputable resort to forbid boys and girls frequenting it; and he can be punished if they are so much as seen there.

We have obtained laws that will permit our probation officers to arrest him; and we can ourselves file a complaint against him if the District Attorney refuses to act. The result is that no man or woman in Denver—no, not the head of the System and king of the corporations himself—has political "pull" enough to save him from the punishments of the law if he offends against the poorest slum child in Denver. No one can know how much that means to the community unless he can remember the horrible traffic in young virtue that used to make our streets and alleys in the dive district the open roads to physical and moral hell; and no one who knows it can doubt that our fight has been a thousand, thousand times worth while—yes, even if this alone had been the one result of it! We have obtained an effective registration law that prevents most of the ballot-box stuffing. We have obtained a probate code that is conceded by lawyers to be one of the best in America. We have obtained amendments to the child-labour laws, affording children better protection and adding a jail penalty for violation instead of a light fine; amendments to the compulsory school law, requiring a complete school year for all children, and providing for the relief of needy children; laws forbidding the prosecution of children for crime and requiring that they be treated, under the chancery jurisdiction, and the rules of equity, as wards of the state, needing "aid, help, assistance and encouragement"; a provision in the city charter and the statutes of the state, forbidding the placing of children under fourteen years of age in jail, and establishing a detention home-school where they may be cared for; a set of laws, enforceable in both chancery and criminal courts, making parents responsible for neglecting their children or setting them a bad example; a law for the special care of dependent children, providing for the inspection of all homes and institutions, public or private, for the care of dependent children; a law requiring parents, who are able to pay, to support their children in state institutions; a law guaranteeing orphan children at least $2,000 from the estate of the parents before creditors are paid; a law giving the judge the right to place orphan children with persons professing the same religion as the parents; a law forbidding any court to take a child away from a parent until the parent's rights have been carefully guarded and adjudicated upon; probation laws for adults; and a dozen other minor laws and amendments of similar purport and effect.

We have helped to obtain night schools in Denver, ungraded schools for backward children, public playgrounds, and public baths. We have failed to obtain trade schools, but we have not ceased our efforts to obtain them. We have established summer camps for poor children in the mountains, obtained work for them in the beet fields and fruit orchards, and found employment and assistance for thousands of city children. Our Juvenile Improvement Association for the betterment and protection of the child has spread over the whole country. Our work for the children has been taken up by President Roosevelt in a message to Congress, by John Hay, Secretary of State, by Herbert Gladstone in a recommendation to the British House of Commons, by Professor Freudenthal, as a representative of the German Emperor, and by officials from countries in all parts of the world. Of all the thousands of children whom we have dealt with, not more than 10 percent have been returned for a second offence; and we estimate that 95 percent have "made good" in the end. No one can know what a saving of young citizens this means. One of the tramway company's detectives is authority for the statement that of 1,000 boys whom he has brought to our court, for acts of lawlessness committed against the railroad, only one class of boys has ever been returned for a second offence—and these were not more than a dozen newsboys who "hopped" on the cars to sell their papers. Under the old methods of criminal prosecution and jail sentence, from 65 to 75 percent of the children were returned to the jail for a second term within five years; and every term in jail meant a term in a public school of crime that made the children worse instead of better.

Very few of these laws—and none of the important ones—could have been obtained without breaking with the political system by which the corporations profit and which their bribes and influence maintain. Few of these laws could have been obtained without first rousing the community to a sense of its responsibilities to the child and stirring up the people by a campaign that was sure to be offensive to the political powers. We should have been false to the child had we failed to point out that the rule of social, economic, industrial and political injustice maintained by the corporations was responsible for much of the child's misfortune and most of the increase in crime; and we should have shirked our duty had we failed to help in educating the public to see that the greatest wrongs to the home, the child and the community are inflicted by the rich criminals of the community. And as for the contributions that we might have obtained from the corporations by kneeling to them, let me boast that by asserting my independence and going on the public platform to obtain our reforms, I have been able in nine years to earn enough as a lecturer to be able to donate $20,000 to our work out of my earnings and my salary; and this is a good deal more than we could have begged from our corporation masters even if we had kissed the ground in front of their feet.

Observe, too, that these results have been gained by the "picayune" fight of a judge of a small county court, without money, without "influence" and for the most part without an organization. Imagine what could have been done by a leader of the people with a political following and a place in the Legislature from which to speak! What defeats might not have been turned into victories! What losses to the people might not have been made unimaginable gains!

Consider these facts: In our first city charter we had provisions giving the city power, from time to time, to "make reasonable regulations concerning the operation and use of all franchise rights and privileges operated and used in the city and county, and to fix reasonable maximum charges for water, light, telephone service, street railway fares and other utilities or properties devoted to the public use." This charter was defeated and these rights denied the citizens by the corporations with the help of Boss Speer and his Democratic city machine and Police Commissioner Frank Adams and his protected "dive element."

By the use of the Legislature, the courts and public officials, the corporations are establishing a power trust that has obtained incredible rights in all the watersheds and power streams surrounding Denver, without any reservation to the state of the people's rights in these natural resources; so that our children and our children's children, for all time, will be compelled to pay the heirs of the Beast for the right to use the water power that should have been an asset of the community instead of an asset of the Beast.

Some of the coal companies have obtained from the State Land
Board hundreds of acres of land devoted by the state to the support
of the schools. Some of this land is so rich in coal that it is worth at
least $2,000 an acre; and the coal companies have obtained it for nom-
inal prices. These frauds have been notorious for years—and not less
notorious has been the recent failure of the courts to punish the guilty
state official who was the tool of the land robbers.

All laws, such as the eight-hour laws, the employer's liability
law, and laws requiring the use of safety appliances have been either
defeated or made ineffective by the corporation control of the Legislatures that should have passed the laws or of the public officials who
should enforce them. The State Railroad Commission has been a pitiful joke. The system of railroad rebates and unjust discriminations
in railroad charges has flourished poisonously. The railroad lobby,
with one of Senator Teller's brothers as attorney for the Union Pacific
Railroad, has strangled every bill that attempted to regulate the railroads for the public good; so that, for example, the son of ex–United
States Senator Dorsey (the other member of the Teller law firm) was
able to boast to the General Solicitor of the Union Pacific Railroad,
in a letter written from Denver in May, 1903: "At the last session of
the Legislature, although many bills were introduced which would
greatly prejudice the railroad company's interests, no legislation was
enacted to our disadvantage. On the contrary several acts were passed
which were favourable to railroad companies, some of which had been
caused to be introduced by the Union Pacific Railroad Company."

One of the bills referred to as prejudicial to the railroad company's interests—according to a previous letter written by Teller and
Dorsey in February, 1903—was "House bill No. 181, by Mr. Frewen,"
which provided "penalties for failure to comply with existing statutes
in respect to safety appliances, etc." Teller and Dorsey reported that
"every effort should be made to defeat" this bill, and enquired, "Will
you kindly advise us whether Union Pacific Railroad Company is willing to pay its share of any reasonable expense incurred in this connection?" President Burt replied that the bill was one of those "more or

less objectionable" and "should be defeated." "Whatever expense," he wrote, "needs to be incurred in connection with legislative matters, you are authorized to make." The bill was killed in committee. And let me add, as a commentary on the defeat of such laws requiring the safeguarding of workmen engaged in dangerous occupations, that in the nation's last generation of childhood, 32,000 children were made orphans by coal-mine explosions alone, and three-fourths of these explosions might have been prevented by the use of safety appliances such as the governments require in Germany, Belgium and other European countries.*

In the last session of the Legislature (April, 1909) all attempts to pass the "platform pledges" on which the Democrats had gained office were defeated by the united corporation legislators among the Democrats and Republicans alike. We could obtain no anti–straight ticket law, no direct nomination law, no corrupt-practices act—no measure designed to restore representative government and over-throw the rule of the Beast by freeing our elections from the con-trol of the corporations. The same Legislature killed the bill giving the people a court in which to contest a fraudulent franchise-election, although the attorneys for the corporations had contended in my court that, until such a bill was passed, there was no court on earth in which the people could recover the hundred million dollars' worth of public property that had been stolen from them by the franchise-election frauds. When the bill was killed, the Legislature was con-trolled by the corporation machine that elected Chas. J. Hughes to the United States Senate; and Chas. J. Hughes was one of the attor-neys who defended the corporations in the franchise-election con-tests. When the bill was killed its fate depended most upon a "Special Orders" committee of three men, of whom two were Senator "Billy" Adams, the most notorious corporation champion in the Senate, and Senator Rodney J. Bardwell, the paid attorney of the Gas and Electric

---

* These figures are on the authority of published government reports, conser-
  vatively estimated.

Company. And this same Bardwell introduced, and the Legislature gaily passed, two bills giving the Gas and Electric Company "special privileges" in prosecuting persons who stole gas or electricity, by practically providing that the accused person in such cases should be required to prove himself innocent or go to jail for as much as ninety days for stealing gas! No bill to protect the people from the steal of a gas franchise worth a fortune—and a special bill to protect the gas company from a steal of gas worth ten cents! A bill to require a citizen to prove himself *innocent* of having tampered with a damaged gas metre—and no bill to allow the citizens the right to prove the gas company *guilty* of having tampered with a franchise election!

The same Legislature defeated a Public Utilities Bill that would have prevented the Gas Company from watering its stocks and bonds twenty-five millions. Twenty-five millions on which the citizens of Denver must pay interest! Money stolen from our homes by a method more refined but none the less criminal than the entry of a "second-story man."

There is no end to it. I might go on in this way to fill a volume with instances of proof that the State of Colorado is exploited and the people robbed by a government by the Beast and for the Beast. A system of corruption that aims to pick the corruptible man for public service, and refuses the honest one an opportunity to serve, has made most of the public life and administration of public affairs in Colorado a gigantic failure, a huge oppression. The functions of government are no longer discharged as against the corporations, except where an error of judgment on the part of the corporations, or an unforeseen frustration of their plans, has permitted an honest man to obtain an opportunity of honestly filling a public office.

The ignorant and the dishonest apologists of the System contend that the men of wealth have, in self-defence, merely corrupted corruption and bought up the politicians who were preying upon them. You might believe it, if there had ever been a case in our courts in which a corporation had prosecuted a legislator for blackmail or attempted to defend itself from a dishonest public official. You might believe it, if you could believe that the boys who steal "junk" are preying upon the junk dealer who induces them to steal it. And even if you believed it, you would have to concede that there is no patriotism in business, no responsibility to the state, no obligation of citizenship to expose dishonesty in public office or oppose the profit of it, and no higher sense in the man of wealth than a criminal self-interest and the cowardice of a knave.

Such an excuse—such an apology—it is impossible to accept. Every man who has had anything to do with politics knows that it is a lie. Our Legislatures have been bought by the corporations not for self-protection; our courts have been corrupted in no struggle against injustice; the "dives" have been subsidized against society not because society oppressed the good. The whole System is an alliance of law breakers against the sources, agents and penalties of the law. It is the alliance of a "plunderbund"—a compact among thieves and criminals, rich and poor, for the subversion of law and the protection of illegal profit.

Even though I had never succeeded in doing anything to check this System, to oppose this corruption, I should still be content that I had fought it. For such a defence of liberty, it is a privilege to fight. It is an honour to be defeated in it. It is a happiness beyond glory to succeed, however obscurely, in the smallest struggle for it. It is my one hope that as long as I live I may be able, I may be found worthy, I may be considered fit, to devote myself to this allegiance, and in this cause to defend my state and its people, my own birthright and our children's inheritance, our right to freedom and our institutions of freedom that are founded in that right.

Well, I have done. I have tried to write without malice—to do no one an injustice—to tell the truth, without fear as without favour, in the firm belief that the truth shall make us free. I shall be called "an enemy of the state," because I have attacked the enemies of the state—for the corporations in Colorado, like King Louis in France, hold majestically, "The state? It is I!" I shall be called a traitor to the community because I have tried to expose the traitors in the community; and the traitorous newspapers of the community will be the first to raise the cry. I shall be called "a blackener of the fair name of Colorado" because I have named the men who have corrupted, debauched and prostituted Colorado—for no men hate the light more than the men who profit by the crimes which the light discloses. Heaven help them!—Heaven help us all. We are struggling toward better things, a happier country, a more perfect civilization. We may never arrive, but, whatever the end, the aim is worth the agony. Let us struggle. Let us hope.

THE END

INDEX

Printed in the United States
219452BV00002B/2/P

9 780870 819537